500 POPULAR

ROSES

FOR AMERICAN GARDENERS

BARRON'S

First United States of America edition published in 1999 by Barron's Educational Series, Inc.

© Copyright by Random House Australia Pty Ltd 1997.

Publisher	Gordon Cheers
Managing Editor	Loretta Barnard
Contributors	Geoff Bryant
	Kevin Hughes
	Richard Walsh
	Trevor Nottle
	Steve Beck
	David Ruston
	Sonja Townsom
	Elizabeth Churchill
	Maureen Heffernan
Page Layout	Joy Eckermann

All inquiries should be addressed to:
Barron's Educational Series, Inc.
250 Wireless Boulevard
Hauppauge, New York 11788
HTTP://www.barronseduc.com

International Standard Book Number 0-7641-0851-4
Library of Congress Catalog Card Number 98-73712

Printed in Hong Kong by Sing Cheong Printing Co. Ltd.
987654321

CONTENTS

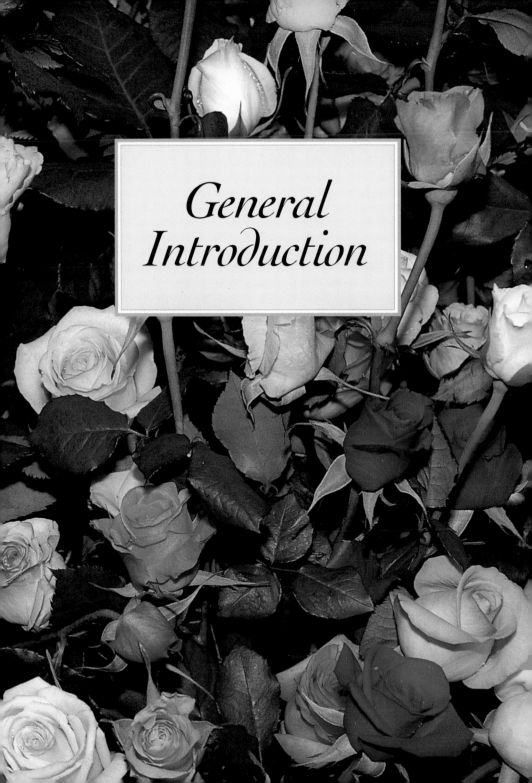

General Introduction

A BRIEF HISTORY OF ROSES

Roses have accompanied the human race since the first red berry was plucked and eaten by some unknown cave dweller in pre-historic times. As medicinal plants, roses were valued for their flowers and fruits by the ancient civilizations of Egypt, China, Greece and Rome, and they were also highly valued for their beauty and perfume. Over 2,000 years ago, roses had been associated with the rituals of life, with myths and legends, and with many religions and their associated ceremonies. By the Middle Ages, thanks to the distilling and pharmaceutical skills of monks and nuns, roses were used to make an enormous variety of products, from eye ointments and salves to scented rosary beads, biscuits and candies. Recipes were not confined to European sources, many were brought back to Europe by Crusaders returning from the Middle East; yet others were transmitted by wandering Gypsies from northern Africa and Eastern Europe. Painted by Renaissance painters in the backgrounds and borders of their works; written about by poets and playwrights, treasured by town housewives and rural peasants, roses moved gradually from their ancient utilitarian purposes in homeopathic medicine, perfumery and cookery to being cultural symbols and objects of beauty. All of these uses for roses are still with us today. More than ever they are valued for their beauty and the ease with which they grow.

This appreciation gained pace in the 18th century and continued in the 19th century, particularly at the hands of French and then British breeders. The Empress Josephine is reputed to have played a leading role in popularizing roses, but more truly it was the rise of the middle classes that ensured that roses became the principal flower in gardens, indoor decoration and exhibitions. By the end of the 19th century, roses were well and truly established as the queen of flowers. Beyond Europe the colonists of the British Empire and the townsfolk, farmers and ranchers of America adopted roses as the mainstay of their gardens. Even the toughest gold miners chose roses for their gardens when they struck it rich; and they knew that roses sent to the stage door would be sure to bring a smile to the face of Lola Montez. Looking back, the peak period of interest in roses may seem to be the early years of the 20th century. Nursery catalogues of the Edwardian era and horticultural magazines of the era show that there were thousands of varieties and large formal rose gardens were the hallmark of gardening excellence everywhere—from the gilded mansions of Newport, Rhode Island to remote Anlaby Homestead in South Australia. As the century progressed the Hybrid Tea (or Large-flowered Rose) came to dominate all other kinds of roses, and while they still remained very

Vita Sackville-West's White Garden at Sissinghurst Castle has an elegant formality.

popular, their habits of growth and the formal way of growing them were not entirely sympathetic to new gardening styles, or to new architectural styles. For a while it seemed the rose had had its day.

Since the introduction of 'Constance Spry'—the first of David Austin's 'English Roses' in 1961—there has been an increasing interest in roses once again. The resurgence has come about because rose breeders recognized the desire among gardeners and landscapers for roses which could be incorporated in flower gardens of mixed shrubs, perennials, bulbs and annuals. Gardens can be informal and cottage-like, or more stylized and designed as in the color-coordinated English flower gardens of Vita Sackville-West and Penelope Hobhouse. As the 21st century nears, gardeners have an enormous range of roses to choose from when making gardens. With a careful selection roses can be found to suit many gardening situations. There is no need to put up with roses that do not flower prolifically or that do not have vigorous healthy growth; there are many roses which do flower well and that are disease and pest resistant. And they are lovely too.

HYBRIDIZING

Since the earliest times rose flowers and fruits were gathered from the wild, and perhaps the first roses taken into gardens were wild roses which were selected because they had semi-double or even double flowers. Medieval monks were among those with the curiosity and inclination to admire and study plants, and from that beginning the rose has become a favorite garden flower. For hundreds of years roses didn't change much, and a few new forms were discovered and introduced by observant but unknown people. But in the 18th century, Dutch gardeners observed that where the best kinds were grown together the resultant crop of seeds produced seedlings with a higher percentage of improved flowers. They soon publicized their wares widely and sold plants across Europe, particularly in France and England where demand was strong for planting the expansive flower gardens being made by wealthy merchants and aristocrats. At this time almost all roses were once flowering and included Gallica roses, Alba roses, Damask roses, Centifolia roses and Moss roses. When Europeans discovered the way to China and Japan, other roses with repeat flowering habits were introduced from the nurseries of Nanking and Yokahama.

When these two main groups of roses were gathered together in nurseries and gardens, it was only a short time before natural hybrids began to appear, and it was from these that today's repeat flowering roses have been developed over the last 100 years or so. The work itself has become much more controlled and scientific. Where once the plants were cross-pollinated by bees, they are now pollinated in strictly controlled conditions so that carefully considered stud lines can be developed and built on generation after generation. There are dedicated amateur breeders at work, and they do have some successes, but most of the roses introduced today come from big commercial organizations because of the high costs and lengthy lead times involved in developing and marketing new roses. Raising new roses is time-consuming, demanding of skill, concentration and patience, and may or may not result in something worthwhile. For gardeners able to take a long-term view, information and demonstrations of the practicalities are usually exhibited at meetings of rose societies from time to time. Selecting potential candidates for naming and introduction is entirely up to the proud hybridizer.

Among the most successful of amateurs was Alister Clark, an Australian who bred over 100 bush roses and climbers in the 1920s and 1930s. He had clear aims and criteria to produce garden roses that would bloom and grow well in the warm, dry climate of Australia. There have been other breeders such as Griffith Buck who aimed to produce cold tolerant roses for countries where winter freezing damages, or kills, many kinds of roses. Such successes should serve to inspire those who feel the urge to take up the hybridizer's scissors, brush and stud book.

THE CLASSIFICATION OF ROSES

Classifying roses is done according to a number of different purposes; botanists classify roses scientifically by the differences and similarities in their floral structures; exhibitors classify them according to criteria which group them by the appearance of their flowers and their breeding; nurseries are beginning

'Climbing Iceberg' is one of the most popular climbing roses.

to classify roses by their habits of growth and landscaping use. For most home gardeners the best classification system is the one which gives them the most useful information. To this end the system of classifying roses by their habits of growth and landscaping purpose coming into use by garden centers and rose nurseries is by far the most sensible. The classifications now being introduced follow these lines:

- Large-flowered/Hybrid Teas and Grandifloras;
- Cluster-flowered/Floribundas;
- miniature roses;
- climbing roses;
- shrub roses;
- ground cover roses (prostrate);
- English Roses® (bred by David Austin);
- old garden (or heritage) roses (members of a class that existed prior to the introduction of the first Hybrid Tea Rose, in 1867, such as Bourbons, Mosses, Damasks, Centifolias, Gallicas, Hybrid Perpetuals, Teas, Chinas, Hybrid Musks and Noisettes and species roses).

Plant labels and nursery catalogs should give more precise information about the dimensions of any particular variety within each classification. The table on page 9 is adapted from the World Federation of Rose Societies.

PLANNING AND DESIGNING A GARDEN WITH ROSES

Choosing the right rose for your garden is the key to a good garden design. All roses need at least six hours of direct sunshine each day to be successful; they

How Roses Are Classified

ROSES

WILD ROSES

CLIMBING
Rambler
Climber

NON-CLIMBING
Shrub

OLD GARDEN ROSES

NON-CLIMBING
Gallica
Damask
Centifolia (Provence)
Moss
Alba
China
Tea
Portland
Bourbon
Hybrid Perpetual
Scotch
Hybrid Sweet Briar

CLIMBING
Rambler
Noisette
Boursault
Climbing Tea
Climbing Bourbon

An informal effect can be created by training climbing roses over posts.

MODERN GARDEN ROSES

BUSH
Hybrid Tea
Floribunda
Polyantha

SHRUB
English Rose
Hybrid Musk
Hybrid Rugosa
Unclassified
Modern Shrub

CLIMBER
Large-flowered
Cluster-
flowered

MINIATURE
Miniature
Climbing
Miniature
Micro-miniature

**GROUND
COVER**

'Roseraie de l'Haÿ', a Hybrid Rugosa, is a favorite among rose growers because of its sweet fragrance and bright color.

A mixture of bright colors and different fragrances makes a stunning rose garden.

Monet's beautiful garden at Giverny was carefully planned and shows the importance of choosing roses that suit your particular area.

will not grow or flower well in the shade of trees and shrubs, or in competition with their roots. As to soils they are adaptable but they will not tolerate boggy, poorly drained soils. Choosing the right rose for any particular garden is easy if you always consider the site first and then find a rose which has the dimensions to fit the space. Never buy a rose looking only at its flowers and then wander around the garden looking for a place to plant it. Pruning a rose to fit a space is a waste of time.

In years gone by, formal rose gardens were considered the only way to grow and display roses. Grown this way, roses are easy prey to the rapid spread of destructive rose pests and diseases. This method of gardening with roses requires regular spraying with chemical poisons and fungicides—difficult in these times of heightened environmental awareness. Fortunately modern gardening, whether in the new cottage style, or the informal mixed borders of small shrubs (including roses) and perennials, means that gardening without heavy chemical warfare is possible and satisfying.

Cottage gardening with roses needs a mix of bright colors, plant forms and perfumes. Old Garden Roses are a popular choice for this purpose, particularly the repeat flowering kinds such as Teas, Chinas, Bourbon and Hybrid Perpetuals; even David Austin's modern English Roses® are suitable for cottage gardens. Grown with a living mulch of low perennials, bulbs and annuals, with an underlay of pea straw mulch, roses of many kinds will be a beautiful addition to the overall plan. Low, shrubby climbers such as Bourbons and Noisettes are ideal for planting on verandah posts and pergolas; Ramblers and Hybrid Musks make a wonderful decoration to a rustic archway or a metal tripod; while large shrubs such as 'Scharlachglut', 'Bloomfield Abundance' or *Rosa chinensis* 'Mutabilis' will add a colorful touch of distinction to a shrub-filled border of cottage flowers. Tall shrubs such as these, make excellent hosts to attractive small climbers such as *Clematis viticella*.

Using roses in an informal flower border offers scope for using a very wide range of varieties to add height without adding dull heaviness to a garden. Roses, with their tall arching growth and fine foliage, are graceful and light. The species are especially attractive shrubs, producing masses of single flowers, followed by heavy crops of berries (called 'hips') which may be red, orange, rusty brown, or black; most are shiny and some are spangled with glistening bristles. In contrast, the Rugosa roses make splendid ground cover. Their deeply veined, glossy dark green leaves provide perfect weed-proof coverage for banks and cuttings, or they can be made into dense, low, informal hedges. Their large, bright scarlet hips spring from large single flowers of magenta, pale pink or white.

Modern shrub roses such as 'Bonica' and many of the new landscaping roses add new color possibilities and flowering seasons to the design of mixed borders. Be aware that dimensions may differ according to climate. In warm climates, such as California and parts of the Southeast, the growing season is long, so they can get much larger than they do in England or the northeastern USA. Allowances must be made in planning a garden with these roses so they have adequate room to grow to maturity.

If an old style formal rose garden is planned, make it simple; the more elaborate the design and planting the greater the expense of making the garden and keeping it up. Use roses of one color and variety to make blocks of color, choose a color scheme which will complement nearby brick or stone work and which will not clash with other planting schemes nearby. Decide that a small garden well kept is to be preferred over a large formal garden poorly maintained. Remember that roses grown in such settings need approximately 3 feet (1 m) between each rose bush in all directions.

SOILS

In the wild, roses grow in a wide range of soils ranging from dry and rocky, to sandy loams and loams stiff with clay. They are intolerant of boggy, or poorly drained soils and they rarely thrive in soils that are saline or rich with other salts. Their root systems are tough and far reaching, but they generally inhabit clearings and the edges of woodlands, or other open spaces such as meadows and sandy grasslands, even the seashore in some instances. Roses are very adaptable as to soil preferences but as a general rule they prefer well-drained, open spaces.

For home gardeners, soils may be enriched by deep mulching supplemented occasionally with animal manures and chemical fertilizers. Sometimes mineral and trace element supplements may be necessary if roses show yellowed, dark veined leaves or reddish purple brown stains around the leaf margins. A general mineral mix fertilizer will usually fix these problems; and local experts may sometimes recommend a specific trace element.

On extremely sandy soils roses will rarely thrive, though *Rosa × fortuneana* used as an understock can sometimes overcome the difficulty of establishing the plants. Even so, careful attention must be paid to ensure an adequate

Poor soils can be enriched with cow manure, blood and bone or compost.

water supply and a replacement for minerals and nutrients leached from the soil by rain and irrigation.

Be careful about planting new roses in soil that has just had an old rose bush removed. To avoid the possibility of the new rose failing to thrive completely, remove the soil taken from the planting hole and replace it with fresh soil from some other part of the garden, or use compost mixed with a good quality potting soil. Otherwise 'rose re-plant disease' may cause a newly planted rose to fail. Growth will be stunted and flowers few. The same advice applies whether the rose is bare-rooted or grown for sale in a pot.

THE INFLUENCE OF CLIMATE

Broadly speaking, roses are adaptable and hardy but they will not grow well in very hot climates, nor will they thrive in really cold climates where the ground freezes in winter, or where frosts are hard and frequent. Of course there are some gardeners who are determined to overcome the limitations imposed by natural conditions. The question is 'how great is the desire to grow roses?'

Roses perform best in climates where there is a long warm growing season with rainfall spread evenly over the growing months, and a short cool dormant season. In similar but some-what drier conditions roses will thrive as long as adequate deep watering by irrigation is possible and affordable.

PREPARATION FOR PLANTING

Roses can now be bought year round. Most nurseries and garden centers offer a range of potted roses, but also offer a larger selection as bare-rooted plants for planting when roses are dormant.

Planting roses bought either as potted plants or bare-rooted follows the same basic rules:

- Check that the roses will be planted where they get at least six hours of direct sunshine every day.
- Check that the soil is free of invasive tree and shrub roots.
- Check that the soil is well drained, that is, water drains away within 10 minutes of the planting hole being filled with water.
- Dig a planting hole wide enough and deep enough to easily accommodate the roots of the plant, including the root ball of potting soil.
- Check bare-root roses for ragged or damaged roots. Cut these off with a sharp knife or hand pruners.
- Sprinkle a dusting of fertilizer in the bottom of the hole if necessary.
- Plant the rose in the hole and back-fill with crumbly soil until the stem is covered to the same approximate depth that it grew at in the pot or nursery field; the bark of the stem changes color at this point from yellowish green to brown.
- Fill the hole with water, let it drain away and top up with soil if necessary. Fill the planting hole with water again.
- Check that the plants are firmly settled in the garden. Tie climbers securely to wherever it is they will grow.
- Mulch the plants well with coarse, loose mulch such as pea straw.

MAINTENANCE

Roses are tough, reliable and able to withstand periods of neglect. However, they will give their best performances if they are cared for with a regular pro-gram of maintenance. Watering, pruning and feeding are low key activities that can be easily managed. As a general rule, gardeners who have no wish to force

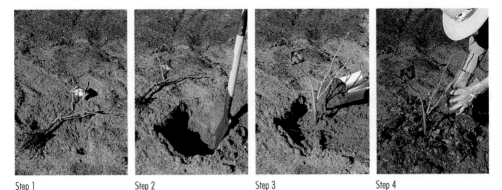

Step 1   Step 2   Step 3   Step 4

When bare-rooting, follow these basic steps: Step 1: check for damaged roots. Step 2: dig a hole big enough to accommodate the roots of the plant. Step 3: plant the rose, back-filling with crumbly soil. Step 4: mulch well.

their plants with substantial doses of fertilizer and water will find a balance can be achieved which maintains healthy plant growth without promoting excessive use of tap water or chemicals. A natural system of no-dig, organic mulching with natural products such as well-rotted manure and straw; or saw dust, wood chips or even shredded tree and shrub branches will suffice, with a little summer watering to keep garden roses happy.

Flowers will be produced in good numbers though they may not be as large as those produced by heavy feeding and watering. Pest and disease control are a matter of choice too. Gardeners have to make up their own minds about balancing environmental concerns about the residual poisons left by pesticides and fungicides, and the benefits of spraying. Environmental controls are now being introduced which severely restrict the availability of garden chemicals to home gardeners, and other means of controlling pests and diseases need to be found. While eco-friendly biological controls may be a solution there is a simpler way. This is to grow roses in gardens mixed with other plants rather than in gardens with roses only. Given present trends for informal gardens and cottage gardens this should be compatible with the general design of a garden for many home gardeners.

PRUNING

It is strongly recommended that you consider the purchase of top quality equipment regardless of how many roses there may be to prune. All roses deserve equipment that will do the job well and prevent undue fatigue in the pruner's arms and hands. A good basic pruning kit includes good hand pruners, a short pruning saw that cuts on the pull and push stroke, a pair of long-handled branch loppers, stout leather gauntlets

Essential tools for pruning roses.

Long-handled pruners for big pruning jobs can prevent fatigue in the pruner's arms.

Rose bushes can be rejuvenated by cutting out old growth.

Old twiggy growth should also be removed.

'Winterizing' with lucerne hay mulch provides insulation from freezing weather.

or gloves, and a sharpening stone.

Pruning roses is largely a matter of personal choice and convenience. Roses are very forgiving and can manage for many years without any pruning. Flower size may lessen but the bushes will not suffer too greatly, and they can be quickly and easily rejuvenated by cutting out completely all the dead growth, all of the non-flowering twiggy growth and trimming back the remaining overgrown bush by approximately two thirds. Given a very light dose of animal manure or complete rose food, regular deep watering and a thick layer of mulch, the neglected roses will bounce back to vigorous growth and flowering.

Such drastic measures should not be necessary as long as a simple regular pruning schedule is adopted. The first objective should be to do occasional pruning when flowers are cut for indoors, or when the faded flowers are removed. It is easy at this time to cut the stems down to a plump dormant bud at the point where the leaves join the stem. As the growing season progresses, growth gets taller and taller. It is possible at this stage to perform summer pruning to lower the bushes. The roses

will put out strong new shoots and flower again before the cooler weather gradually induces winter dormancy. Then all that remains is to give a further light pruning before new growth begins in the spring. At this time any dead branches and non-flowering twiggy growth can also be cut out. Treatment such as this should keep most garden roses growing well for many years. Roses that only flower once a year, including the species and the old European roses (Gallicas, Mosses, Damasks, Albas etc), can be pruned immediately after their flowers have faded. New growth will develop and ripen well in time to flower again next year.

Bear in mind that any pruning should be done in consideration of the vigor and growth habits of any particular variety. Modification of pruning techniques will also be necessary in areas where winter freezing and prolonged heavy frost can damage growing roses. In these areas pruning should be confined only to those times of the year when there is no danger of frost or late snows killing growth. In these areas too, dormant roses may need 'winterizing'. This is a process of mounding up leaves, straw, or other light dry mulching material to cover the roses and insulate them from the freezing weather. Remove the insulating mulch only when the danger of late cold snaps is past. At this time winter killed growth can be cut off and the roses pruned.

Roses can also be pruned with a far more casual approach than is outlined above and still produce abundant healthy growth and many flowers. 'Pruning' with hedge clippers, electric shears and even chain saws can be done. The results can be an eyesore but once growth begins, it is soon hidden under a canopy of leaves and flowers.

In contrast to this are the exacting pruning techniques used by rose growers who exhibit at flower shows. Their prescriptive methods are useful for producing championship blooms but are not necessary to the production of a good garden display or to have lovely cut flowers. For information about pruning roses this way, contact your local rose society.

Whichever method is selected for use the same basic idea applies — to completely renew the branch structure of the bush within a time frame of about four or five years.

A final point about pruning is that no amount of pruning will make a rose grow in any other way than is natural to the habit of that particular variety. There is no way a large growing shrub can be trained to fit a confined space; a climber cannot be made into a low bush any more than a miniature be encouraged by pruning to grow large. If a rose is wanted to fit a particular garden site a rose which has the approximate dimensions required must be chosen.

But be reassured that it is almost impossible to kill a rose by pruning it.

PROPAGATION

Roses are propagated in three main ways — by seed raising, by planting cuttings and by budding a desired variety onto a selected rootstock.

Seed raising is used by hybridists seeking to raise new varieties and by botanically minded rose collectors who have acquired seed of species roses. The seed-raising process requires the seed to be stratified in a sterilized, damp soil mix, exposed to chilling and then to warmth which triggers germination. It is not difficult but does require time and patience. Small seedlings need protection from pests, diseases and drought, but are tough once they get going. Species roses from seeds collected in the wild should be true to type, but hybrid seedlings will be extremely variable, so they will need to be planted in some sunny out of the way corner and grown for several years before deciding which are worth keeping. It is not unusual for commercial rose breeders to raise 100,000 seedlings every year from which they may keep as few as five for further assessment. Hybridizing can be an absorbing pastime for amateur gardeners, and some do enjoy a degree of success, but it takes a lot of time, dedication and a considerable amount of garden space. Within each rose society there are usually a few amateur breeders with knowledge and skills to pass along to anyone interested.

By comparison, growing roses from cuttings is simple. All that is required is a small space free of tree roots in an area that is lightly shaded and has free movement of air. Rose cuttings can be planted at almost any time, as long as there is no likelihood of frost or snow, but the best time is in early summer.

Select cuttings from stems that are about pencil thick and long enough to

Seed raising requires time—and patience!

Select your cuttings from stems that are about the thickness of a pencil.

When propagating by budding, the first step is to cut the T.

The T is then cut vertically.

The blade is levered out . . .

. . . and the bud is inserted.

The top part of the budding piece is cut, so that it fits flush with the T.

The final step is to tape the budding, and hope for the best!

have five to seven sets of leaves. Cut the stems using sharp hand pruners just below the lowest leaf stalk; trim off, or gently pull off, all the sets of leaves but the topmost set. Six cuttings of each variety wanted should be collected and bundled together with a name tag. Have handy a bucket of water, some damp rags or newspapers and store the just harvested cuttings in a cool and damp place at once. Never let them get heated, wilted or dried out. Set the bucket with the cuttings in a shady place while a planting hole is made ready. Plunge a sharp spade into the soil as far as it will go and move it backward and forward slightly to make a narrow hole. The cuttings can now be planted or it may be thought worthwhile to dip the ends of

the cuttings in a root-promoting hormone powder before they are set in the soil. Some growers also advocate dribbling a small quantity of sharp sand into the bottom of the hole as an additional aid to root formation. When the cuttings are all planted they should be gently firmed in the ground by watering and stepping lightly on the soil on either side of the row of cuttings. There is no need for heavy stamping.

A similar process can be used to raise cuttings in pots. In both cases it is important that cuttings do not touch. After several months, fresh growth should appear on the cuttings which have made roots. Feed the young plants regularly with a weak solution of water soluble fertilizer. Transplant the new plants into their permanent positions after about six months by which time the root system should be well-established. Remember that the young plants will need careful nurturing for the first year; watering, feeding, weeding and pest control is critical if the plant is to settle in and grow.

As a general rule two plants could be expected to grow from a batch of six cuttings, although some varieties are more reliable and some are almost impossible. The big advantage of cutting grown roses is that they never grow unwanted suckers; the disadvantage is that the bushes take longer to reach their full potential.

Budding roses is the most popular commercial method of propagating roses. It is possible for home gardeners to use this method but many commercial rose nurseries offer a custom budding service so that even old favorites from grandmother's garden can be propagated for distribution to family members more certainly than an amateur could easily manage. Rose society members some-times demonstrate the skill for those eager to learn how. Basically the process involves inserting a growing point, or bud, of a desired variety under the thin bark of another rose selected for the superiority of its adaptable and strong root system. Judging the right time to do this and developing the necessary fine motor skills takes much practice and time.

PESTS AND DISEASES

Rose pests and diseases are many and varied. Over the last century or so, ingenious chemists and enterprising horticulturalists have invented and developed all manner of means of conducting a kind of control of these problems that amounts to little less than warfare. However the home gardener who wants to grow roses need not adopt over-kill strategies if a little forethought is put into plans to make a garden with roses:

- Plan mixed plantings of roses with other shrubs, perennials, annuals etc.

- Always see roses growing in a garden or nursery so an assessment can be made about growth, foliage and resistance to pests and diseases.

- Always choose roses which have strong growth and leathery foliage.

- Avoid roses which have a tendency towards getting fungal diseases such as rust and mildew.

- Use natural predators whenever possible.

- Plant roses well apart.

- Ask your local rose society for advice on how to prevent or mitigate the effects of common rose pests, such as Japanese beetles.

- If chemicals must be used follow the directions thoroughly, use protective clothing and breathing gear, and shower immediately afterwards.

Black spot is a fungus which attacks damp leaves. If you live in a humid climate, avoid roses which are susceptible to this disease.

CHAPTER 1

Species or
Wild Roses

There are around 120 true species roses and around the same number that are classified as species but are generally garden forms or hybrids. These roses are often known as wild roses.

Rose fossils have been found on all three northern hemisphere continents — North America, Europe and Asia — dated at around 35 million years. Species of the genus Rosa occur naturally only on those three continents. To understand why, we must consider the theory of tectonic plates. But first the question 'what is a species rose?' must be answered.

To produce another rose, pollen from one flower is rubbed onto the stigma of another, thus cross-fertilizing. When the petals drop, a rose hip forms. This contains seeds which fall to the ground and germinate. Because two different roses are required to produce fertile seeds, the offspring will be different in certain aspects from the two parent roses, due to the differing ways that the chromosomes unite in pairs.

However, the first roses were self-fertile. The stigma was receptive to the pollen of the same flower. This phenomenon occurs throughout the plant kingdom — all species will produce identical offspring from seed. Offspring produced by cross-fertilization from a different plant of the same genus will then require cross-fertilization from another different plant to produce seed, and the offspring will differ from the parents.

So why is there not just one species rose? Evolutionary theory dictates that different forms evolve to suit particular conditions. Thus the North American species roses differ notably from those found in Europe and those from Asia.

Wild or species roses can be classified into different sections, the most notable being the **Pimpinellifoliae**, the **Gallicanae**, the **Chinenses**, the **Cinnamomae** the **Carolinae** and the **Synstylae**, but it is sometimes difficult to place wild roses into categories because of their varying ancestries.

Now to return to the tectonic plate theory. The Earth's surface is made up of many different forms of hard rock, overlaying a very hot liquid core or magma. Magma is released when a volcano erupts and hot molten rock flows out. This cools to form solid rock, which in turn weathers to form soil. Because of varying underlying pressures and atmospheric temperatures, the rock surface splits up to form many separate plates, with each continent forming its own plate. These plates are forced to move over the underlying magma by the same varying pressures, the movements almost undetectable, but making a considerable impact over time.

Around 225 million years ago, all the continents joined together to form one large land mass, referred to today as the continent of Pangaea. This land mass persisted for some 35 million years, when the continents started to move apart again. Laurasia, made up of the present continents of North America, Europe and Asia split from Gondwanaland, made up of Central and South America, Africa, Australia, Antarctica and the sub-continent of India. It was probably during the several million years between the splitting of Laurasia and Gondwanaland and the start of the formation of the Atlantic Ocean, that roses evolved and spread across the northern continents. This would appear to make the age of genus Rosa around 150 million years and many of our present species would date from that time (although this is not yet scientifically proven). Other forms and hybrids would have evolved in the intervening years.

This is a simplified explanation of why roses occur naturally on only three continents. That roses are found all over the world today, except on the very cold land masses, is a tribute to human endeavor.

Over the millions of years of rose evolution, plant propagation was from seed and the spread of seed was by animals who ate the ripe hips and voided the seeds. There were a few rambling species roses that also propagated by layering, where the tips of the rose canes rooted where they touched the ground. This was mostly restricted to *R. wichuraiana, R. luciae* and *R. setigera*. Also, many roses will grow suckering shoots off their root systems and form vast clumps in the wild.

Since the end of the 18th century, with the increasing demand for garden plants, propagation has been from cuttings and by budding onto an understock. Both these methods of reproduction, while very effective, are unnatural to the rose plant. Prior to the 18th century, propagation was generally by division of the plant stools.

Most of the roses in our gardens today flower throughout the spring, summer and autumn. For those living in warm climates with mild winters, roses will flower all year round. The original wild or species roses flower generally in the spring, set seeds through the summer, which mature in the winter when the plants defoliate and are dormant, until the warmth of the next spring starts them into activity again. So why bother to grow species roses in our gardens today, when we can have flowers for most of the year by growing modern hybrid roses? The answer lies in their delicate beauty.

Rose hips are a distinctive feature of wild roses.

Most modern rose flowers have up to 50 petals, whereas the species or wild roses generally have only five petals (or four in the case of *R. sericea*). The five-petalled rose with its very prominent stamens, in great masses of flowers and often heady fragrance in the spring, is a sight to be relished. After the petals have dropped, the unique foliage, thorns and wood become the feature of the plant — with the bright color of many of the rose hips in late summer, followed by rufous foliage in autumn. During winter the color of the bark and the form of thorns or bristles are evident. The shape of the species plant varies from a small bush, to a large shrub, a spreading rambler or a great climber, depending upon the species grown. Some of the species roses such as *R. rugosa* and *R. bracteata* carry both flowers and hips on the plant at the same time, increasing the plant's beauty. Most of the shrubs we grow in our gardens flower only once and species roses can be treated as shrubs in the garden. They tend also to be more drought and disease-resistant than modern roses.

Species roses are difficult to find in garden centers so it is worth visiting a specialist nursery to find the wild rose that best suits your garden.

Rosa bracteata

Rosa banksiae lutea

Rosa banksiae banksiae

ROSA BANKSIAE BANKSIAE
R. banksiae Alba Plena, The Lady Banks Rose
Rambler

This rose is a garden variety of *R. banksiae normalis*, which is the true species rose. It was discovered in a Canton garden, by William Kerr, and named after the wife of Sir Joseph Banks, director of Kew Gardens. The plant has long arching, thornless canes. Leaflets are slender, pointed, dark green, smooth and leathery, with three or five to a stem; foliage is evergreen and disease free. The sweetly scented, small white flowers appear in spring, are double and grow in clusters of three to seven flowers. It rarely bears hips,

which are small and dull red. It requires a warm sunny environment but will thrive on neglect, although it can be frost tender. It can be severely cut back immediately after flowering.

ROSA BANKSIAE LUTEA
Rambler

This is a native of central and western China. It was introduced to Scotland in 1796 by Robert Drummond but not distributed until 1877. The plant has long, arching, thornless canes and can grow to a great size if allowed. Leaflets are slender and pointed, evergreen, smooth, dark green, leathery and disease free. The double, yellow spring flowers with prominent stamens are sweetly scented and grow in clusters, produced on spur growths off second year wood. The hips are small and dull red. The rose has a spread of over 30 feet (10 m). It is also a variety of the *Normalis* species.

ROSA BRACTEATA
(The Macartney Rose)
Climber

Introduced to England from China in 1793, this rose is evergreen, with dark

Rosa chinensis viridiflora

Rosa davidii var. elongata

green, glossy, healthy foliage. The leaflets have a blunt or rounded apex, unique among roses. New growth is covered with soft gray-brown hairs and red bristles with double hooked thorns at each node. It flowers from late spring through autumn, with five petalled white flowers with very prominent orange-yellow stamens. The flowers are either in clusters of three to seven, or single, with only one flower out at a time. The globular orange hips are carried with the flowers. *R. bracteata* can grow up to 20 feet (6 m), and prefers warm climates. It has produced the hybrids 'Mermaid', 'Marie Léonida' and 'Schneezwerg' reported to be *R. bracteata* × *R. rugosa*.

ROSA CHINENSIS VIRIDIFLORA
(The Green Rose, Monstosa)
Shrub
Thought to be a form of *R. chinensis* 'Old Blush', its origin is unknown. It is reported to have been in cultivation in England as early as 1743. The bush is typical of a China rose, with mid-green smooth foliage and somewhat twiggy, prickly growth. The bush has clusters of three to seven small oval buds of soft blue-green, which open to flowers with

long thin bracts, light green streaked reddish brown, in place of normal rose petals. Each flower is some $1^1/_2$ in (40 mm) across, with about 35 bracts and a muddled hairy reddish brown center where the stamens would normally be. As far as is known, the rose is completely sterile. It is popular with flower arrangers due to its unique form.

ROSA DAVIDII VAR. ELONGATA
(Père David)
Shrub
Named for Père David, who collected *R. davidii* flowering in mountain scrub, this rose is a tall open shrub of around 10 feet (3 m), with strong, straight, smooth shoots and a few straight prickles. Leaflets are broad and oval shaped, smooth and dark green. The flowers appear in spring only, are bright pink some $2^1/_2$ in (6 cm) across, and appear in clusters of three to seven. They have prominent golden stamens and long sepals. The hips are orange-red and elongated. It will tolerate poor soils, shade and dry conditions. This rose should not be confused with *R. davidii*, which has smaller leaflets, up to 12 flowers in loose corymbs and bottle-shaped hips.

ROSA ECAE
(R. xanthina var. ecae)
Shrub

Discovered by Surgeon-Major Aitchison in Afghanistan in 1880, and named after his wife's initials — E.C.A., this rose occurs naturally in an area from Pakistan to Northern China. The plant is very dense, with many twiggy branches and grows to a 5 feet (1.5 m) suckering shrub in the wild, and larger in cultivation. The brown stems are covered with straight flat thorns. The leaflets are small, fernlike and elliptical. The small golden yellow five-petalled flowers are carried singly at each node. The petals often do not overlap. The hips are oval and red-brown. The rose prefers a dry, sunny situation, and will not thrive in wet, humid conditions.

ROSA × ECAE 'GOLDEN CHERSONESE'
Shrub

This is one of the few cultivated roses included in this chapter. It is a hybrid of *R. ecae* × 'Canary Bird' and was produced by E. F. Allen of the UK in 1963. The plant makes an attractive shrub up to 6 feet (2 m) high with arching thorny canes and twiggy lateral growths. The seven to nine leaflets are larger than those of *R. ecae* but retain the fernlike appearance. The flowers are also much larger than *R. ecae*, up to 2 in (5 cm) across, and are golden yellow, with overlapping petals and prominent golden stamens. In spring, the flowers are produced singly along the canes at each node. This rose can be intolerant of wet, humid conditions.

ROSA ELEGANTULA 'PERSETOSA'
(R. farrari Persetosa, The Threepenny Bit Rose)
Shrub

Named 'Persetosa' after the mass of hairlike prickles on the rose stems, this rose was discovered in a batch of seedlings of *R. elegantula*. The plant grows to nearly 6 feet (2 m) high and can spread to twice that dimension. The growth is light brown and the hairlike prickles give it a mossed effect. The fine fern-like foliage of seven to nine leaflets gives the plant a delicate appearance. The foliage is mid-green and smooth, but can burn to a reddish hue in hot sunshine. Lilac-pink flowers appear in spring, and are no more than $1/2$ in (15 mm) across. The profusion of orange-red hips are bottle-shaped, making a charming autumn shrub. The rose does best in a shady spot.

Rosa × ecae 'Golden Chersonese'

Rosa ecae

Rosa filipes 'Kiftsgate'

Rosa foetida

ROSA FILIPES 'KIFTSGATE'
Rambler

The Kiftsgate clones of *R. filipes* are extremely vigorous and when mature can reach around 50 feet (15 m), although the plant is very slow to establish. The reddish tinted new growth has many hooked thorns and can grow up to 20 feet (6 m) in a season. The foliage is large, profuse and glossy mid-green, tinted copper on new growth, and rich russet in autumn. The late spring flowering is profuse, the fragrant single white flowers being small, but carried in huge corymbs, which can be 10 in (25 cm) across with upwards of 80 flowers. The flowers are borne on slender stems, which is the meaning for 'filipes'. The hips are orange-red and round. It is not recommended for a small garden.

ROSA FOETIDA
(R. *lutea*, Austrian Briar, Austrian Yellow)
Shrub

This rose was grown in Europe prior to 1542 under the name *R. lutea*. The plant grows to 8 feet (2.5 m) tall with smooth young growth and numerous slender straight thorns on the reddish-brown older wood, that ages silvery gray. The foliage is dull, with light to grayish green leaves. The rich golden yellow flowers appear in spring, are borne singly, and measure some 3 in (8 cm) across. The stamens are prominent. To some the fragrance can be offensive, although some others will call it 'over-sweet rose'—hence the specific name. *R. foetida* thrives on poor soils but dislikes hot, humid conditions and being pruned. It is prone to black spot.

Rosa gallica

Rosa foetida bicolor

ROSA FOETIDA BICOLOR
(R. lutea punicea, Austrian Copper)
Shrub

This rose was known prior to 1590 and probably originated as a sport of *R. foetida* in Turkey or Central Asia. The growth is very similar to *R. foetida* and with similar foliage. The flowers are single, and are golden yellow reverse with the yellow showing through the thin petal texture of the intense nasturtium red of the flower face. They are quite dazzling when at their best. Some of the flowering lateral growth can revert to the golden yellow flowers of *R. foetida* and the effect can be quite striking. Like *R. foetida*, 'Bicolor' thrives on poor soils, dislikes hot, humid conditions and is prone to black spot.

ROSA FOETIDA PERSIANA
(Persian Yellow)
Shrub

This rose probably originated in Western Asia and was introduced to England by Henry Willock around 1837. It is similar to *R. foetida*, except that the flowers are very double, cupped, opening flat and in a lighter shade of yellow. It is also less vigorous, growing to around 6 feet (2 m). It thrives on poor soils, dislikes hot, humid conditions and is prone to black spot. This rose caused a sensation when it was introduced, with its double yellow flowers being a great improvement on the decorative yellow roses then available. But it is best remembered for its contribution to modern roses, when Pernet-Ducher used the pollen of *R. foetida* 'Persiana' to produce 'Soleil d'Or' in 1883, from which modern yellow roses are descended.

ROSA GALLICA
(R. provincialis, The Provins Rose, French Rose)
Shrub

R. gallica was thought to be in cultivation prior to 1500, and is the ancestor of garden roses in Europe. The plant is a sprawling, suckering shrub around 30 in (80 cm) high, which can cover a large area. Prickles on the stems are usually found on the older wood. There are three to seven leaflets, which are oval and often with a rounded apex, smooth and bluish-green in color. The spring flowers are five-petalled, clear pink in color but lighter pink to the center with golden stamens. They are sweetly scented. The hips are oval to round. *R. gallica*, like its offspring, is resistant to the leaf diseases that afflict modern roses, such as black spot.

ROSA GIGANTEA
(Giant Rose)
Climber

As its name suggests, this is a vigorous climber growing up to 50 feet (15 m). It has strong hooked prickles. The leaves are oval, dark green, smooth and have reddish stems. The pale apricot bud is tall and slender, and the creamy white flowers are very large. The subtle fragrance is of tea, said to be of the leaves of green China tea. With favorable weather conditions, after the hips have fallen in autumn, it will have a late flush of flowers. It is frost tender. *R. gigantea* was possibly a parent of 'Park's Yellow Tea Scented China' and 'Hume's Blush Tea Scented China', imported to England from China as garden roses and used in the hybridization of the tea roses.

ROSA GLAUCA
(R. rubrifolia)
Shrub

This rose is native to central Europe and was introduced to cultivation prior to

1830. The plant is spectacular, growing to around 14 feet (4 m) high, with arching canes and purplish red wood. There are five to seven gray to purplish leaves, which are long and slender. Flowers appear in spring, usually in groups four to six. They are pink with delicate pale pink centers, golden stamens and a subtle fragrance. The brownish red oval hips are around 1 in (20 mm) long. The rose has become very popular in recent years as a subject for flower arrangements, due to the striking colors of the foliage and wood. It makes a very attractive garden shrub.

Rosa gigantea

Rosa glauca

ROSA HOLODONTA
(R. moyesii rosea)
Shrub

The synonym for *R. holodonta* is now incorrect, as it is related to *R. davidii elongata* (based on the number of chromosomes), not *R. moyesii*. This rose makes a spectacular shrub, growing to some 10 feet (3 m) high and 6 feet (2 m) across. The plant is upright with arching reddish-brown canes and few straight prickles on the old wood. The leaflets are dark green and wrinkled, taking on rufous colors as they age. The spring flowers are a deep rose pink, and have prominent stamens. The hips are orange-red and bottle-shaped. The size of the hips, up to $1^{1}/_{2}$ in (35 mm) long, resulted in the incorrect alliance of *R. holodonta* to *R. moyesii*.

ROSA HUGONIS
(R. xanthina forma hugonis, Father Hugo's Rose)
Shrub

Native to central China, this rose was introduced from seed sent to Kew by Hugh Scanlon, a missionary known as Pater Hugo. It grows to a tall shrub, up to 8 feet (2.5 m) high and as much across. The mature wood is gray and has flattened thorns, while the new growth is reddish-brown and has a few hairs and bristles. Mature shrubs can often be thornless. The foliage is very fine and fernlike, with light green, smooth leaves. Pale buttercup yellow flowers appear in spring in small sprays. They are five-petalled and cupped, with golden stamens. The hips are small, oval and maroon-colored. It will tolerate poor soils and is subject to die-back at times.

ROSA LAEVIGATA
(R. sinica Alba, The Cherokee Rose)
Climber

R. laevigata was introduced to cultivation from southern China in 1769 but being very frost tender it did not survive the cold winters in Northern Europe. A vigorous climber, it grows to 20 feet (6 m) with green new wood and many hooked thorns; old wood is silvery gray. Leaflets are smooth, shiny, light green and oval in shape with a long pointed apex. The large flowers show in late winter and depending upon weather conditions, produce continuously for up to three months. The flowers are single, white with prominent golden stamens, and are slightly fragrant. Debate continues as to how *R. laevigata* became naturalized in the United States. Some believe that the Native Americans, in their original migration across what is now the Bering Sea, brought seeds with them.

Rosa hugonis

Rosa laevigata

Rosa × macanthra

ROSA × MACRANTHA
Shrub

This rose is not a species and is thought to have originated in a cross of *R. gallica* with a form of *R. canina*, although there are variations on this hypothesis. It was introduced to cultivation around 1880. The plant is a vigorous and arching shrub with many thorns, growing 5 feet (1.5 m) high and 6 feet (2 m) across. The mid-green foliage has five leaflets each around $1^{1}/_{2}$ in (40 mm) long. The single flowers are borne in clusters of three to five, and are cream pink fading near white, with conspicuous stamens and a delicious fragrance. The hips are orange. This shrub requires little maintenance, and can be naturalized in a medium sized garden.

ROSA MACROPHYLLA
(Large-leafed Rose)
Shrub

Native to the Himalayas, this rose was discovered in China in 1817. It has delicate, soft pink, sweetly fragrant flowers, with golden yellow stamens on a

Rosa macrophylla

very large free-growing shrub which grows to some 16 feet (5 m). The leaves are mid-green, and the plant has deep red to purple stems. It is thornless. It flowers in late spring, and flowers are followed by large, bottle-shaped, scarlet-colored hips, which in the right conditions, can be almost 3 in (8 cm) long. Distinctive hips, such as those of *R. macrophylla*, display their colors best in cold climates.

ROSA MAJALIS
(R. cinnamomae, The Cinnamon Rose)
Shrub

A native of Europe and western Asia, this rose was in cultivation prior to 1600. It is an upright shrub to around 6 feet (2 m) high with light green canes, having a reddish-brown hue (the probable origin of the cinnamon connection) and slightly hooked prickles and bristles on the old growth. The foliage is long, oval and gray-green in color. The fragrant single spring flowers are an attractive pink, with prominent golden stamens produced singly or in clusters of three. There is a double form of the rose *R. majalis* Plena, also known as 'Rose de Mai', 'Rose de Saint-Sacrement' or 'Rose des Pâques', which was in cultivation in 1659, and which many consider a better garden form.

ROSA MOSCHATA
(The Musk Rose)
Shrub

A sweetly fragrant rose—of musk—*R. moschata* was probably introduced to cultivation early in the 16th century. It is generally grown as a shrub 10–14 feet (3–4 m) high, though some describe the rose as a robust climber to 30 feet (10 m). It has smooth branches with very few prickles. The mid-green foliage is smooth and shiny on the face and downy on the reverse with oval leaflets in groups of seven. The single white flowers, in loose corymbs, open cream and fade white, and are produced in late summer. The hips are oval and hairy. This rose at one time became almost extinct, its place in botanic gardens being taken by the more spectacular *R. brunonii*, which is often sold for *R. moschata*.

ROSA MOYESII
Shrub

Native to western China, this rose was introduced to cultivation in 1894 by E. H. Wilson. It is a robust upright shrub growing to 10 feet (3 m) high, often with many stems shooting from the base. The mature wood is yellowish tan colored and has a few straight thorns near the base. The leaflets are smooth and oval. The fragrant spring flowers are produced singly or in groups of up to four, and are red, with golden anthers. The most spectacular feature of the rose is the hips, which are bottle-shaped,

Rosa moschata

Rosa majalis

Rosa moyesii 'Highdownensis'

orange-red and, although not so large as those of *R. holodonta*, are produced in far greater profusion. *R. moyesii* often produces pink flowers in the wild, and has many hybrids.

Rosa moyesii 'Geranium'

ROSA MOYESII 'GERANIUM'
Shrub

The rose was raised by the UK Horticultural Society in 1938 from an *R. moyesii* seedling and is the most commonly grown of the *R. moyesii* seedlings. The rose forms an open shrub with stiff canes growing to 8 feet (2.5 m), being more compact than the parent and with more copious fresh green leaves. The flowers are variously described as 'blazing red' or 'bright orange-red' and with a waxy texture and creamy anthers. It has a good display of hips and is often preferred as a garden plant to its parent because of its compact growth.

ROSA MOYESII 'HIGHDOWNENSIS'
Shrub

A seedling of *R. moyesii* which occurred in Sir Frederick Stern's garden at Highdown, Sussex, England in 1928. This rose is also thought by many to be a better garden plant than *R. moyesii* due to its more compact, busy growth and a

Rosa moyesii

greater profusion of flowers. The single flowers are displayed in conspicuous clusters of vivid cerise-crimson. 'Highdownensis' appears to have the best display of hips of all the *R. moyesii* progeny.

ROSA NITIDA
Shrub

This rose is native to eastern North America and was introduced to cultivation in 1807. It is a suckering shrub growing to around 3 feet (1 m) high, with dark green upright canes covered with tan colored bristles and a few straight prickles. The leaflets are shiny dark green, narrow and elliptical. The single, fragrant flowers are produced singly or in clusters of three to five in early summer, and are deep rose-pink. The red hips are shiny and round. *R. nitida* presents a fine display of autumn foliage, when the leaves turn deep crimson. It also occurs naturally in boggy areas and is therefore very tolerant of wet conditions and shade.

ROSA PIMPINELLIFOLIA
(*R. spinosissima,* The Scotch Briar, The Burnet Rose, The Scotch Burnet Rose)
Shrub

This rose forms a suckering low thicket up to 3 feet (1 m) high with bristles and prickles the full length of the stems. The smooth leaflets are small and fern-like with good autumn coloring. The prolific, single flowers are creamy white often

Rosa nitida

Rosa pimpinellifolia

shaded pink, and have golden yellow stamens. The hips are purple to shiny black and round and make almost as good a display as the spring to early summer flowers. It will grow in any soil, provided it is not wet or sticky. It hybridizes freely and a few 'Scotch Burnet' roses are still available today, although at the peak of their popularity, in the mid-19th century, over 200 different forms were available. Kordes' 'Frülings' series of roses was developed from *R. pimpinellifolia*.

Rosa pimpinellifolia altaica

ROSA PIMPINELLIFOLIA ALTAICA
(R. pimpinellifolia Grandiflora, R. spinosissima Altaica) Shrub

This rose forms a large suckering shrub up to 6 feet (2 m) high and across. The new growth has straight prickles, and is reddish brown, aging silvery brown. The foliage is fern-like, grayish light green, with five to nine leaflets. The early spring flowers are produced singly or in clusters of three, from short spurs along the stems. The flowers can be quite large, varying from $1^1/_2$–$2^1/_2$ in (40–70 mm) across. They are ivory white but suffused with primrose yellow on opening and make an attractive shrub when in full bloom. They are fragrant. The hips are round, shiny dark maroon to black. There is some dispute among botanists concerning the correct naming of this rose.

Rosa rugosa

Rosa roxburghii

ROSA ROXBURGHII
(Chestnut Rose, Burr Rose, R. roxburghii Plena, R. roxburghii roxburghii)
Shrub

This rose was introduced from the Calcutta Botanic Garden in 1824 by the garden superintendent, William Roxburgh. It forms a large suckering shrub 6 feet (2 m) high and across, with many upright stems, light silvery brown in color with flaking bark (giving off a pungent aroma) and very sharp, straight thorns in pairs at the nodes. The mid-green foliage is quite striking. The flowers are produced singly throughout summer and are very double, opening flat and reflexing, with upwards of 80 petals. The color of the petals varies from white to deep mauve pink. The buds open from a prickly calyx and sepals that have the appearance of small horse chestnut casings (hence the common name). It tolerates poor soils and shade.

ROSA RUGOSA
Shrub

This rose makes a large suckering shrub to 8 feet (2.5 m) high, with stout prickly stems. The foliage is bright glossy green and wrinkled ('rugosa' means wrinkled), and displays good autumn colors. The very fragrant flowers are produced throughout summer, either singly or in clusters of three. The flowers are large, up to $3\frac{1}{2}$ in (9 cm) across, and vary from purplish-rose to violet-carmine. The large tomato-like hips are a feature of the rose. *R. rugosa* used to be used as an understock for standard roses, because of its strong, straight stems and in old gardens, large clumps of rugosa still persist long after the scion has died out. Its tolerance of salt laden winds and poor soils highly recommends it for coastal plantings.

ROSA RUGOSA ALBA
Shrub

The foliage, prickles and hips of *R. rugosa alba* are similar to *R. rugosa*, although this rose is not quite as vigorous, growing to around 6 feet (2 m). The flowers are pure white, but open with a pale pink flush to the petals. As with many wild roses, the stamens are a very prominent golden yellow. It makes an impressive shrub when in full flower and with the shiny red hips displayed. *R. rugosa alba* is probably the most popular form of all the rugosas and is often used for hedging. Rugosa foliage is disease resistant and retains the glossy green color until the yellow and orange colors set in around autumn. It is bare of foliage throughout the winter months.

ROSA SERICEA VAR. PTERACANTHA
(The Maltese Cross Rose, R. sericea subsp. omiensis forma pteracantha)
Shrub

The last of the synonyms is no longer applicable, as subspecies *omiensis* is now united under *R. sericea*; it is included here for record. It is an upright shrub growing to 10 feet (3 m) high with strong arching canes, which are adorned with an almost continuous array of large red winged thorns. The thorns are most attractive and are popular in flower arrangements. New wood is gray-green with a reddish hue and is often covered with fine hairs. The foliage has a fern-

like appearance. The flowers are white with four petals only which are borne singly at the nodes. The hips are oval and red. Pruning in autumn is recommended. This rose tolerates poor soils and shady conditions.

ROSA SETIGERA
(The Prairie Rose)
Climber

A rose much overlooked for the garden, *R. setigera* forms a rambling shrub which can climb up to 15–17 feet (4–5 m) if supported. Because it suckers readily, the shrub can become quite extensive. The new wood is light green, becoming red as it ages and the prickles at the nodes are red and hooked. The leaflets grow in threes, and have a shiny darkish green upper surface that is wrinkled and broad with a fine tapered apex. The leaf stems are red, which continues through the center of the stipule. The fragrant early summer flowers are produced in clusters, and are crimson, paling to white at the center. The hips are small and red. It flowers when most once-flowering roses are finished.

Rosa setigera

Rosa sericea var. pteracantha

Rosa rugosa alba

ROSA × VILLOSA DUPLEX
(Wolley-Dod's Rose, R. Wolley-Dod, R. pomifera Duplex)
Shrub

The latter synonym is no longer used— the name has changed to villosa. 'Wolley-Dod' is the Reverend Wolley-Dod in whose garden Ellen Willmott first saw the rose, which she included in her book *The Genus Rosa*, published in 1914, although the rose first appeared before 1797. It is probably a hybrid of *R. villosa*, also known as 'The Apple Rose'. It forms a shrub 10 feet (3 m) high and 14 feet (4 m) across of arching prickly canes, silvery gray-green in color, ageing reddish brown. The leaflets are grayish-green. The flowers are semi-double, clear rosy pink, have soft yellow stamens and are slightly fragrant. The hips are large, red, bottle-shaped and hairy. It tolerates poor soils and shade, and is a popular garden plant.

ROSA WICHURAIANA
Rambler

This is a prostrate, creeping rose with long (10 feet (3 m)) pliable, smooth green branches with curved prickles, which are red on new growth. The foliage is shining green and smooth. The flowers are in loose corymbs of three to 15, and are white with five petals and golden yellow stamens. The flowers open in succession in early summer, later in cooler climates. The hips are small and orange-red. It tolerates shade and poor soils. This species can be difficult to identify today as some modern ground cover roses appear similar. *R. wichuraiana* has contributed to the development of many modern rambling and climbing roses.

ROSA WILLMOTTIAE
Shrub

Named for famous rose gardener, Ellen Willmott, this very delicate shrub grows to 10 feet (3 m) high. The new growth is pale mauve to lilac with fine straight prickles. Older wood is plum colored. The leaflets are fine, light gray-green and slightly fragrant. The small, fragrant flowers are produced in spring, and are lilac pink with yellow stamens. The hips are bright red and bottle-shaped, and fall off when ripe. Phillips and Rix are of the opinion that there are three forms of

Rosa wichuraiana

Rosa × villosa duplex

Rosa xanthina 'Canary Bird'

Rosa woodsii var. fendlerii

R. willmottiae — this one, 'Haddon's Variety' with smaller and deeper pink flowers, and 'Wisley' with narrower leaflets, deeper pink flowers and hips that do not fall off as soon as they are ripe.

ROSA WOODSII VAR. FENDLERI
Shrub

Native to North America, this rose was introduced to cultivation in 1888, although it is not commonly seen in gardens. It is an upright shrub with arching canes some 6 feet (2 m) high, and has wide flat thorns at the nodes which are red on the new growth. The wood is grayish-green to light brown with a reddish hue. The leaflets are long and mid-green. Flowers appear in clusters of three and are pale lilac pink, about $1^1/_2$ in (40 mm) across with yellow stamens. The round buds have long sepals. The hips are round and turn orange-red. *R. woodsii* var. *fendleri* tolerates shade and poor soils.

ROSA × XANTHINA 'CANARY BIRD'
Shrub

A clone of *R. xanthina* of unknown origin, this rose is a possible hybrid between *spontanea* and *hugonis*. It is a tall, angular shrub 8 feet (2.5 m) high and 6 feet (2 m) across, with reddish brown

Rosa willmottiae

wood and a few prickles near the base. The stems carry many warty growths. The foliage is bright, fresh green and the leaflets small, oval and fern-like. The spring flowers are borne singly, and have five petals, which are rich canary yellow, with prominent stamens. They are moderately fragrant. In favorable weather conditions, there can be a repeat flush of flowers late in the season. 'Canary Bird' can suffer from die-back and dead wood should be pruned out. The rose grows at its best under fairly dry conditions.

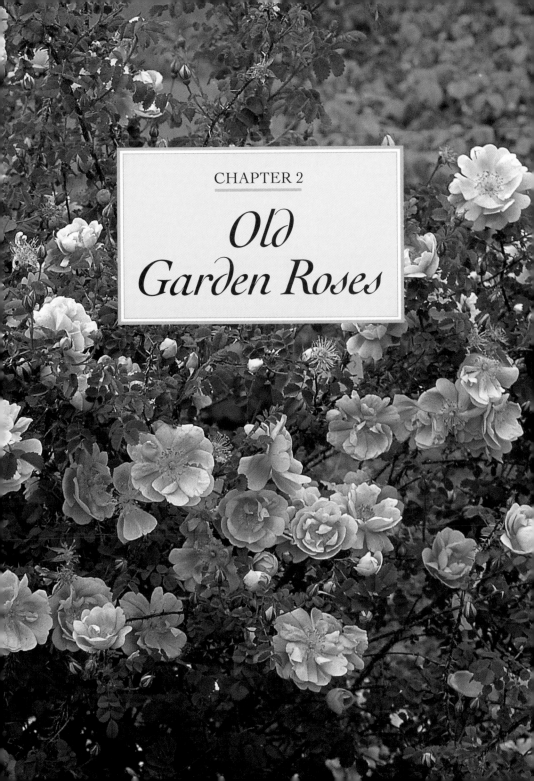

CHAPTER 2

*Old
Garden Roses*

The Old Garden Roses were grown in the gardens of Europe and Asia for many hundreds of years. They were derived in the first place by selection from some of the 120 or more species of wild roses which have evolved and grown for millions of years across the temperate regions of the northern hemisphere. These, in general, bore single five-petalled flowers, but from time to time doubling occurred as an aberration, usually by the transformation of stamens into petals. Further changes came about with hybridization between forms which were not contiguous in nature but were made so by human intervention. So by a long

Rosa 'Tuscany Superb', a gallica rose, in all its glory.

process of selection and crossing over the years, many beautiful new garden roses were created.

The main group in Europe and Western Asia were the **Gallicanae** and the main member of the group was *Rosa gallica*, the French Rose. This has single red flowers in the wild, but many semi-double and double forms developed, ranging from pink to deep purple. They are slender arching plants to 3–6 feet (1–2 m) in height with prickly stems, much given to suckering, creating big stands.

In the course of time, crosses took place between the Gallicas and *Rosa phoenicea* a single white rose of Asia, producing a group now known as the **Summer Damasks**, as if of Damascus, where they were possibly prevalent. They are white and pink in color, stronger and bigger than the Gallicas, even more scented, and perhaps more lax in growth. Their leaves are a lighter green.

A cross of Gallica with the Musk Rose, *Rosa moschata*, another Asian, produced the similar **Autumn Damasks** which were the only ones to deliver a limited second flowering. All the others flowered only once, in early summer.

Further hybridization between the Damasks and *Rosa canina*, the wild dog rose of the English hedgerows, created a further group, the **Albas** or white roses. Some are pink but there are only pastel shades—no purples like the Gallicas. They are more upright like Canina and make noble shrubs. The leaves have a characteristic blue-green appearance.

Later came the **Centifolias** or 100-petalled roses, raised from the others in the 17th century by Dutch hybridists, and to be seen in the great Dutch flower paintings of the period. Finally, there were the **Mosses**, which are really aberrant Centifolias which have devel-

Rosa 'Madame Alfred Carrière' is a particularly beautiful Noisette rose.

oped a mossy excrescence on the stems and sepals.

All the above should not be taken as ultimate truth but as an attempt to classify and explain the origins of the various forms. They existed in limited numbers until about 1800 but thereafter many new varieties were created by hybridists, mainly in France. Most of these have since been lost.

Meanwhile, in China and East Asia, separated to some degree from the West by climatic and physical barriers, another group of garden roses had developed—the **China Roses**. These were more gracile plants with twiggy growth and more delicate flowers and most importantly, flowering was re-peated throughout the season. In the late

18th and early 19th centuries four kinds, in particular, were brought to Europe. Two were low to medium bushes and, in England, were named 'Parsons' Pink China' (or 'Old Blush' or 'The Monthly Rose') and 'Slater's Crimson China' (or *R. sempervirens*). They had both been developed from a wild China rose, *R. spontanea chinensis*. The other two— 'Hume's Blush Tea Scented China' and 'Park's Yellow Tea Scented China'— were short climbers with fragrant flowers, one repeat flowering, the other not. They were, in fact, hybrids between the wild China rose and a tall strong growing wild 'tea scented' climber with large single creamy white flowers— *R. gigantea*. They are now known botanically as *R.* × *odorata*. In the early days, they were known not as 'chinensis' but as 'indica', many having come via India. The French still call them 'Roses de Bengale'.

Inevitably, the Chinas and Gallicas were hybridized to produce new forms with new characteristics, including the hardiness and appearance of the one with the repeat flowering propensity of the other. So began the rose revolution of the 19th century with the creation of a great many new types and ending with the advent of the modern roses—the Hybrid Teas.

The first of the new types were the **Bourbons** from a cross between 'Old Blush' and the Autumn Damask, which occurred initially in the Île de Bourbon in the Indian Ocean. Then there were the **Portlands** named for a Lady Portland and also known as **Perpetual Damasks**, from a Gallica/Damask/China cross.

At the same time, the two tea-scented Chinas were being further developed and a whole new race of **Tea Roses** was introduced mainly in France, since they were somewhat tender and unsuited to colder climates by virtue of their *Gigantea* ancestry. They were, and are, beautiful graceful roses with typical high centered pointed buds and flowers.

Crossing between the Chinas and the Musk Rose gave rise to a race of Climbers known as the **Noisettes**. Their story is told in the entry on 'Champney's Pink Cluster'.

As the century progressed, intense

The Ramblers are well-loved because of their delicious fragrance, which comes not from the petals, but the stamens.

Rosa 'Chapeau de Napoleon'—popular since 1827.

Rosa 'Lamarque' is an old favorite.

hybridization and selection involving many thousands of seedlings, mainly in open field cultivation gave rise to a further group, a new hardy and semi-remontant race, the **Hybrid Perpetuals**, rather coarse growing big shrubs of a number of types, with large flowers in a wide range of colors. This was the dominant class in Victorian England. The Teas were confined to sheltered spots or to greenhouses.

Eventually, towards the end of the century, hybrids were produced between the two groups, creating the **Hybrid Teas** (or **Large-flowered Roses**)and their allies the **Floribundas** (or **Cluster-flowered Roses**), which combined the best qualities of both kinds. These swept away all before them and many of the older roses ceased to be grown and were lost; some to be recovered later through the efforts of old rose enthusiasts.

A further group was developed during Victorian times — the **Ramblers** — a class that was greatly extended in the early 1900s by the introduction of two wild rambling roses from the Far East, *R. multiflora* and *R. wichuraiana*. These and the **Scotch Roses** (described later) complete the group known as the Old

Garden Roses in the new simplified system of classification adopted by the World Federation of Rose Societies in 1979. In the descriptions which follow in this chapter, however, the old terminology has been retained in designating Hybrid Teas, for example, in order to be historically correct. They are also called 'Large-flowered Roses'.

The Old Garden Roses are also known widely as Heritage Roses or Historic Roses.

The developments continue with many new groups having come into existence in recent years. We should not forget, however, that had it not been for that repeat flowering gene in the Chinas, our modern roses would still be as seasonal as daffodils and camellias. Many of the individual rose descriptions in this chapter have more details about the historical process involved in the story of the Old Garden Roses.

AIMÉE VIBERT
Noisette

Named for the breeder's daughter, this rose is a cross between 'Champney's Pink Cluster' and a *R. sempervirens* double form (see 'Felicité et Perpétue'), so it is a mixture of China, Musk and Evergreen roses. The small double white flowers are borne in clusters which come late in the season but which repeat continuously. The respected rosarian Graham Thomas called it 'the only perpetual white climber of any quality', which is perhaps going a little far. It can be trained on supports or left free standing where there is room for its long arching, almost thornless shoots. Alternatively, it can be used for a ground cover but it is not as dense as *wichuraiana*. The scent is musky. Sometimes it is a little shy of flowering.

ALBA MAXIMA
(Jacobite Rose, Bonnie Prince Charlie's Rose)
Alba

Worn as an emblem by the Jacobites in the insurrection of 1745, the once blooming white roses are thought to have been derived long ago from a combination of Damask and a form of Canina (the dog rose of the English hedgerows). The leaves are gray or blue-green. The flowers are pure white, although the later ones are shades of pink. 'Alba Maxima', the great white rose, has double white flowers with some 50–60 petals, on a large, tall, rather gaunt bush to 10 feet (3 m). The white form of Canina in the ancestry of this rose could be a type called 'Laxa' which is used as a stock rose in Europe nowadays.

ALBÉRIC BARBIER
Rambler

Most rambling garden roses are derived from two wild 'rambling' roses—R.

Rosa 'Albéric Barbier'

Rosa 'Alba Maxima'

Rosa 'Aimée Vibert'

Rosa 'Albertine'

Rosa 'Alfred de Dalmas'

multiflora and *R. wichuraiana* — crossed with garden roses. Many were created early in the 20th century, this one by 'Barbier of Orleans', a *wichuraiana* cross with 'Shirley Hibberd' (a yellow Tea Rose of 1874 named for a famous horticultural writer and journalist). It is a very dense and vigorous ground cover, or rambler to 23 feet (7 m) or more and could cover a house. The small creamy yellow flowers are borne in clusters and are fragrant. The foliage is a glossy dark green, characteristic of *wichuraiana*, which is known also as the 'Memorial Rose' in America for its use on graves, where the trailing shoots can make a dense covering.

ALBERTINE
Rambler
English gardens are resplendent with 'Albertine' in June. Among the best of the ramblers, it was bred by Barbier in 1921 from *R. wichuraiana* and 'Mrs. A.R. Wadell'. It is a most rampant, well-armed large leafed plant and is covered in midsummer with large semi-double salmon pink flowers, which are very large for a rambler (25 petals). The foliage is typically glossy and the plant

will grow to 20 feet (6 m) on a wall, fence or the side of a house (not recommended), or to 10 × 16 feet (3 × 5 m) if left as an unsupported cascading shrub. This would be appropriate only in a large garden and it could be interplanted with a repeat flowerer, for example 'New Dawn'.

ALFRED DE DALMAS
(Mousseline)
Moss
This popular rose was introduced in 1855 by Jean Laffay and should not be confused with another rose of this name, which was introduced by Robert et Moreau in 1881. Sometimes it happens that the name of a rose is changed, either because the original is perhaps too difficult to pronounce, or because a new name is patriotic (like the famous 'American Beauty' which was renamed from 'Madame Ferdinand Jamain'). This rose has blush pink flowers and is said by some to smell of honeysuckle, by others, of sweet peas. Moss is an aberration which occurs on Centifolia roses, or on some of the Damasks from which they are derived. The moss is slight on this rose.

ALISTER STELLA GRAY
(Golden Rambler)
Noisette

This rose was raised by Alexander Hill Gray of Bath and introduced by George Paul in 1894. The provenance was not recorded. It grows to 8 feet (2.4 m) as a shrub, and up to 16 feet (5 m) on a wall or trellis or at the back of a border, for which it is very suitable. It blooms continually from summer to late autumn, the double flowers being pale yellow with an orange center and borne in small clusters. There is a pronounced musk scent. It is slow in starting and does best in warm spots. The shoots have a kind of zig-zag growth which is found in some of the Musks.

AMADIS
Boursault

The Boursaults are a small group of thornless once-flowering climber-ramblers, created in France in the early 19th century. They are generally considered to have been a cross between the China Rose and *R. pendulina*, a small pink alpine thornless rose of southern Europe. An alternative theory proposes

R. blanda, the 'Hudson's Bay Rose' as the second parent. In any event, the Boursaults are sterile, do not set seed, nor repeat flower, except perhaps for an odd bloom. They were once called *R.* × *l'heritierana*, but were later named after Henri Boursault another French botanist. 'Amadis' climbs with long arching shoots to about 14 × 10 feet (4 × 3 m) with smallish semi-double reddish-purple rather raggedy and variously shaped flowers. It flowers early.

AMELIA
Alba

This is a smaller Alba, introduced by Vibert in 1823. It has large pink semi-double flowers with glossy golden stamens. It grows to just over 3 feet (1 m) tall, and has a strong perfume. It is not so vigorous and possibly contains some admixture of Damask. Another of the Albas is 'Alba Semi-plena', the White Rose of York, which has semi-double white flowers (8–12 petals), and is slightly smaller than 'Alba Maxima' but more vigorous and is found growing wild in some areas. It is used in Bul-

Rosa 'Alister Stella Gray'

Rosa 'Amadis'

garia, along with 'Kazanlik', in the creation of rose attar. Alba roses benefit from some winter pruning, cutting back the main shoots by about one third, and trimming the side shoots.

ANAÏS SÉGALES
Gallica

This is classified as a Gallica but is probably a Gallica/Centifolia introduced by Vibert in 1837. It forms a small rounded bush to 3 feet (1 m). If it is grown on its own roots or from a cutting, or if the graft is planted below the ground level, it will sucker freely and make large strands. This is characteristic of all the Gallicas. The flowers are variously described as rosy purple, rosy lilac, or deep pink. They are smallish, compact and rosette shaped in a formal way. It is extremely easy to grow and pops up throughout the garden, but the flowering period is short.

Rosa 'Amelia'

Rosa 'Anäis Ségales'

Rosa 'Anna Olivier'

Rosa 'Archiduc Joseph'

ANNA OLIVIER
Tea

This strong branching bush with mid-green leaves was introduced by Ducher of Lyons in 1872. The young growth of teas is an attractive red. The flowers are high centered and a mixture of flesh pink and rose. It blooms freely and continuously. Tea rose flowers tend to have weak necks and so hang down, which is not a bad fault in rain. Tea roses are so called, either because they have the scent of a freshly opened tea packet, or because they were brought to Europe from China in tea clippers. Known botanically as *R.* × *odorata*, they are hybrids between the wild China rose and *R. gigantea*, a single cream-flowered, tender climbing rose native to China, which has the tea scent.

ARCHIDUC JOSEPH
(Monsieur Tillier)
Tea

'Archiduc Joseph' was introduced by Gilbert Nabonnand, and is a look-alike of 'Monsieur Tillier', introduced by Bernaix in 1891. Discussion rages in the old rose world about whether or not they are the same rose. Any difference is certainly hard to spot. This is a vigorous shrub 5 feet × 5 feet (1.5 × 1.5 m) though it can grow to 14 feet (4 m) in shrubbery conditions. Flower color is deep rose to purple with orange and russet shades, and the flowers open flattish. The first Tea roses are of French origin, and most are too tender to survive very cold winters. It was once customary in North America to lift them in autumn, winter them in frames and re-plant in spring!

AUTUMNALIS
Noisette

'Autumnalis' has been described as an early Hybrid Musk of unknown date and origin, but grown as early as 1812. It has also been equated with 'Princesse de Nassaut' attributed to Laffay in 1835. It grows to 10 feet (3 m). The flowers are of musk rose style but are semi-double, creamy white with a slight scent. The leaves are light green and the shoots have a zig-zag shape (see 'Aimée Vibert'). As the name implies it flowers late in the season. There are many forms of the musk rose, all of considerable but varying vigor. They tend to have gray leaves and all share the musk perfume.

BARON GIROD DE L'AIN
Hybrid Perpetual

A splendid name, this rose was introduced by Reverchon in 1897. The flowers are an unusual and attractive bright red, the petals wavy-edged and blotched white, like a carnation. The bush is upstanding. Flowers are bountiful in summer and repeat later. It is a sport of 'Eugene Furst', a Hybrid Perpetual of 1875 from 'Soupert et Notting', to which it can revert. It is said to be more vigorous than the other rose of this type, 'Roger Lambelin'. Watch for the worst pest of roses, which are tiny thrips. These can appear in large numbers in early summer, get into the buds and cause disfigurement and discoloration of the flowers. There are no satisfactory cures.

Rosa 'Baron Girod de l'Ain'

Rosa 'Autumnalis'

BARONNE HENRIETTE DE SNOY
Tea

Raised by Bernaix of Lyons in 1897, this rose is a cross between 'Gloire de Dijon' (1853) and 'Madame Lombard' (1877). It grows to between 4–5 feet (1.4–1.5 m). The flowers are globular, high centered, and flesh pink, with a deeper reverse. They are borne on stiff stems. They are produced throughout the season but in flushes, which is the normal way with tea roses. This rose tolerates the cold well, but is also suited to warm climates where it will usually flower well in the winter. Crossed with the hardy Hybrid Perpetuals, the teas originated the Large-flowered Roses to which they brought the high centered flowers.

BARONNE PRÉVOST
Hybrid Perpetual

'Baronne Prévost' was raised by Desprez in 1842. He sold it for about

Rosa 'Baronne Henriette de Snoy'

100 francs to Scipion Cochet, who introduced it. It was a very good buy, for it became one of the best known roses of its time. The shrub grows to $3^{1}/_{2} \times 3$ feet (1.3×1 m) or more and makes a handsome bush. The flowers which come throughout the season, are large and bright rose, flat in shape with a green button eye. It is still very vigorous if a little coarse. Vigor in roses seems to be greatest in those nearer in make-up to the wild or species form. A wild rose seedling can make an enormous growth, where a complex garden rose would fail completely.

BELLE AMOUR
Alba

This rose was 'discovered' by Nancy Lindsay in 1950, in a French convent garden. It grows vigorously to 6 feet (2 m). The flowers are semi-double and salmon pink in color, with pronounced yellow stamens. Some place it among the Damasks. Its claim to fame lies in its scent, described variously as spicy, aniseed, or by Graham Thomas as of myrrh. The flower color and the scent

Rosa 'Baronne Prévost'

Rosa 'Belle Amour'

Rosa 'Belle de Crecy'

resemble the Hybrid Scotch Rose 'Ayrshire Splendens', and also the Gallica 'Belle Isis', which was used by rose breeder David Austin as a parent of 'Constance Spry', which does not repeat flower, although it was the first of Austin's great race of English Roses — roses which look like old fashioned roses but repeat flower.

BELLE DE CRECY
Gallica

Attributed to Alexandre Hardy and introduced by Roeser of Calais in 1829, this is a very fragrant rose changing from cerise to a soft violet on exposure to the sun. The growth is lax with thin shoots to about 5 feet (1.5 m) and is practically thornless. The flowers are wide reflexing and flat with a pronounced button eye. It is not a sturdy rose and needs support from its neighbors. The Chateau de Crecy was a home of Madame de Pompadour, mistress of Louis XV, and the rose is probably named for an historic connection. It is not a pure Gallica and it displays China characteristics.

Rosa 'Blush Damask'

BLUSH DAMASK
Damask

The origin of this rose is unknown, but literature dates it to 1759. It resembles a

Gallica in many ways and also *R. pimpinellifolia* in its bristly stems, but is placed in the Summer Damasks. Like a Gallica, it grows to 6 feet (2 m) making a large bush. It suckers freely. Flowers are lilac pink, multitudinous, and nodding. They are rather fleeting and dead-heading is needed to ensure an attractive bush. It grows very easily, will put up with any treatment and is best placed in a raised, even dry position, such as a bank where it can arch down. The Summer Damasks are thought to be hybrids of *R. gallica* and *R. phoenicea*, a musk-type wild rose of Asia Minor.

BLUSH NOISETTE
Noisette

This seedling of 'Champney's Pink Cluster' was the first Noisette to be sold to the public and it is still highly regard by rose gardeners. It started its life in South Carolina. Loosely double, perfectly formed blush-pink blooms open from dark pink buds. The dainty petals are supported on glossy, green foliage. Many declare that the perfume is strongly clove-like. It is often seen on pillars or as a hedge. The rose is vigorous, healthy, and continues to bloom into the autumn. It does not mind light shade. Redouté, who published a series of portfolios entitled *Les Roses* between 1817 and 1824, has portrayed it as *Rosa noisettiana*.

BLUSH RAMBLER
Rambler

A Multiflora rambler introduced in 1903 by Cant's of Colchester and bred from 'Crimson Rambler' × 'The Garland', Turner's 'Crimson Rambler' was brought from Japan and distributed by Turner's of Slough. It was also called 'The Engineer' because it was an engineer, Albert Smith, who sent it home to Edinburgh. It was a sensation in its day and set a trend but has now been discarded for better varieties. 'Blush Rambler' is almost thornless, grows to 16 feet (5 m) and has small, light pink scented flowers. All these ramblers can be grown on pillars, trellises or arches or as weeping standards.

BOTZARIS
Damask

This Summer Damask is dated to 1856 but unfortunately, the parentage is not recorded. It makes a small bush to 3 feet (1 m) high. The very double flowers are creamy white with a button eye. The leaves are light green and would seem to indicate some Alba content. The fragrance is quite pronounced. The Albas themselves are thought to be derived from the Damasks and *R. canina*. Much of the work investigating rose origins was done by Dr C. C. Hurst (1870–1947) and published by Graham Thomas. The Damask roses are notable for their strong perfume. They are undoubtedly complex and it is reasonable to accept that they did in fact originate around Damascus in Syria.

Rosa 'Blush Rambler'

Rosa 'Boule de Neige'

BOULE DE NEIGE
(Snowball)
Bourbon

This rose was introduced by Lacharme of Lyons in 1867. The flowers are pure white and symmetrical, borne in small clusters and reflexing almost to a ball, hence the name. There is a hint of crimson in the bud and the flowers are borne over a long season. The growth is slender to 6 feet (1.8 m), with dark green glossy foliage. For best effect it should be planted among other low bushes. It was bred from a Bourbon and a Perpetual Damask. The Bourbons were named for the Île de Bourbon in the Indian Ocean where the first

Rosa 'Botzaris'

accidental cross between a Damask and a China heralded the great rose revolution, the resultant 'Rose Edouard' (1817) being the first Bourbon rose.

Rosa 'Bourbon Queen'

Rosa 'Bullata'

BOURBON QUEEN
(Queen of the Bourbons, Souvenir de la Princesse de Lamballe)
Bourbon

'Bourbon Queen' was introduced by Mauget of Orleans in 1838. The flowers are rose pink semi-double and cupped, and the shrub grows to 6 feet (2 m). It is vigorous and long-lasting. It can maintain itself in the wild and so is an old cottage garden favorite. It flowers plentifully but cannot be relied on to do so in autumn. The Bourbons are notable for their large silky petals, making circular cupped flowers and have rather large leaves on compact and bright green vigorous canes. They were bred throughout the 19th century. Their era was really from about 1834–1870 and they gave way eventually to the more spectacular Hybrid Perpetuals, which were bred from them and the Perpetual Damasks.

BULLATA
(Lettuce-leafed rose)
Centifolia

'Bulla' is Latin for bubble, and 'bullata' means blistered or puckered, which describes the very large leaves of this rose. In all other respects it is the same as *R. centifolia*, the 'Provence Rose'. Centifolia means literally 'hundred leaves' which is a misnomer—in this context, it refers to the petals, the pink flowers being exceedingly double. 'Bullata' is very double, very fragrant, very straggly and droopy. This rose used to be thought of as very ancient, but it has in fact been shown that it is the product of the Dutch breeders of the 17th century, being an amalgam of Gallica, Phoenicia, Moschata and Canina roses.

CAPITAINE JOHN INGRAM
Moss

This is one of Laffay's roses, and was introduced in 1856. It forms a vigorous dense thorny bush to 6 feet (2 m) with dark purple pompon-like flowers, which are very strongly scented. It is worth a place in a collection for its extreme darkness. Moss is a kind of a fragrant glandular growth on stem and bud. There are no literary references to it before about 1700, but it seems preposterous to assume that such a pronounced aberration is so recent. It seems confined to the Centifolias and the Damasks. Moss-less plants can sport in part, or whole, to mossiness and vice versa. The amount of moss can be variable. Moss roses were very popular in Victorian times.

CARDINAL DE RICHELIEU
Gallica

This rose was introduced in 1840 by Laffay of Auteil who, it is said, got it from a Dutch grower. It is not a true Gallica, showing some China characteristics. It grows to 6 feet (2 m) and is very bushy with dark purple double flowers, which are lightly fragrant. This rose needs good cultivation, and careful pruning, which with Gallicas, is best done after flowering, because they will

not repeat in the same season; the next year's best flowers will be on new growth. Laffay named it for Duc Armand Jean du Plessis, the Cardinal de Richelieu (1585–1642), chief minister of Louis XIII.

Rosa 'Capitaine John Ingram'

Rosa 'Cardinal de Richelieu'

CELESTIAL
(Celeste)
Alba

'Celestial' is said to be of Dutch origin. The flowers are a delicate soft pink and semi-double on a vigorous bushy shrub, growing to 6 feet (2 m) or more. The Albas, unlike the Damasks, are rigid shrubs. Graham Thomas writes that he has heard tell that this rose features in the history of the Suffolk Regiment. After the Battle of Minden on August 1 1759, during the Seven Years War, soldiers of the regiment, following the retreating French, passed through a rose garden and plucked roses to put in their hats. This is commemorated each year on Minden Day. It seems that the Albas bloomed late in that year! They are all, of course, once blooming only.

CÉLINE FORESTIER
Noisette

Some classify this as a Climbing Tea since the Tea side of its ancestry seems particularly apparent. It was introduced in 1842 by Trouillard of Anger and named for a close friend. It is similar to 'Lamarque' of which it may be a seedling. It is not, however, as vigorous as 'Lamarque', but the flowers are a little deeper in color, being pale yellow and quartered, borne in clusters and fra-

Rosa 'Céline Forestier'

Rosa 'Celestial'

Rosa centifolia muscosa

Rosa 'Champion of the World'

grant. Growth is to about 10 feet (3 m), and flowering is repetitive. Because the Noisettes and Teas became terribly mixed up, it is sometimes hard to know where to draw the line.

CELSIANA
Damask

A characteristic Damask, tall to about 5 feet (1.5 m) with arching canes bearing light green foliage. The silky flowers, light to medium pink, fading to white, are borne in clusters and are wide and open, showing bright yellow stamens. It is a mid-18th century rose created in Holland and introduced to France by M. F. Cels. It was painted by both Van Huysum and Redouté. Gwen Fagan in her magnificently illustrated book of personal anecdotage *Roses at the Cape of Good Hope* writes of its prevalence there in old gardens where it was no doubt introduced by Dutch settlers in the 18th century. It is not to be confused with 'Celeste' or 'Celestial'.

CENTIFOLIA MUSCOSA
(Old Pink Moss)
Centifolia

The Centifolias are prone to give sports with mossy excrescences and this rose is *R. centifolia* with moss. The flowers are very double, and mid-pink. The effect of moss is created by an enlargement of the glands over the flower stalk and sepals; the latter are quite enlarged in the Centifolias. This 'moss' is sticky and fragrant. 'Centifolia Muscosa' was the first of the Mosses, originating about 1700, and was followed, particularly in the 19th century, by a succession of Mosses of varying value and color. Ralph Moore in California has bred miniatures with moss.

CHAMPION OF THE WORLD
Hybrid Perpetual

Some classify this among the Bourbons. The name has been described as presumptuous by Peter Beales, and the rose as quite meek by Graham Thomas. It was raised in 1894 by a Mr. Woodhouse, from 'Hermosa' and 'Magna Charta'. There is a very similar rose, 'Madame Degraw', a Hybrid Bourbon of 1885 which may be the same. The medium sized flowers can be described as refined; they are rosy lilac in color. The bush is low-growing to 6 feet (2 m) and sprawling. Nomenclature can get mixed up over the years, either by accident or design, but a well-chosen name for a rose can improve its marketability considerably! It might be thought, however, that Mr. Woodhouse has overdone it in this case.

Rosa 'Champney's Pink Cluster'

Rosa 'Chapeau de Napoleon'

CHAMPNEY'S PINK CLUSTER
Noisette

The accepted story of this rose is that in 1812 John Champney of Charleston, South Carolina, crossed *R. moschata* with 'Old Blush' ('Parsons' Pink China'). The resultant seedlings were climbers, showing characteristics of both parents, and were named for the grower. They flowered once only. However, Philippe Noisette, also of Charleston and later of Paris, sowed seeds of this rose and obtained seedlings which were short and denser but flowered repeatedly like the Chinas. This was due to the segregation of the recessive gene, a mechanism discovered by Mendel later in the century, but not then known. They were introduced in France in 1817 as 'Blush Noisette' (Redouté's *R. noisettiana*). Crossed with the Tea Scented Chinas they gave rise to the Noisettes.

CHAPEAU DE NAPOLEON
(Centifolia Cristata, Crested Moss)
Moss

This rose was introduced in 1827 by Vibert. Although mossy, it is not strictly a moss rose. Rosarian Roy Shepherd, who died in 1962 (he was famous for 'Golden Wings') wrote that it was discovered growing on top of a ruined tower in Switzerland about 1820, and must therefore have been a seedling from a bird, a theory enhanced by the fact that the whole plant bore the same blossoms. The 'moss' in this rose appears only on the edges of the sepals giving a ferny effect. In bud, the whole plant resembles a cocked hat and hence the name 'Napoleon's Hat'. The flowers are deep pink and 'cabbage like' and the parent was clearly a *R. centifolia* variant.

CHARLES DE MILLS
Gallica

The origin of this rose is not recorded. It may be supposed, however, that many of these old roses were growing in gardens from time immemorial and were taken to, or selected by, nurserymen for propagation during the Age of the Gallicas. This is a true Gallica. The flatness of the flowers is a notable characteristic. It is large, rather coarse not unlike a carnation, rosy purple in color with a central green hollow eye. It is a very compact shrub to 5 feet (1.5 m) with lush green foliage and is considered by some to have very little fragrance.

This rose will make great thickets of growth which are spectacular for a short time in summer and are suitable for large or wild gardens.

CHEVY CHASE
Rambler

This rose was bred from *R. soulieana* × 'Eblouissant'. It has small, full, dark crimson blooms with 65 petals that are borne in great clusters and cover the vigorous canes, which can grow 15 feet (4.5 m) in one season. These are rather stiff and difficult to train. When in full flower this is a spectacular Rambler, although it is a high maintenance plant that needs to be pruned for best effect. The foliage is light gray-green, wrinkled and dense; the prickles are hooked. After its early summer blooming, it should be deadheaded. It is prone to rust. It was named after Chevy Chase, Maryland, where it was raised by Hansen in 1939. It won the Dr W. Van Fleet Medal in 1941.

CHLORIS
(Rosee du Matin)
Alba

This rose is known poetically as 'Dew of the Morning'. It grows to 6 feet (2 m)

Rosa 'Chloris'

Rosa 'Charles de Mills'

with very dark green leaves and few thorns. It is very ancient. The flowers are similar to those of 'Celeste'. Dog roses, from which the Albas are in part derived, are very variable due probably to the unusual arrangement of 28 chromosomes in the female germ cell and seven in the male. The introduced types found in the wild in Australia and New Zealand are usually rather small-flowered, and do not compare with the beauty of those in the English hedgerows in June.

COMMANDANT BEAUREPAIRE
(Panachée d'Anger)
Bourbon

'Panachée' means variegated or mixed. This rose was introduced by the French

Rosa 'Commandant Beaurepaire'

firm of Moreau et Robert in 1874. The ample large fragrant flowers are bright rose pink, streaked or striped purple or violet and marbled white. They repeat occasionally. The plant can be very vigorous with long arching shoots and long pointed leaves, almost in the style of a banksia. Graham Thomas remarks that the name 'Beaurepaire' was given in error, but does not elaborate. The growers stated that 'Panachée' was remontant and 'Beaurepaire' was not. However, the one we grow nowadays is—at least sometimes! Names are changed in the rose world from time to time, either by error, by design, or for marketing reasons.

COMPLICATA
Gallica

This is not at all like a conventional Gallica, growing rampantly to 10 feet (3 m) with strong arching branches. It bears deep pink single flowers as much as 4¹/₂ in (12 cm) wide, with a white eye and prominent yellow stamens. It is probably a Gallica/Canina cross. It is

Rosa 'Complicata'

Rosa 'Conditorum'

best grown scrambling up a tree, or at the back of a border. It is very beautiful in its brief season but the hips are not worth waiting for, so it is best pruned after flowering. The flower is not at all complicated, the word in Latin meaning merely 'folded' or 'furled'.

COMTE DE CHAMBORD
Portland

This rose was introduced by Robert et Moreau in 1860. An alternative name for this group of roses was 'Damask Perpetual'. Their origin is unclear but they probably came from Italy to England and then to France, where they were named for the Duchess of Portland, a rose enthusiast. The first, the 'Portland Rose', is a red rose derived from a Damask or Gallica and 'Slaters Crimson China'. 'Comte de Chambord' has clear pink, medium size, double flowers, somewhat repeating, flat and full, in the old style. The canes are whippy and arching to 6 feet (2 m). Chambord is a castle on the Loire River.

Rosa 'Comte de Chambord'

The Comte was a pretender to the French throne calling himself Henri V. This rose seems identical to 'Madame Boll'.

CONDITORUM
(The Hungarian rose)
Gallica

This is a very old Gallica resembling, in style, 'Officinalis' and 'Tuscany'. The shrub is bushy to 5 feet (1.5 m), the flowers seem double, rather loose, deeper than the 'Officinalis' red and lighter than the 'Tuscany' purple, with showy yellow stamens. The petals are said to keep their scent and color when dried, a characteristic which perhaps led to the name. 'Conditorum' refers to storage and the petals were used in the making of conserves, presumably in Hungary. Rose petal jam is still made extensively in the countries of south-eastern Europe. The Gallicas had their heyday in the first half of the 19th century before the advent of the Bourbons and Hybrid Perpetuals.

CRAMOISI SUPÉRIEUR
(Lady Brisbane)
China

This rose was raised by Cocquereau in France in 1835, released by Vibert and originally named 'Agrippina'. It is a typical China, petite and wiry with thin stems and small leaves, building up to a small bush to 3 feet (1 m). The flowers are small, crimson, semi-double and cupped. They repeat regularly throughout the year. The foliage is rather sparse, but can be cut back regularly to promote bushiness and continual flowering. There is also a climbing form which first

appeared in 1885. These roses retain their color well in sun. 'Cramoisi' is French for crimson or scarlet.

DE MEAUX
(Centifolia Pompona)
Centifolia

This is one of a number of miniature Centifolias growing to about 3 feet (1 m) with tiny light green leaves and pink pompon-type double flowers. It was known in 1700 and may have been named for a gardening Bishop de Meaux, and is likely to have been a sport of a normal Centifolia. It is, in fact, a charming old fashioned miniature and should be grown in a suitable situation, for example in a rock garden (unless you are an Alpine purist). There is also a white version and both are a little addicted to black spot. But black spot comes and goes and is by no means the bogey that some imagine.

DESPREZ À FLEURS JAUNES
Noisette

The name is usually shortened to 'Jaune Desprez', as it is 'Desprez' with yellow flower. It is not unlike 'Céline Forestier'

Rosa 'De Meaux'

but the flowers are a darker shade of yellow-orange-apricot. It has been known for stocks to have been mixed and one sold for the other. It was grown from seed by Jean Desprez from 'Blush Noisette' and 'Park's Yellow' around 1828. These two have had a remarkable variety of offspring. Desprez sold it for 3,000 francs, an enormous sum. It has retained its vigor and can grow to 20 × 20 feet (6 × 6 m). It is a remarkably fragrant rose. Desprez was an enthusiastic amateur, and not averse to perpetuating his name.

DEVONIENSIS
Tea

This English Tea rose was introduced by Foster in Devonport in 1841, and released in 1858 in climbing form. The flowers are creamy white, very double, large and very fragrant, commencing

Rosa 'Devoniensis'

Rosa 'Desprez á Fleurs Jaunes'

Rosa 'Duchesse de Brabant'

Rosa 'Duchesse de Montebello'

early and produced throughout the season. It is also known as the 'magnolia rose'. There are three versions—a low growing rather weakly bush found in England, a medium strong bush described in the literature but not easily found, and the climbing form available in Australia. It is truly enormous with strong thick thorny branches reaching 14 feet (4 m) and very vigorous. The seed parent is presumed to be 'Park's Yellow', the pollen parent 'Smith's Yellow'. 'Park's Yellow Tea Scented China' was one of the original four China roses brought to Europe.

DUCHESSE DE BRABANT
(Comtesse Ouwaroff, Comtesse de Labarthe)
Tea

One of the famous teas, this rose was raised by Bérnede in France in 1850. The flowers are soft rosy pink, double with 45 petals and cupped, this cupping being a distinguishing characteristic. The bush has a spreading habit growing to 5 feet (1.5 m), or higher in a shrubbery. It also looks good as a standard. 'Duchesse de Brabant' is very repeat flowering. It does best in a mild to warm climate.

DUCHESSE DE MONTEBELLO
Gallica

Raised by Laffay before 1838, this is another Hybrid China classified with the Gallicas. The china-like flowers are a very pretty rose to flesh pink, but the bush is characteristically gallica-like with prickly stems to 5 feet (1.5 m) suckering widely. If you don't want it to sucker, place the graft well above the ground level. The flower has been described as very feminine, the petals like chiffon. The Duc de Montebello was one of Napoleon's marshals and acquired the castle of that name near Milan. Laffay was a very successful nurseryman in Paris and was responsible for some of the early Hybrid Perpetuals, including the famous 'La Reine' in 1842.

EMPRESS JOSEPHINE
(Frankfurt Rose, R. francofurtana)
Gallica

'Empress Josephine' is a practically thornless rose with large stipules, grayish leaves and hips. It is well-branched growing up to 6 feet (2 m). It has also been named *R. turbinata*, the hips being reminiscent of the tops of turbans. The flowers are slightly fragrant, and are purple. This rose has been recognized as a hybrid between *R. gallica* and *R. cinnamonea* (now named *R. majalis*) a wild rose native to southern Europe and west Asia. The nomenclature of this rose is a little obscure and our knowledge of it has been enhanced by a good deal of detective work by Graham Thomas, the noted English rosarian. It was, of course, named for the rose loving Empress Josephine.

FANTIN-LATOUR
Centifolia
Named for the illustrious French painter, Henri Fantin-Latour, this is a

Rosa 'Empress Josephine'

Rosa 'Fantin-Latour'

very handsome shrub rose. It is fragrant, vigorous and bushy to about 6 feet (2 m), and flowers only once. The provenance is unknown, though it originated as late as 1900. The flowers are unusual in color, pale pink with a touch of lilac and are of characteristic old rose shape, full and cupped with the outer petals later reflexing. It is not a true Centifolia, having aspects of Gallica and China but not, alas, to the extent of repeat flowering. This rose is considered to be among the most fragrant of all.

FÉLICITÉ ET PERPÉTUE
Rambler

Dated to 1828 and named by the Duc d'Orleans for his twin daughters, who themselves were named after two Christian virgins, Felicitas and Perpetua, martyred in Carthage in AD 203. A good deal has been written on the subject of this name, the 'Perpétue' connoting perpetual, and this rose is not. The cognoscenti omit the 'et'. Some misguided writers have added an accent to the final 'e'. This is incorrect. This rose is neither *wichuraiana* nor Multiflora, but derived from *R. sempervirens* a wild evergreen rose of southern Europe

with fragrant single white flowers. Tall and vigorous to 6 feet (2 m) with small white rosette flowers with a touch pink, it flowers in summer only.

FÉLICITÉ PARMENTIER
Alba

This rose is said to date from before 1834 (which is probably the first catalog mention date), but the origin is unknown. The Parmentiers were Belgian nurserymen. This rose is a low grower to about 3 feet (1 m) with plentiful, rather flat reflexing, very light pink flowers, full petalled. The scent is not strong. The Albas are said to tolerate shade and they will do so more than some roses. Generally, however, roses require full sun and plenty of space and air. Their origin was in the temperate grasslands of the northern hemisphere, where they had to survive a number of ice ages. Roses are not found in equatorial rainforests!

FERDINAND PICHARD
Hybrid Perpetual

This is quite a late comer in its class, having been created in 1921. It is a richly

Rosa 'Félicité Parmentier'

Rosa 'Félicité et Perpétue'

Rosa 'Ferdinand Pichard'

scented striped rose, carmine and white with medium luscious almost double flowers on a vigorous bush to 6 feet (2 m) of compact growth. It has been compared with 'Commandant Beaurepaire'. This rose will repay 'pegging down' (see 'Madame Isaac Pereire') a process which will stimulate many more blooms on short stems. The same effect, to a lesser degree, can be obtained by encouraging arching. A feature of this rose is its ability to produce flowers continuously into autumn, that is, it is repeating or 'remontant'.

FISHER HOLMES
Hybrid Perpetual

'Fisher Holmes' was introduced by E. Verdier of Paris in 1865. A seedling of 'Maurice Bernadin', which in its turn was a seedling of 'Général Jacqueminot', this rose has camellia-like reddish scarlet flowers, shaded velvety crimson. The

Rosa 'Fisher Holmes'

blooms are recurrent, the bush upright and the scent is good. A problem might be lack of vigor. Very popular roses tended to get over-propagated, or sometimes there is poor bud selection by growers anxious to raise as much stock as possible to satisfy the market, with consequent degeneration over the years. So care should be taken when buying such roses and there must be good cultivation. Overcrowding or root competition is fatal.

Rosa 'Général Kléber'

FRANÇOIS JURANVILLE
Rambler

The late Jack Harkness praised this rose as the most beautiful of all the *wichuraiana* hybrids. It was bred by Barbier in France in 1906 from *R. wichuraiana* × 'Madame Laurette Messimy'. The bright salmon-pink blooms appear as clusters over a long summer flowering period. They are a deeper pink in the center with a yellow base. The quilled and quartered petals appear brighter in the shade. It has an apple fragrance. Reaching almost 25 feet (8 m) at maturity, it has upright, very vigorous canes with shiny dark leaves, which are bronze-green at the edges, and a few prickles. It seems happiest climbing a tree although it is often used as a ground cover.

GALLICA OFFICINALIS
Gallica

This is a double form of the old single wild Gallica, the French rose, native of southern Europe and west Asia. Doubling occurs when stamens are transformed to petals and such forms were selected for gardens long ago. It is also known as the 'apothecary's rose' because it was used in medicine, the 'Rose of Provins' because it was grown there for conserves, perfumes and pots-pourri, *R. rubra* because it is red, and the 'Red Rose of Lancaster', a badge in the Wars of the Roses. It is a spreading suckering dense bush up to some 4 feet (1.3 m). The flowers are semi-double, red and fragrant with few thorns.

GÉNÉRAL KLÉBER
Moss

This rose was introduced by Robert in 1856. Robert succeeded Vibert at Angers, and continued, with Moreau, the production of first class roses. The French were as much given to calling roses by the names of their military heroes as they were to erecting triumphal arches in Paris to commemorate their successes. Général Kléber commanded Napoleon's army in Egypt and was assassinated in Cairo in 1800. This rose has bright shiny pink flowers in a moderate, almost thornless, bush with light green moss extending to the tips of the sepals. The flowers are particularly beautiful and are said to resemble crumpled tissues.

GÉNÉRAL JACQUEMINOT
Hybrid Perpetual

A famous rose from which many others are descended, it was known affectionately in Victorian times as 'General Jack'. Most experts agree that this was the first Hybrid Perpetual. It was introduced in 1853 by Rousselet of Meudon, and is said to be derived from a famous early Bourbon, 'Gloire des Rosomanes' (1825) crossed with 'Geant des Batailles' (1846). The flowers are a rich crimson, full and cabbage-like, very fragrant and with long stems borne on a moderately vigorous bush, less so now perhaps than in 1853. Jacqueminot was a French general of the time, who also founded a brewery in Paris. This may have helped the sale of both products.

GEORGES VIBERT
Gallica

Jean-Pierre Vibert was a Parisian, a soldier under Napoleon, a hardware dealer and finally a grower of roses and vines, mainly at Angers in the Loire. He and Laffay were the two 'greats' of the period, Vibert, it is said, doing the spade work, notably in creating 'Gloire des Rosomanes', and Laffay the later developments. Vibert started his collection in 1815 moving another nurseryman's stock from Paris during the occupation. Shortly before his death he said he had only two real loves — Napoleon and roses, and two profound hatreds — the grubs which ate his roses and the English who overthrew Napoleon! This rose was named for his son. It is a typical Gallica but with purplish red flowers streaked white, prettily quilled and quartered.

GHISLAINE DE FÉLIGONDE
Rambler

Bred by Turbat in 1916 from 'Goldfinch' × seedling, this rose has small, fragrant yellow-white blooms tinted flesh. They are borne in clusters of 10-20. The flowers may change their colors from yellow to pink, orange, salmon and red. It grows to 8 feet (2.4 m) high. There are few prickles and an attractive crop

Rosa 'Général Jacqueminot'

of red hips. If it is treated as a shrub or climber, it will do equally well on rich or poor soil as well as in the sun or the shade. It looks stunning tumbling down an embankment or over a wall. It produces blooms profusely in early summer and occasional clusters in autumn.

GLOIRE DE DIJON
Climbing Tea

Dean Hole (see 'Rambling Rector'), the great Victorian rosarian, wrote in his *A Book About Roses* '... if ever for some heinous crime I were miserably sentenced for the rest of my life to possess but a single rose-tree, I should desire to be supplied, on leaving the dock, with a strong plant of 'Gloire de Dijon'.' 'Strong plant' is to the point. It is difficult to find one nowadays. It was

Rosa 'Gloire de Dijon'

bred from 'Desprez a Fleur Jaune' and 'Souvenir de la Malmaison', and has rich, large buff-pink flowers, shaded orange in the center and fragrant. They are borne on a climbing shrub to 16 feet (5 m) with a long flowering season.

GLOIRE DE FRANCE
(Fanny Bias)
Gallica

The grower is not known although this rose is dated to 1820. It is low growing with reflexed pompon-type double flowers, lilac rose in color. The shrub is almost thornless. This is one of the few Gallicas which has survived from the 500–1,000 which were produced in the enthusiasm of the first half of the 19th century, in the wake of the revolution in the rose world, caused by the introduction of the China rose and the subsequent burgeoning of hybrids of all kinds.

Crosses were then made by growing hundreds of plants in proximity, collecting the seeds, and selecting the best of the progeny. Only later in the century were more scientific methods adopted.

GREAT MAIDEN'S BLUSH
Alba

This is a large arching shrub up to 8 feet (2.4 m) known since the 1400s. The blush pink informal flowers are finely perfumed, the color aptly described in the name. The foliage is grayish in the Alba fashion. The French call this rose, among other names, 'Cuisse de Nymphe', Nymph's Thigh, which is indicative of an alternative Gallic approach to nomenclature. It is also sometimes known as 'La Virginale', a name which seems quite appropriate, given its delicate color. There is, as one might expect, also a 'Small Maiden's

Rosa 'Great Maiden's Blush'

Rosa 'Hermosa'

Blush' which was recorded and perhaps raised at Kew Gardens in 1797. This is slightly smaller in all respects. These roses are apt to sport variations and there is a deeper flowered version which the French have named 'Emue' or 'stirring'! Thrips and wet weather can damage this rose considerably.

HÉNRI MARTIN
Moss

Hénri Martin was not a general but an historian. He is commemorated by Laffay with this rose of 1863. It is a red rose of shiny crimson with semi-double camellia-like blooms produced plentifully on a medium vigorous bush growing to 6 feet (2 m). The shoots are wiry and seem to be able to tolerate some shade. Heavy pruning is not

Rosa 'Henri Martin'

recommended. The mossing is moderate but attractive. The rose is worth a place in any garden, but, of course, does not repeat flower. Some mosses, however, including 'Madame Louis Léveque' and

'Soupert et Notting', do repeat; repeat flowering depends on the degree of China rose in the ancestry.

HERMOSA
China

'Hermosa' is sometimes classified with the Bourbons from which it may be a reversion. It is a low growing plant to about 3 feet (1 m), and is tidy and compact, with small clear mid-pink symmetrical double flowers. It was bred from 'Old Blush' × 'Madame Desprez', a seedling of 'Rose Edouard' ('Old Blush' × 'Autumn Damask') and distributed in 1834. It is a classic stylish rose suitable for the front of a border, or for growing in a pot. Although the China roses are hardy, their hybrids were bred mostly in France, because the climate there was more favorable for the ripening of seeds in large numbers of plants grown in the field. This was before more scientific breeding methods were introduced.

HIPPOLYTE
Gallica

The provenance of this rose has been lost. It is a vigorous shrub growing to 6 feet (2 m) and is practically thornless. The flowers are small and flat, rosette-like and come in various shades of carmine violet and gray. They tend to make little balls. It is once flowering only, and should be pruned by cutting out old wood after flowering and shortening the remaining stems according to individual judgment. There are no hard and fast rules about this. The object is to make a shapely shrub. The ultimate growth, and the floriferousness of all roses depends on the amount of light, air and shade in their environment. Hippolyte was queen of the Amazons and the wife of the Greek hero Theseus.

HONORINE DE BRABANT
Bourbon

The introducer and the date for this rose are unknown. It is a very healthy shrub over 6 feet (2 m) round with large broad light green leaves, somewhat like a coarse 'Commandant Beaurepaire'. It can be used on a column, as a shrub climber or as a shrub. The flowers are double, blush pink, cupped and quartered with stripes in red, violet and mauve. The particularly special qualities of the Bourbons are the petals which have been described as silky and translucent, and the habit of growth which is compact and vigorous. They are also usually very good in autumn provided there has been a hot summer to stimulate growth.

Rosa 'Honorine de Brabant'

Rosa 'Hippolyte'

IPSILANTÉ
Gallica

There is no record of the introduction of the grower of this rose, apart from a mention in old catalogs indicating 1821. It is later flowering than most. The flowers are sweetly scented, lilac pink, quartered and quilted, and not repeating. The plant grows vigorously to 6 feet (2 m). It is often stated that the old roses do not need to be pruned. This is to some extent true and they can be left awhile. A stage can be reached however, when the only flowers are confined to the tops of tall stems. Sometimes drastic cutting down can produce spectacular results in rejuvenation. Not all appreciate this, however, so trial and error is called for.

Rosa 'Ipsilanté'

IRÈNE WATTS
China

This rose was introduced by Guillot of Lyons in 1896. It grows to no more than 24 in (60 cm) high and wide, with soft apricot orange flowers fading to white. It is free flowering with a strong tea scent. It is not a common rose, and belongs to the heyday of the smaller Chinas, before they were replaced in fashion by Polyanthas and Miniatures. The first of the Polyanthas is considered to have been 'Paquerette', a cross between *R. multiflora* and a China or Tea rose. The second generation seedlings gave dwarf repeat flowering plants without much scent, and heralded a new class of Polypoms early in the 20th century.

Rosa 'Irène Watts'

Rosa 'Ispahan'

ISPAHAN
(Pompon des Princes)
Damask

Somewhat further east than Damascus, Ispahan is a city of Iran. This rose was probably in cultivation earlier than the 19th century. The compact flowers are warm pink, very fragrant and last well when cut. It is a tall, vigorous shrub to 6 feet (2 m), is very free flowering and is said to have the longest season of all the Damasks, commencing early in the season and continuing for longer than others, but there is no repetition. So many of these old roses were grown for so many years that the opportunities for divergence by way of sporting, or by seed, were considerable.

Rosa 'Irish Rich Marbled'

Rosa 'Jacques Cartier'

Rosa 'James Veitch'

IRISH RICH MARBLED
Scotch

This is one of the many varieties of the Scotch Roses, hybrids of a species known as *R. spinosissima* or *R. pimpinellifolia*. The former name is descriptive of the bristles, the latter derives from a resemblance of the leaves (8–9 leaflets) to a wild plant, the Burnet or Pimpinella. The species is widespread across the northern cool temperate regions of Europe and Asia, and the plants range from 6 feet (2 m) to 6 in (15 cm) growing in sandy coastal areas of North Britain. In the 19th century, they became popular and many varieties were raised but most of them are now lost. They are hardy and flower once only. This variety is semi-double, deep cherry pink with lilac reverse and a yellow center full of stamens.

JACQUES CARTIER
Portland

This was introduced by Moreau et Robert in 1868. It flowers a little later than 'Comte de Chambord' which it resembles, but the recurrent flowers when developed are less cupped and more carnation-like. It is an offspring of 'Baronne Prévost'. It has been alleged that this rose is the same as 'Marquise de Boccella' which was introduced in 1840, so eyebrows may have been raised. Jacques Cartier was a 16th century French mariner who explored the St. Lawrence river. Portlands and Damasks tend to bear their flowers on the tips of tall shoots, which is good only if the shoots are hidden by other plants. Otherwise, a solution is to bend the shoots over to stimulate inter-nodal growth, or to prune heavily.

JAMES VEITCH
Moss

This rose was raised by Verdier of Angers in 1865. It is low growing to only 3 feet (1 m), good for the front of the border, very thorny with bristly moss on dark magenta flowers. It is very free flowering and is one of the 'perpetual' forms, flowering throughout the season, provided dead-heading is carried out. It is important, though, to feed roses after the first flush if good second flowering is to be expected. The rose is named for James Veitch (1792–1863) the son, or James Veitch (1815–1869) the grandson, of the founder of Veitch's, a famous English firm of nurserymen in both Exeter and Chelsea, which was responsible for many plant hunting expeditions, notably those of Wilson and Lobb.

JEAN DUCHER
Tea

This rose was raised by Claude Ducher of Lyons in 1873. This is one of the best of the Teas, certainly in warmer climates, making a strong upright branching shrub to 6 feet (2 m). The flowers are in shades of yellow-salmon and red, and are fragrant, simple and unostentatious. It is among the hardiest of the Teas with good foliage and not liable to mildew. Claude Ducher died in 1874 and the firm was then managed by his widow, under the title of Veuve Ducher (Widow Ducher). In due course Ducher's daughter married Joseph Pernet, who under the name Pernet-Ducher, produced many of the outstanding roses of the 20th century, including the famous yellow Pernetianas. But that is another story.

Rosa 'Jean Ducher'

KATHLEEN HARROP
Climbing Bourbon

'Kathleen Harrop' is a sport of 'Zéphirine Drouhin', as also is 'Martha'. The flowers are soft pink, deeper on the reverse, and have a strong fragrance. It repeats, and the plant has the added bonus of being thornless. It is not as popular as its parent, but makes a lovely addition to the garden. Watch for mildew.

KÖNIGIN VON DANEMARCK
(Queen of Denmark)
Alba

The flowers are deeper in color than most Albas, a vivid carmine, cupped, quartered and full petalled. It was a seedling of 'Maiden's Blush' raised by John Booth and distributed in 1826. The flowers are well-scented and the shrub grows rather leggily to 6 feet (2 m), so some tidying up and pruning is recommended after flowering. People are accustomed to thinking of pruning as a winter occupation but with roses that flower only once, pruning should be done directly after flowering, though winter shortening may also be advisable.

Rosa 'Königin von Dänemarck'

There is a story that there was a violent quarrel over 'Jacques Cartier', a Professor Lehmann, Director of the Hamburg Botanic Gardens, alleging that this rose had long been grown in France, but he apparently failed to prove his assertion.

KRONPRINZESSIN VICTORIA
(Von Preussen)
Bourbon

This rose is a sport of 'Souvenir de la Malmaison' introduced by Spath in Berlin in 1888. It is similar in all respects to its parent except in color, which in this case is creamy white, with lemon shadings. It grows only to 4 × 3 feet (1.3 × 1 m) and is particularly suitable for small gardens. It is fragrant. It repeats well and is continually in flower. The flower is camellia-like and lasts well. Its main disadvantages are spoiling in wet weather and the need for good cultivation. David Austin recommends not growing it. This could be a challenge! The Princess was Queen Victoria's daughter and the last Kaiser's mother.

Rosa 'Kronprinzessin Victoria'

LADY HILLINGDON
Tea

This hardy rose was introduced in 1910 by Lowe and Shawyer at Uxbridge near London, and was named, presumably, for one of their customers, since the Hillingdons had a place at Uxbridge Court. It is known in England mainly as a climber, but in Australia and New Zealand as a shrub, which grows elegantly to 5 feet (1.5 m) or more. The flowers are informal, of soft apricot yellow, and strongly tea-scented. The young plum colored leaves turning dark green are particularly beautiful. It is one of the most repetitive of roses and grows well in poor soils. Lady Hillingdon has been credited with creating the phrase 'to lie back and think of England'! Lord Hillingdon was Governor-General of Canada in the early 1930s.

LADY HILLINGDON, CLIMBING
Climbing Tea

This sport of 'Lady Hillingdon' looks exactly like its parent, but is superior in some ways. In the right climate it blooms

Rosa 'Lady Hillingdon'

Rosa 'Lady Mary Fitzwilliam'

Rosa 'La Reine Victoria'

this rose, lost for many years, was rediscovered by his friend Keith Money in a Norfolk garden. Its main claim to fame is that it is the ancestor of many famous roses, including 'Madame Caroline Testout'. It might be hard to find a vigorous specimen nowadays. Lady Mary Fitzwilliam herself was descended from William IV, in an illegitimate line.

LAMARQUE
Noisette
Named after a Napoleonic general, 'Lamarque' was raised from 'Blush Noisette' and 'Park's Yellow Tea Scented China' around 1830 by an amateur called Marechal, a cobbler who grew it in a pot in his window! It is a very vigorous climber with great thick stems and long trailing shoots. Suitable for warm climates, it grows well into trees or over arches. The flowers which repeat well are large and in clusters; they are white, double, quilled and quartered with a yellow center. They tend to hang down, which is no disadvantage as one looks up to them. It is

from late spring until the approach of winter. The nodding flowers are especially effective on an arch or trellis. The flowers have blowzy appearance. They stay cupped on plum-colored canes. This climber will reach 10 feet (3 m). There is plenty of dark green foliage and some prickles. Although it is easy to train on a structure, it takes time to establish itself.

LADY MARY FITZWILLIAM
Tea
This rose was raised by Henry Bennett (see 'Grace Darling') in 1882 from 'Devoniensis' × 'Victor Verdier'. It is usually classed among the early Hybrid Teas. The flowers are flesh colored, globular, large and very fragrant. The plant is by no means over vigorous, but is quite bushy. It has been accused of exhausting itself by producing too many flowers. Peter Beales has described how

Rosa 'Lamarque'

similar to 'Jaune Desprez' which is of the same parentage but 'Lamarque' is more of a Tea.

LA REINE VICTORIA
Bourbon
'Found' by Labruyere, this rose was introduced by Schwartz of Lyons in 1872. The plant is classic, tall, slender and erect to 6 feet (2 m) in the gracile China style. The flowers are cupped, shell-like, rose colored and translucent. Perfectly grown flowers are like porcelain but they come at a price. This rose must be well grown and requires a dry atmosphere. Humidity and rain can easily spoil the flowers and black spot and mildew are constant menaces. In a hot, dry summer climate it can be superb.

LA VILLE DE BRUXELLES
(The City of Brussels)
Damask
This rose was raised in 1849 by Vibert. It is another Summer Damask with very

Rosa 'La Ville de Bruxelles'

large clear rich pink flowers, somewhat heavy for the stems, but very full and fragrant. They are flat and quartered with an incurved center. It blooms for about six weeks in summer and some shade will enhance the color of the flower. The bush grows to 6 feet (2 m), is large and vigorous with large, glossy light green leaves. In 1849 Vibert was at Angers, but in 1851 at the age of 74 he sold out to his foreman Robert and moved back to Paris. Robert went into business with Moreau and they were responsible for many successful later introductions.

LÉDA
(Painted Damask)
Damask

There are two forms of this rose, different only in color, one white, the other pink and the names seem to be confused. They are both very fragrant and although it is classed as a Summer Damask there are some flowers in autumn. The foliage is dark green and the flowers have the reflexing character-istics which produces ball-like blooms. It is a low grower to only 3 feet (1 m). This rose originated in England, and it seems likely that 'Léda' is the French version. In Greek mythology, Leda was seduced by Zeus in the form of a swan, and became mother, among others, of Helen of Troy. The rose has been known since 1827.

Rosa 'Louise Odier'

LORD PENZANCE
Hybrid Sweet Briar

The Sweet Briar is known botanically as *R. rubiginosa* (formerly *R. eglanteria*). It is a form of *R. canina*, from which it differs mainly in having a very distinctive smell of apples, noticeable after rain or when the leaves are crushed. In the 1890s, 'Lord Penzance' created some 14 hybrids. They all have an arching growth to 10 feet (3 m), very suitable for making a hedge, with thorns to deter, and oval red autumn hips to delight, or for planting in the wild garden. The Sweet Briar has clear pink single flowers, 'Lord Penzance', a cross with 'Harison's Yellow', is a soft rosy yellow, paler at the base. 'Lady Penzance', primrose colored, is more manageable.

LOUISE ODIER
(Madame de Stella)
Bourbon

This rose was a seedling of 'Emile Courtier' and was introduced in 1851 by Margottin (France). It is a first-rate cut flower and a reliable repeat-bloomer. The round buds open to reveal large, very double, warm pink flowers. It is a perfect shape for a Bourbon—cupped at first, then becoming flat and round. The ragged center petals have a lavender tint and a rich perfume. This is one of the most floriferous of the old roses and the flowers are held on long stems. The arching canes are covered with soft, olive green leaves and maroon prickles. If left unpruned it can be used as a climber, but more often it is a valuable addition to the border. It is the parent of many popular French roses.

MADAME ALFRED CARRIÈRE
Noisette

This rose was introduced in 1879, which is later than most of the Noisettes. It is, without a doubt, one of the greatest

Rosa 'Madame Alfred Carrière'

Noisettes, its most famous site being on the high wall of the cottage which it covers in Sissinghurst Castle Garden in Kent (see photograph). The foliage is light green, the flowers are double, flattish, a little muddled and are white with some pink, particularly in autumn. Growth is strong and flowering is almost perpetual. The individual flowers have long stems making them good for cutting. This rose can be recommended without reservation. It is probably still the best white climber and should be left pretty well unpruned.

Rosa 'Madame Hardy'

MADAME HARDY
Damask

Alexandre Hardy was chief horticulturalist at the Luxembourg Palace in Paris, which in 1848 contained the most splendid collection of roses in France. He created many varieties, this one in 1832, which he named for his wife. This is a famous and classic rose with white flowers having a pronounced green eye. It is not a typical Damask, having leanings to Albas and Centifolias. The flowers are flat and reflexed, perfectly formed and medium sized, the bush upright to 6 feet (2 m) with mid-green lush foliage. Although the name sounds English is should be pronounced 'Ardy', without the 'H', in the French manner.

MADAME ISAAC PEREIRE
Bourbon

This rose is perhaps the last of the Bourbons, and the breeder did not divulge the lineage. It has aroused strong differences of opinion, the color being variously described as 'pretty' and 'revolting'. It is a kind of shocking pink heavily overlaid with magenta. What cannot be in doubt is the very intense fragrance and large size of the flowers, borne on very short stems on a strong bush to 10 feet (3 m). This rose is often grown pegged down, horizontal to the soil, thus promoting a greater number of flowering side stems. There is a pink sport, 'Madame Ernst Calvat' which is the same in all respects. Jack Harkness recommended planting both where they could face and annoy the neighbors!

Rosa 'Madame Isaac Pereire'

MADAME LEGRAS DE ST. GERMAIN
Alba

St. Germain is a suburb of Paris, but Madame Legras must remain anonymous as all that is known is that this rose pre-dates 1846. It makes a tall upright shrub to 10 feet (3 m) and is suitable for the back of a shrubbery or border, where it will get some support. It can also be grown as a climber. The flowers are rather formal, flat and quartered, ivory white, with a hint of yellow, unusual in an Alba, which seems to suggest some Noisette in its make-up. Some pruning is recommended after flowering and with a lot of luck there might be a flower or two later in the autumn.

MADAME LOUIS LÉVEQUE
Moss

This is another of the 'perpetual' or repeat flowering Mosses produced by Léveque in France in 1898 and more of a Moss/Hybrid Perpetual hybrid. The flowers are very large, fragrant and pale pink, held erect on mossy stems. Balling, a condition in which large or full petalled roses fail to open, is a common result of wet weather, and militates against the growing of such roses in wet summer climates. They are more suited to dry Mediterranean type summer climates. Balling in wet weather is to be expected from this rose, though a later autumn flush of flowers will be satisfactory, particularly if disbudding and summer pruning has been done.

MADAME PIERRE OGER
Bourbon

A sport of 'Reine Victoria' discovered by Oger (or his gardener) of Caen and introduced by Verdier of Paris in 1878. The shrub is upright and identical to the parent. The flowers, however, are of a distinctly paler color, shell-like, translucent and flesh colored. It has become more popular than its parent and is a classic where conditions suit it, that is hot dry summers and good cultivation. In the Wallace Collection in Manchester House (behind Selfridge's in London) there is a picture of the Marquess of Hertford with Madame Pierre Oger. It would be interesting to know the status of the Ogers and why the rose was so named.

Rosa 'Madame Louis Léveque'

Rosa 'Madame Legras de St. Germain'

MADAM PLANTIER
Alba

This hybrid Alba was created by Plantier of Lyons in 1835, and has been variously classified as a Noisette, a Hybrid China and a Damask. It is now thought to be an Alba/Moschata (musk rose) cross. This is not a wholly satisfactory theory, though, since Plantier did not go in much for Albas. It is a lax shrub with few thorns bearing smallish white flat flowers, and it can be grown as a shrub, on a column or as a climber. Apple trees in the garden at Sissinghurst Castle are filled with this rose which produces a sheet of white blossom and is in flower for a long time. The petals suffer in wet weather.

MAMAN COCHET
Tea

This rose was raised by Scipion Cochet of Coubert in France in 1892 from two Tea roses, 'Marie van Houte' and 'Madame Lombard'. It is a vigorous bush with very large blowzy flowers, which are pale pink with a deeper center and a yellow-lemon base. The buds are very pointed; the flowers very double and very beautiful, unless visited by thrips and/or rain, when they can be balled and ruined. This is why Teas do so well in mild dry winters or in greenhouses. It grows quite well in poor soil. There is also a white form. Mother Cochet was in her 87th year when this rose was named for her in 1892!

MARIE LAMBERT
(Snowflake, White Hermosa)
Tea

'Marie Lambert' was introduced by Elie Lambert of Lyons in 1886. It is a sport from 'Madame Bravy'. The bush grows to 3 feet (1 m) and bears pure white formal full petalled flowers in the style of 'Hermosa'. It would be suitable for pot culture. The first Tea roses to be grown in England were 'Park's Yellow Tea Scented China' and 'Hume's Blush Tea Scented China', both climbers to about 6 feet (2 m). These were derived from the wild Tea rose in China and started the race of Teas in Europe. The first new Tea created in Europe was said to be 'Adam' (1833) so called, not because it was the first, but after its breeder, M. Adam of Rheims.

Rosa 'Martha'

Rosa 'Madame Plantier'

MARTHA
Bourbon

This is a sport of 'Zéphirine Drouhin', and was introduced in 1912. This is a climbing Bourbon to 6 feet (2 m). It is thornless and long flowering, the color being a paler pink than the parent. Like its parent, it is vigorous, long flowering, and healthy, but not commonly found. A better known sport of 'Zéphirine Drouhin' is 'Kathleen Harrop', which is a shell pink. All these roses are thornless, which in view of the propensity of roses to attack passers by, is a very desirable characteristic, particularly in such good roses. These roses can be grown well on a west wall as they will stand some shade, or on an arch.

Rosa 'Maman Cochet'

Rosa 'Maman Cochet'

MRS. FOLEY HOBBS
Tea

This is a latecomer, created by Dickson of Newtownards in Northern Ireland in 1910. It has upright vigorous growth, with soft ivory white flowers, tinged with pink at the tips. It is said by Jack Harkness to be purely an exhibition variety, the flowers being too big for the stems in the garden. The original two Tea roses from China were later lost, having been superseded by the new Teas and Noisettes bred from them. They have, however, been rediscovered, and are again available. The Tea rose is said

to smell of a freshly opened packet of light China tea.

MRS. JOHN LAING
Hybrid Perpetual

A famous rose which has not declined in vigor and is still an asset to any garden, this rose was raised by Henry Bennett in 1887. The buds are pointed, the flowers are pink, large, cupped and double (45 petals). The bush is comparatively dwarf to 4 feet (1.2 m) and will grow in poor soil. Growth is upright and the flower stalks are long and strong. Bennett is said to have received $45,000 for the US

Rosa 'Mrs. Foley Hobbs'

distribution rights. It was a seedling from 'Francois Michelon', which itself was a seedling of 'La Reine', one of the first Hybrid Perpetuals from Jean Laffay who is generally credited with creating the class. John Laing was a London horticulturalist who died in 1901.

MUTABILIS
(Tipo Idéale)
China

'Mutabilis' has been known since 1896, but was introduced to horticulture in 1932 by a Swiss botanist, Henri Correvon of Geneva, who got it from Prince Ghilberto Borromeo's garden at Isola Bella. How it got there is not known, but it seems probable that it came from China. It normally makes a large spreading bush 3×6 feet (1–2 m) high, but can climb to 25 feet (8 m). The flowers are butterfly-like and borne in masses. They open yellow, turn pink and then crimson, which is the opposite way to normal. There is a very long period of

flowering. In many ways it is a curiosity, but a beautiful one. The modern rose 'Masquerade' seems derived from this.

OLD BLUSH
(The Monthly Rose, Parson's Pink China)
China

This is the most common of the four original Chinese roses brought to Europe in the late 18th century, initiating the great revolution in rose breeding by introducing the repeat flowering

Rosa 'Old Blush'

Rosa 'Mutabilis'

Rosa 'Mrs John Laing'

factor into the once-flowering old European roses. It is said to be Thomas More's 'Last Rose of Summer'. The bush grows slowly to 3 feet (1 m) or more; it is twiggy, gracile and practically thornless. The light pink flowers are smallish, muddled and semi-double. There is a slight fragrance reminiscent of sweet peas.

OMAR KHAYYAM
Damask
This is a true Summer Damask but unlike any of the European type. A seed was reputedly taken from a rose growing on the grave of the celebrated poet Omar Khayyam, in Nashipur in Iran, and planted on the grave of his translator, Edward Fitzgerald. The original seed was said to have been collected by William Simpson of the *Illustrated London News* and was grown at Kew. It is a romantic story for a rose! The plant grows up to 6 feet (2 m), and has fragrant pink cupped flowers, which are complemented by the soft green foliage.

Rosa 'Omar Khayyám'

PAPA GONTIER
Tea
This rose was introduced in 1883. The flowers are bright coppery pink with the reverse carmine red; they are semi-double, loose and fragrant. The growth is rather wiry and twiggy to 3 feet (1 m) but it can grow into a large shrub with age and suitable conditions. It flowers well in winter and grows easily from cuttings. It is a parent of 'Lady Hillingdon', and a climbing form appeared in 1904. Many of the Teas and Hybrid Teas (Large-flowered) mutate at some time from bush to climber, though the climbers tend to be not so floriferous. There are, of course, also other climbers in their own right which were never bushes. Papa Gontier himself was a noted horticulturalist.

PAUL NEYRON
Hybrid Perpetual
This is what many people think of as the 'cabbage rose', a name first given to the Centifolias. The flowers of a clear rose pink can be up to 8 in (20 cm) across, containing as many as 50 petals which are cupped, fragrant and recurrent, and resemble peonies. The bush is still

Rosa 'Paul Transon'

Rosa 'Papa Gontier'

vigorous although introduced as long ago as 1869. It was derived from 'Victor Verdier' and 'Anna de Diesbach', both with rose pink flowers. It grows to 6 feet (2 m) and the stems are upright and strong. The flowers are good for cutting, and better for it. Paul Neyron was a medical student who died in 1872, a result of the Franco-Prussian War.

PAUL TRANSON
Rambler

'Paul Transon' was introduced in 1900 by Barbier of Orleans. It is a medium flowered rambler-climber bred from *R. wichuraiana* (some say *R. luciae*, a lookalike) and 'L'Ideal'. The flowers are quite large and full in clusters of three to five. They are slightly fragrant. The color is bright salmon-pink, the shape flat and pleated. There is some repetition in autumn. It grows to about 14 feet (4 m). *Wichuraiana* itself carries only very small single white flowers with a scent of violets. Not only is it the progenitor of the better ramblers but also the ancestor of the many recently developed carpet roses, which inherit its trailing habit.

PETITE DE HOLLANDE
Centifolia

This rose is a scaled down version of *R. × centifolia* which it resembles. It was introduced from Holland in 1838. It grows to over 3 feet (1 m). 'Petite de Hollande' is fragrant and upright, and praised by all the authorities as the best of the smaller Centifolias. Jack Harkness has pointed out some of the misconceptions about the Centifolias. They acquired the name of 'Provence roses' because they grew so well in the south of France, although they originated in Holland. Gallicas were also

Rosa 'Petite de Hollande'

Rosa 'Phyllis Bide'

called roses 'de Provins' a different place altogether, so there is more confusion! Antiquarians, too, have recalled ancient writers who spoke of 100-petalled roses and thought they were Centifolias. But they are Dutch and of the 17th century.

PHYLLIS BIDE
Rambler

Said to be a cross between 'Perle d'Or' (or 'Yellow Cécile Brunner') and 'Gloire de Dijon', this rose was introduced by the Bide Nurseries in Farnham in Surrey in 1923. 'Phyllis Bide' has small leaves and small mixed yellow, cream and pink flowers in clusters and flowering is continuous throughout the season. It is not very high, climbing perhaps to 6 feet (2 m), and looks best on a column or a standard, or as a free standing shrub.

POMPON BLANC PARFAIT
Alba

The translation is 'perfect white pompon'. The rose was introduced by Verdier in 1876. It is recommended chiefly for its small, compact lilac white flowers, nicely scented and produced in small, tight clusters. It grows in a slender way to about 5 feet (1.5 m). It starts late in the season and flowers over

Rosa 'Pompon de Bourgoyne'

a long period, and the flowers are long lasting. It is possibly an Alba/Multiflora hybrid. The pompon roses were very popular until the advent of the Polyanthas, which combined small flowers with clustering and repeat flowering but in many cases, with loss of scent.

POMPON DE BOURGOYNE
(Burgundy Rose)
Centifolia

Also known as 'Parvifolia' (small leaves), this rose is another lovely miniature dating to the early 1600s, or perhaps earlier. It has erect growth and pompon style reddish purple flowers. It is classified by some as not a Centifolia

at all, but a Gallica. The ancestry of all these roses has become so mixed that the line of demarcation is difficult to establish in some cases, thus providing a great deal of scope for experts and purists to argue about it. This rose must be grown in full sun or there will be no flowers.

PRÉSIDENT DE SÈZE
Gallica

This lovely rose is said to have been produced before 1836. 'Président de Sèze' is reputed to be one of the most beautiful of the Gallicas with the usual loose bush form to 5 feet (1.5 m). The flower is two-toned pale lilac, pink

Rosa 'Pompon Blanc Parfait'

Rosa 'Président de Sèze'

around the circumference and crimson in the center. They are very double, cup-shaped and tend to the convex. The flowers are borne in clusters and change color with age. Graham Thomas considers this rose to be the same as 'Jenny Duval', a rose still sold under this name and of unknown provenance. Gallicas went out of fashion for so long that many identifications are difficult.

PRINCE CHARLES
Bourbon
'Prince Charles' was introduced by Hardy around 1842. It is a vigorous shrub to 6 feet (2 m) with dark foliage and, like most Bourbons, few prickles. The flowers are three-quarters double, crimson with a white base, loose and crinkled. It does not repeat. It is worth trying by those who are interested in uncommon acquisitions. The factor in the China roses for repeat flowering is in a recessive gene. Consequently, when a repeat flowering rose is crossed with a summer only flowering rose, the offspring are all summer flowering. When seed is taken from these, in the next generation, approximately a quarter will contain only the recessive gene and will therefore be repeat flowering, but other characteristics will be segregated differently.

QUATRE SAISONS
(R. × damascena bifera)
Damask
This ancient rose was known and grown in Greek and Roman times and is mentioned by ancient writers. It is also known as the 'Autumn Damask'. It is thought to be a hybrid of Gallica and Moschata, the musk rose, another old

Rosa 'Prince Charles'

Rosa 'Rambling Rector'

Rosa 'Quatre Saisons'

world rose of great vigor with single white flowers. It was the only old European rose to flower again in autumn—hence its name. An upright bush to about 5 feet (1.5 m) with clear pink, rather loose double and very fragrant flowers, it was highly regarded in the days before the China roses brought in the repeat flowering factor to modern roses. It is a variable rose given to sporting to white and mossy types.

RAMBLING RECTOR
Rambler
Clergymen were very much to the fore in the 19th century rose world. Perhaps they had the time and, of course they had their large vicarage gardens. The celebrated Samuel Reynolds Hole, Dean of Rochester, was President of the (Royal) National Rose Society from its inception in 1876 to his death in 1904. The wonderfully named Rev. Henry Honeywood d'Ombrain was its secretary for 25 years. The origin of this rose is not known but it is probably a Multiflora/Musk hybrid, and is merely dated to 'before 1912', more recently

than one would expect. It will ascend far and wide through trees, bearing masses of small semi-double white flowers in clusters in summer only.

REINE DES VIOLETTES
(Queen of the Violets)
Hybrid Perpetual
This well-known and popular rose is oddly classed as a Hybrid Perpetual, although it looks rather like a Bourbon. It makes a medium to tall, full bush with Gallica-like purple flowers fading to violet, and filled with 75 quilled and quartered petals, each with a button eye. It flowers in the summer and repeats in autumn and is well scented. The foliage is smooth green and it is almost thornless. The vigor of this bush has enabled it to survive successfully through the years. This rose is one of the 'musts'.

RÊVE D'OR
Noisette
This rose was introduced in 1869 by Veuve Ducher of Lyons. It is descended from 'Lamarque' via 'Madame Schultz'.

The large flowers are semi-double, buff yellow, fragrant, frilly and quartered, and the plant climbs to 20 feet (6 m) with strong branching stems, large hooked red thorns and plentiful foliage. The name, of course, means golden dream, which is quite poetic and, one hopes, not mercenary! It is a handsome rose and in 1878 it produced a well known sport, 'William Allen Richardson' which is more orange in color. Richardson was apparently a rich American and a customer of the Duchers.

ROSA CENTIFOLIA
Centifolia

The type rose of the group, the rose of 100 petals, the 'Rose of Provence', the

Rosa 'Rêve d'Or'

'Rose des Peintres', this rose was probably created by the Dutch in the 17th century. It features in many of the famous Dutch flower paintings. The English called it the 'Cabbage Rose' because its opening shape resembled an unopened cabbage, and because it was quite big. This has led to some misconceptions, however, because what most people think of cabbage roses nowadays are some of the very big Hybrid Perpetual roses of the 19th century, like 'Paul Neyron', which came, of course, much later. This is a tall, floppy, but sturdy bush with large droopy leaves and deep pink flowers, very double, cupped and fragrant.

ROSA MUNDI
(Rose of the World, R. × rosamundi, Rosamund's rose)
Gallica

A rose of the world or Rosamund's rose? One name seems meaningless, the other romantically apocryphal. Rosamund was the mistress of Henry II. The problem can be solved by using its other name 'Versicolor'. It is just a striped form of 'Officinalis', pale pink splashed with

Rosa centifolia

crimson and it sometimes reverts to it. 'Rosa Mundi' is sometimes confused with 'York and Lancaster', also called 'Versicolor', but this is a Damask, quite different, and indeed inferior. The branches in these roses tend to flop over with the weight of the flowers and require support. This can be solved by pruning halfway in spring, giving a better effect. They are good roses for hedging and grow to a height of about 5 feet (1.5 m).

ROSE DE RESCHT
Damask

This rose is said to have been found in old garden in Iran by Nancy Lindsay and brought to England. Although it is classified as a Damask because of its strong scent, it does not fit easily into any category. It is, however, continually in flower, making a small compact bush with light green dense foliage. The rosette type flowers are cerise and magenta, small and pompon-like. It is of great garden value (like 'Gloire de Guilan', another Lindsay introduction). Romantics may imagine its forebears immigrating by caravan from China, but Brent Dickerson, an American horticultural writer, has advanced the theory that it was imported to Iran from France about 1807 and is the true 'Rose du Roi'.

Rosa mundi

ROSE DU ROI
Portland

A splendid name, and a splendid rose. The flowers are an intense bright red, quite large, semi-double and very fragrant. The shrub grows to 3 × 3 feet (1 × 1 m). It is similar to the 'Portland Rose' but it flowers continuously without the special treatment which that one requires. It might be difficult to get good stock nowadays. It is sometimes classified as the first of the Hybrid Perpetuals and was raised in 1815 by Ecoffay, a gardener at Sevres, marketed by a florist named Souchet, who took it to the Comte Le Lieur, Director of the Royal Gardens, who named it for himself. Later it was renamed for Louis XVIII who was restored to the throne on the fall of Napoleon.

Rosa 'Rose du Roi'

SAFRANO
Tea

Not long on the heels of 'Adam', 'Safrano' was introduced in 1839 by an amateur, Beaurepaire of Angers. He bred it from 'Stud Tea', 'Park's Yellow' and 'Madame Desprez'. The flowers are apricot-yellow or saffron, semi-double large and fragrant. It is remarkable how vigorous these early roses continue to be when many later Hybrid Teas (Large-flowered) have faded away. 'Safrano' blooms freely and repeatedly and resists weather damage. It is perhaps at its most beautiful in the bud stage and used to be very popular as a gentleman's bouton-nière. Unfortunately, the flowers fade rather badly during a sunny day and by the evening little remains of the glory of the morning's gold. It is said that this

Rosa 'Rose de Rescht'

rose was the result of the process of hand pollination, which was an extremely innovative exercise in the mid-19th century.

SISSINGHURST CASTLE
Gallica

This is said to be the same as an old garden rose, 'Rose des Maures', named presumably for the darkness of its complexion. The famous literary couple, Harold Nicolson and Vita Sackville-West, created the wonderful Sissinghurst Castle garden in Kent, which is one of the great gardens of England, if not the world, and are said to have found this striking rose when they were clearing the debris and rubbish around the castle grounds in 1930. The flowers are a lovely plum color. They are semi-double and have the usual Gallica style of growth.

Rosa 'Safrano'

SOMBREUIL
Climbing Tea

The flowers of this rose typify the old rose style. They are white, flat, quilled, quartered and very double, with an occasional touch of rose and yellow, and can best be described as refined. It was introduced by Robert (France) in 1851 and is said to be a grandchild of 'Park's Yellow' via 'Gigantesque'. The flowers have a wonderful sweet fragrance and the rose is in every way a classic. It climbs to 14 feet (4 m) high and has the added bonus of being repeat flowering. It was named for Mademoiselle de Sombreuil who was a popular heroine of the French Revolution. She is reputed to have drunk a glass of the blood of an aristocrat to prove her father's non-aristocratic status. 'Sombreuil' is said to be reasonably hardy for a Tea.

SOUPERT ET NOTTING
Moss

Another of the perpetual form of the moss rose, 'Soupert et Notting' was a firm of rose growers in Luxembourg. They did not, however, introduce this rose, which was released in 1874 by Jean Pernet of Lyons, the father in-law of Pernet-Ducher, the creator, at the turn of the century, of the famous Pernetiana class of yellow Hybrid Tea (Large-flowered) roses. This is a well-formed moderately mossy rose with fragrant pink blossoms and being remontant, flowers again in the autumn. The attractive flowers are deepish pink, small and dense, rounded and flat. The plant grows to 3 feet (1 m) high. Mildew can be a problem and preventative measures ahould be taken early in the season to ensure a fine display of flowers and foliage.

Rosa 'Soupert et Notting'

Rosa 'Sombreuil'

SOUVENIR DE LA MALMAISON
Bourbon

The most famous and perhaps most beautiful of the Bourbons, Beluze of Lyons bred this rose in 1843 from 'Madame Desprez' and possibly 'Devoniensis'. It is named for the Empress Josephine's rose garden at Malmaison. The flowers are characteristic of the old roses, wide quartered, full of petals and very fragrant. The color is pale flesh pink, fading paler on exposure. Flowering is in bursts. It grows to 6 feet (2 m). There is also a climbing form, introduced in 1893, reaching 14 feet (4 m) or more, but it is not so remontant. The autumn blooms are better than the summer ones, and balling is to be expected in wet weather.

SOUVENIR DE MADAME LEONIE VIENNOT
Climbing Tea

This rose was bred from 'Gloire de Dijon' by Viennot of Dijon and introduced by Bernaix of Villebanne-Lyons in 1898. It bears quite large, loosely shaped flowers, light rose pink with yellow and coppery orange tints, a little gold perhaps and reminiscent of 'Lorraine Lee'. It grows particularly well in warm temperate areas and will ascend through trees to great heights of 33 feet (10 m) or more. It has a long flowering period, putting on a glorious show with an occasional later repeat. It flowers on the old wood, so the less pruning the better. A long lived rose, there are specimens alleged to be 100 years old in New Zealand.

Rosa 'Souvenir de la Malmaison'

Rosa 'Souvenir de St. Anne's'

Rosa 'Souvenir de Madame Leonie Viennot'

SOUVENIR DE ST. ANNE'S
Bourbon

This is an almost single sport of 'Souvenir de la Malmaison', which occurred in 1916 in Dublin and was preserved for many years by a Lady Moore of Rathfarnham. It was introduced in 1960. This story is told by Graham Thomas in his *Rose Book* (1994) and he is credited elsewhere with the introduction. Having few petals, it stands up to rain better than its parent but is not so spectacular. It is, however, even more fragrant, the scent residing in the stamens, according to Thomas, of which there are, of course, many. The shrub is bushy to 6 feet (2 m) and the flowers are continuous.

SOUVENIR DU DOCTEUR JAMAIN
Hybrid Perpetual

Introduced in 1865 by Lacharme, this rose was a seedling of 'Charles Lefebre', which had been bred from 'Général Jacqueminot' × 'Victor Verdier'. The fragrant flowers are rich and dark, the color of port wine. They are semi-double, showing yellow stamens and need some shade from strong sunshine, to avoid burning. The plant grows to 10 × 6 feet (3 × 2 m) and is not over-vigorous. Lacharme was a great 19th century rose breeder. His 1887 obituary stated that he 'was modest to the extreme; indeed he did not believe it was his place to perpetuate his name by giving it to any of his varieties' (quoted by Dickerson and repeated here, as the memory of such a rarity in the rose world should not be lost).

STANWELL PERPETUAL
Scotch

This is probably the best known of the Burnet rose hybrids. It occurred as a chance crossed seedling between a Burnet and probably an Autumn Damask in a Mr. Lee's garden in Stanwell in Middlesex in 1838. It makes

Rosa 'Stanwell Perpetual'

Rosa 'The Bishop'

of tree roots. The advent of the new granular slow release fertilizers has greatly facilitated this.

THE BISHOP
Centifolia

'The Bishop' is really a Gallica/Centifolia hybrid, and its name, classification and origin are uncertain. The flowers are flat of closely packed rosette form, cerise magenta in color verging on blue in certain lights. The shrub is slender and erect to 6 feet (2 m) with smooth stamens. Graham Thomas compares it with 'Tour de Malakoff'. He places it in the Centifolias. Although the classification system is meant to impose order and perhaps to simplify some complexities, there will always be borderline cases and exceptions that prove the rule! This rose was illustrated by Redouté the famous early 19th century flower artist as 'L'Eveque'.

TUSCANY SUPERB
Gallica

'Tuscany' was Gerard's 'Old Velvet Rose' and this name describes it superbly. It has blackish crimson to deep purple, semi-double, large, flattish blooms with conspicuous yellow stamens. The plant is upright and vigorous

a lax thorny bush up to 6 feet (2 m) with pale blush-pink, double, flat, quilled and quartered petals. For some reason it flowers repeatedly if not exactly perpetually. The foliage is very small and ferny, burnet-like with nine leaflets, and the stems are very prickly. Several bushes can be grown together with advantage. Old wood should be cut out from the base each season to stimulate new growth. The fragrance is delicious. It is highly recommended.

STRIPED MOSS
(Oeillet Panachée)
Moss

'Oeillet Panachée' means 'variegated pink' or 'carnation', which it resembles. It looks like a mossy Gallica. It is a small upright shrub to 3 feet (1 m) and is suitable for growing in a pot. The flowers are small, pale, pink, and striped with vivid crimson. It is said not to be very vigorous. In many cases roses can be grown better in pots than in the open ground, particularly in the neighborhood

Rosa 'Tuscany Superb'

Rosa 'Trigintipetala'

to 5 feet (1.5 m) and is of ancient origin. It is one of the most characteristic Gallicas, but the scent, to some, is less pronounced than in most. 'Tuscany Superb' is an improved version, larger in every respect and seems to have originated as a seedling, or sport, in the mid-19th century. Height in shrub roses is a very variable characteristic and often depends on location. Shade or neighboring shrubs will cause the plants to grow higher seeking the sun. In such cases blooming is often diminished.

TRIGINTIPETALA
(Kazanlik)
Damask

'Trigintipetala' in Latin means '30 petals', and Kazanlik is a town in Central Bulgaria where this rose is grown commercially to provide a considerable attar of roses industry. Roads out of town meander through the rose fields and serve the occasional distillery where the perfume is manufactured. Tourists flock there on the first Sunday in June when a Rose Festival is held in the town and rose fields. The perfume of this rose is, perhaps, the most intense of all the Damasks. The

Rosa 'Variegata di Bologna'

flowers are the usual informal double pink type. The bush grows to 5 feet (1.5 m) and is rather straggly. The origin of the attar industry is probably Turkish, the origin of the rose lost in antiquity.

VARIEGATA DI BOLOGNA
Bourbon

This Italian rose was introduced in 1909 by Bonifiglioli of Garisenda. The fragrant flowers are white, striped purplish red, double and globular and

Rosa 'Veilchenblau'

Rosa 'William Lobb'

lot in old gardens. It was derived in 1910 from a cross between the famous 'Crimson Rambler' and 'Erinnerung an Brod', a purplish semi-climbing Hybrid Perpetual of 1886. It was introduced by Schmidt of Erfurt in Germany. The flowers may be described as violet streaked with white, fading to gray. The yellow stamens are prominent and the flowers are small and incurved. The blooms are fragrant and are borne in clusters on short stems. The plant is vigorous to 16 feet (5 m) and is best with a little shade to delay fading.

VICK'S CAPRICE
Hybrid Perpetual

This was introduced by James Vick of Rochester, New York, in whose garden it sported from 'Archiduchesse Elisabeth d'Autriche'. The flowers (25 petals) are lilac rose, striped white and carmine, cupped, large and fragrant. The plant is vigorous to some 4 feet (1.2 m). It can revert to the original as is the way with such sports. 'Vick's Caprice' is inclined to ball in wet weather. The Hybrid Perpetuals were a very complex and mixed class of roses derived mainly from the Bourbons but also from a medley of earlier roses—Gallicas, Damasks, Chinas, Portlands etc. Consequently they vary greatly in style and are grouped in 12 different classifications, requiring differing treatments. Serious collectors should consult specialist literature.

WILLIAM LOBB
(Duchesse d' Istrie, Old Velvet Moss)
Moss

'William Lobb' was raised by Laffay in 1855. This is perhaps the most vigorous of all the mosses, growing to 10 feet (3 m). It bears dark crimson-purple flowers in various shades and in heavy clusters

are borne in clusters. It is tall and lax to 12 feet (3.5 m) and very handsome but repays good cultivation. It is a sport of 'Victor Emmanuel', which has shorter growth and the same colored flowers but without the stripes. It occasionally reverts back to this. All plants that sport can do so both ways. There are few repeat flowers after the main summer flush. Black spot can be a problem, but it is a moot point whether one should spray for black spot or just accept it. Like mildew, it will come and go.

VEILCHENBLAU
Rambler

This is the best known of the three violet purple Multiflora ramblers, and is seen a on long stems, which need support, so it is best grown inter-mingled with other shrubs or with ramblers; or perhaps on a pillar. It is not very mossy, but very fragrant, and flowers only in midsummer. Thomas and William Lobb were Cornishmen and gardeners who became plant hunters for Veitch (see 'James Veitch'). William was responsible for the introduction of many trees and shrubs to England from South America. He is credited with the popularization in England of the monkey puzzle tree, *Auraucaria araucana*, from Chile.

YORK AND LANCASTER
Summer Damask

This rose is also known as 'Versicolor' to increase the confusion with 'Rosa Mundi'. The bush is tall and straggly to 6 feet (2 m). The rose is unusual in the inconsistency of its rather informal double flowers, some blush white, some pink, some flaked or mixed, but not striped like 'Rosa Mundi'. It is an old rose thought by some to be the shrub from which the opposing factions

plucked their different roses at the onset of the Wars of the Roses, but Shakespeare's lines are ambiguous and it is more likely the roses were on different bushes, probably 'Officinalis' and 'Alba Semi-plena'.

ZÉPHIRINE DROUHIN
The Thornless Rose
Climbing Bourbon

'Zéphirine Drouhin' should be in every garden! It is thornless and can be grown as a pillar, over an arch, or as a shrub to about 14 feet (4 m). The flowers are semi-double, loose-petalled, medium size, cerise pink with a white base and sweetly scented. The plant is vigorous and of easy cultivation, Zéphirine Drouhin was the wife of an amateur gardener living at Semur on the Côte d'Or. 'Kathleen Harrop' is a pink sport of this rose. Both make good hedge roses, but should be kept away from walls for fear of black spot. This rose will tolerate some shade, for example, on westerly aspects. It was introduced by Bizot of Lyons in 1868.

Rosa 'Zéphirine Drouhin'

Rosa 'York and Lancaster'

CHAPTER 3

Modern Garden Roses

In 1867 a new rose was introduced, and not just any rose, but the first in a long line which would become known as Hybrid Teas (also known as Large-flowered Roses), a type that would dominate rosedom for many years to come. Its name was 'La France', bred by Jean-Baptiste Guillot. It had been selected, from among more than 1,000 submissions, by a panel of 50 members set up by the Society of Horticulture of Lyons in France to choose a rose worthy to carry the name of its country. It was from this rose that the modern garden roses we know today are descended.

But how did the first Hybrid Tea rose come about? The Hybrid Teas became possible when roses from China were brought back to Europe by traders and adventurers between 1750 and 1825. Their value was immediately recognized, as they flowered regularly throughout the warmer months, unlike most of the European roses, which only flowered once in early summer. Many of these roses were found in the Empress Josephine's garden, and André Dupont, one of many experts attracted to her unparalleled collection, was able to use them in his developing breeding pro-

'Coral Meidiland' is popular with landscapers.

gram. It is generally agreed that he was the first person to make carefully planned crosses by hand pollination when most of his colleagues relied on honey bees. The robust growth of the Hybrid Perpetuals was combined with the repeat flowering qualities and delicately pointed bud form of the Teas. The culmination was 'La France'.

The Empress Josephine had a great love for plants, particularly roses, and she did much to popularize the rose through her comprehensive collection at Malmaison. She made the rose a symbol of romance and peace, and ships carrying roses for Josephine were granted safe passage during the Napoleonic Wars. This marked a huge change in the way people thought about roses. In the Middle Ages, for instance, roses were associated with the decadence of the latter days of the Roman Empire. And in Britain, the rose was inextricably associated with The War of the Roses, the bloody conflict between the families of York and Lancaster. (Interestingly, the symbols adopted by those families were *Rosa gallica officinalis*, the Red Rose of Lancaster, and *Rosa alba*, the White Rose of York.)

While Modern Roses began with the first Hybrid Tea (Large-flowered Roses) in 1867, not all roses bred since then are classified as Modern. Roses classed as Hybrid Perpetual or Tea roses bred after that time remain Old Garden Roses. But the great popularity enjoyed by 'La France' and other Hybrid Tea (Large-flowered) varieties, meant that by the beginning of the twentieth century, the roses known as Modern garden roses were the favored rose among growers.

Modern garden roses are divided into Bush, Shrub, Ground Cover, Miniatures and Climbers. The **Bush Roses** are the most significant of the modern roses, and

The effect created by the masses of blooms of Cluster-flowered Roses can be quite striking.

these are the ones people are most likely to grow in their own gardens. The Bush roses are divided into Hybrid Teas (Large-flowered), Floribundas (Cluster-flowered) and Polyanthas.

The **Hybrid Tea (Large-flowered) Roses** are probably the most widely grown class, and are considered the more 'classic' rose. The beautiful individual blooms are borne singly or in groups of three or four. Depending on the climate, the flowers can be anything from 4–7 inches (10–18 cm), and grow from 3–5 feet (1–1.5 m) high.

The **Floribunda (Cluster-flowered) Roses** produce their flowers in clusters. They are generally bushier and the effect created by the masses of blooms can be quite striking. They are free-flowering and largely trouble-free.

As more crosses were made between the Hybrid Teas and Floribundas, it became more and more difficult to discriminate between them. There were Large-flowered Roses with bigger

clusters than some Cluster-flowered Roses and Cluster-flowered Roses with bigger flowers than some Large-flowered Roses, and there are still the in-between varieties that make the classification confusing and sometimes inadequate. In the United States, these in-between roses are often classed as **Grandifloras**, a term not commonly used outside America.

A dwarf variety of *R. polyantha* (about 24 in (60 cm) high) was discovered in Japan by Robert Fortune late last century and brought back to Europe. From it Jean-Baptiste Guillot developed a low growing rose with small, double, white flowers borne in clusters, introduced as 'Paquerette' in 1875. This is generally accepted as the first of the roses classified as **Polyanthas**. Polyantha flowers are small and are produced in clusters. Although they are not much grown these days, some like 'The Fairy' have never really lost their popularity.

There was another class called

Pernetianas after the breeder, Joseph Pernet-Ducher. The roses in this class are primarily yellow. Pernet-Ducher admired the strong yellow of the *Rosa foetida* 'Persian Yellow' and set out to breed its color into Hybrid Perpetuals, Teas and Hybrid Tea (Large-flowered) Roses. The Pernetianas were eventually absorbed into the Hybrid Tea and other classes, giving us the bright yellows and oranges we have today, but bringing also the curse of black spot with them.

There are roses which are perhaps a little bigger, more vigorous or spreading and defy attempts to classify simply, so we call them **Shrubs**. They range in color and fragrance, but because they are easy to grow they are popular with both beginning rose growers and experienced rosarians. Shrub roses are divided into Hybrid Musk, Hybrid Rugosa, English roses and Unclassified Modern Shrubs.

The first **Hybrid Musks** were released in 1913 by the Reverend J. H. Pemberton, an English clergyman and rose enthusiast. These vigorous roses bear very attractive flowers throughout the season, and can be trained to grow around pillars if desired.

The **Hybrid Rugosas** are attractive, large bushy shrubs, growing to some 6 feet (2 m) and have a strong resistance to disease. They respond well to a good pruning.

The **English Roses** were bred specifically by David Austin to capture the fragrance and charm of Old Garden Roses on plants with the vigor, health, color range and repeat flowering of modern roses. They capture the wave of fervor for all things historical that we experience as we approach a new millennium. Old-fashioned has become fashionable!

Ground Cover Roses do not always

Climbing Roses can be trained to grow over walls and verandas.

Modern Garden Roses are popular as they flower regularly throughout the warmer months.

live up to the name. They do not grow as thickly as other ground cover plants and as such do not suit all gardens.

Miniature Roses are small replicas of the Large-flowered Roses, and are described more fully in the introduction to Chapter 4.

Climbing Roses are classified as either Large-flowered or Cluster-flowered. They are often bred from Bush roses, and when this happens, they have the same name, with the word 'Climbing' going before the cultivar name, as in 'Climbing Peace'. Climbers can be trained to grow over walls or verandas. They usually flower in spring.

When selecting roses to grow, do not be seduced by glossy photos or glowing descriptions in books or catalogues. Contact your local rose society for a list of the roses that perform in your area and preferably ask to see them growing.

The ever popular 'Duet' looks great in any garden.

If you are not sure how to classify or name a rose, don't worry. A name does not make it less beautiful, fragrant or romantic. Ultimately, it does not matter what we call it. Don't forget that Shakespeare said: 'A rose by any other name would smell as sweet.'

Rosa 'Abraham Darby'

ABRAHAM DARBY
English Shrub

Named for a founder of the industrial revolution, 'Abraham Darby' was bred by David Austin in 1985 from two modern roses, 'Yellow Cushion' × 'Aloha'. His self-imposed mandate, to create roses with the charm of old garden roses and the strengths of modern ones, meant that he had mainly included old garden roses in his breeding program, but not this time. 'Abraham Darby' is a tall shrub, almost a pillar rose, with classic old rose-shaped blooms of a coppery apricot color, fading towards pink on the outer petals as they age. The flowers are very fragrant, and are borne freely on a healthy, vigorous plant which has spreading, arching growth if not supported.

ADOLF HORSTMANN
(Adolph Horstmann)
Large-flowered/Hybrid Tea

This rose was bred by Kordes (Germany) in 1971 from 'Color Wonder' × 'Dr. A. J. Verhage', and is deep amber yellow, almost gold, with some orange and red flushes in warmer weather. The blooms are moderately fragrant, large, double and ruffled, on long stems with glossy, mid-green foliage. 'Adolf Horstmann' makes an excellent cut flower and is popular with florists because the blooms keep well after cutting. The bush is upright and about 5 feet (1.5 m) tall with bronze-tinted new growth and this free blooming variety makes a good garden rose. It was named after a friend and colleague of the breeder.

AGNES
Hybrid Rugosa

One of the first old fashioned roses in this color, 'Agnes' was bred by Saunders (Canada) in 1922 from *R. rugosa* × *R. foetida* 'Persiana'. It was the result of a search for a winter-hardy yellow rose and certainly fulfilled that requirement. The plant is typically Rugosa, with its rough but shiny, bright green, mint-like leaves and many fine prickles. The flowers are amber yellow, fading to cream with a flat old rose shape. It has a delicate and unusual fragrance, which seems to be a combination of the perfumes of its parents, the sweet perfume of the *rugosa* and the not very pleasant perfume of *foetida*. Unfortunately, it seems to have inherited a habit of black spot from its yellow parent.

ALCHYMIST
Climber

This rose was raised in 1956 by the great German rosarian, Wilhelm Kordes. It was bred from a Large-flowered Climber 'Golden Glow' and a Sweet Briar.

Rosa 'Agnes'

Kordes used the latter and also Scotch Roses to ensure suitability for cold climates. Alchemists tried to turn base metal into gold and, true to its name, this much admired rose is golden. The flowers are large, double and quartered in the old style. They are very fragrant. The plant is strong and can be grown either as a climber or as a large shrub. It will go happily into trees. If it has a fault, it is that the flowers can fade into something less than gold. It is not recurrent.

Rosa 'Alchymist'

Rosa 'Alec's Red'

Rosa 'Alexander'

ALEC'S RED
Large-flowered/Hybrid Tea
Bred by Cocker (Scotland) in 1970 from
'Fragrant Cloud' × 'Dame de Coeur',
this is a free-flowering, healthy, vigorous
plant about 3 feet (1 m) tall with matte,
dark green foliage. Flowers are cherry
red in color and are big, very double,
globular, and last well when cut. The
raiser, Alexander (Alec) Cocker, allowed
several growers to trial it, and his
colleagues affectionately referred to it as
'Alec's Red'. The name stuck. In Britain
it won the Royal National Rose Society's
premier awards for both merit and
fragrance, gaining a 9 out of 10 rating
for the latter from Jack Harkness.
When it was first introduced, it filled a
gap in the red rose stable, with no
significant ones being introduced for
some time.

ALEXANDER
Large-flowered/Hybrid Tea
'Alexander' was bred by Harkness
(England) in 1972 from 'Super Star' ×
('Ann Elizabeth' × 'Allgold'). 'Super
Star' was a new color in roses when it
was first introduced in 1960 but
'Alexander' surpasses its forebear in
both color and health. The luminous
vermilion, semi-double blooms with 22
petals sometimes have scalloped edges
and are borne on long stems. It is a tall,
healthy grower (up to 6 feet (2 m)),
flowering continuously throughout the
growing season. It was named in honor
of Earl Alexander of Tunis, who was an
outstanding British general of World
War II and under whom the breeder had
served.

ALPINE SUNSET
Large-flowered/Hybrid Tea
The name aptly conveys the coloring of
this delightful rose, a restful combination
of peaches, pinks, apricots, creams and

yellows. The large, sweetly scented blooms are borne on firm stems close to the foliage on neat, compact plants. The combination of big bloom and limited growth makes for a wonderful color impact. The leaves are light green and shiny. Although repeat-flowering, there is usually a pause between the summer flowering and the next flush because the plant needs time to recover the energy expended in producing its large blooms in quantity. New stems are not made freely, and die-back will affect it in

severe winters. This award-winning rose was bred from 'Dr. A. J. Verhage' × 'Grandpa Dickson'.

ALTISSIMO
Cluster-flowered Climber

This rose was bred by Delbard-Chabert (France) in 1966, and is a climber in its own right. Flowers are single, large, have seven petals and an intense blood red color opening to show golden stamens. Growth is upright and bushy, and it is disease resistant. Flowers are

Rosa 'Alpine Sunset'

produced continuously in clusters over a long period if spent blooms are removed. 'Altissimo' looks good as a pillar rose on veranda posts, and can even be grown as a huge free-standing bush in the border or shrubbery. Height is to 10–14 feet (3–4 m), but it can be kept lower. Petals sometimes fall quickly after flowering. The single flowers keep well when picked and look good with driftwood or arranged with fruit. Fragrance is slight.

AMBASSADOR
Large-flowered/Hybrid Tea
This rose was bred by Meilland (France) in 1979 from an unnamed seedling × 'Whisky Mac'. It has large, well-formed, double blooms in shades of light orange with yellow shadings, which turn apricot as they age. The long, upright stems make it a good cut flower. Flowers are borne on a tallish bush which grows to 5 feet (1.5 m), and has healthy, dark, semi-glossy foliage. It is not to be confused with the earlier (1930) well-perfumed American Large-flowered rose with the same name.

Rosa 'Altissimo'

AMBER QUEEN
Cluster-flowered/Floribunda
'Amber Queen' was bred by Harkness (England) in 1983 from 'Southampton' × 'Typhoon'. The plump buds develop into large, double (40 petals), fragrant, amber yellow blooms borne in clusters of three to seven. It is a free-flowering, low-growing plant about 24 in (60 cm), and is vigorous and bushy with copper-red to medium green foliage. It makes an attractive, neat, bedding plant, in spite of a propensity to black spot, so spraying is essential in a humid climate. It does appear to have some potential for breeding, as it boasts some valuable progeny (including 'Savoy Hotel'). It won an All-American Rose Selection award in 1988 when it was introduced into the United States.

AMBRIDGE ROSE
(AUSwonder)
English Rose
This is an English Rose of modest size, producing a good continuity of bloom through summer and autumn. The fragrant flowers are rounded, well filled with petals which crowd into each other in the manner of an old Centifolia, and are carried in small clusters. They are

Rosa 'Amber Queen'

Rosa 'Angel Face'

Rosa 'America'

cupped at first, expanding to form rather loose rosettes, the color changing from apricot to apricot-pink and paling towards the outer edges. Growth is short, bushy and upright; the leaves are dark green and somewhat glossy. It was named after a long-running English radio program called 'The Archers'. An episode was written wherein one of the characters went to see this rose at the Chelsea Show and talked to the breeder David Austin.

AMERICA
Large-flowered Climber

Bred from 'Fragrant Cloud' × 'Tradition', this rose was introduced in 1976, and won that year's All-American Rose Selection award. The fragrant flowers are a bright salmon, with a paler reverse, and are borne in clusters. 'America' is a very reliable repeat flowering climber, and dead-heading is recommended to boost repeats. It grows upright to about 8–10 feet (2.4–3 m) and prefers well-drained soils. It does not like humidity and does best in cool climates. Its name suggests that it is very popular in the US, but in fact, 'America' is popular around the world for its exhibition quality blooms and glossy foliage.

ANGEL FACE
Cluster-flowered/Floribunda

This beautifully fragrant rose was bred by Swim and Weeks (United States) in 1968 from ('Circus' × 'Lavender Pinocchio') × 'Sterling Silver'. The pointed buds open to double (30 wavy petals), high-centered blooms of deep mauve-lavender, with darker edges on the petals. If this rose had no other attributes than its fragrance, then it would be worth having, as the fragrance is sweetly intense. The blooms are borne singly and in clusters on a vigorous, upright, bushy plant about 3 feet (1 m) high, with dark green, glossy foliage. 'Angel Face' won an All-American Rose Selection award and a John Cook Medal. It needs a little pampering.

Rosa 'Anne Harkness'

ANNA PAVLOVA
Large-flowered/Hybrid Tea

Named after the famed Russian ballerina, 'Anna Pavlova' was bred by Beales
(England) in 1981. Its breeding is either
unknown or not declared. The blooms
are large, double and highly perfumed,
having broad petals of the most delicate
pink color with deeper overtones. They
make good cut flowers. The bush is free-
flowering and healthy with upright
growth to about 4 feet (1.2 m). It prefers
warm climates and the flowers do not
like rain very much, as they have a
tendency to ball in wet weather.

ANNE HARKNESS
Cluster-flowered/Floribunda

Named for the breeder's niece, this rose
was bred by Harkness (England) in

1979 from 'Bobby Dazzler' × ('Manx
Queen' × 'Prima Ballerina') ×
('Chanelle' × 'Piccadilly'). The globular
bud opens into medium, double (28
ruffled petals), cupped flowers in an
appealing shade of deep but pastel apricot.
The lightly perfumed blooms are borne
in evenly-spaced trusses on a tallish
upright plant to about 5 feet (1.5 m),
with medium-green, semi-glossy foliage.
Harder pruning prevents it from
becoming too tall. It may need protect-
ing from mildew but is not affected by
rain. It makes an excellent cut rose.

ANTIGUA
(JACtig)
Large-flowered/Hybrid Tea

Bred by Warriner (United States) in
1974 from 'South Seas' × 'Golden

Masterpiece', this rose has large blooms which are an interesting blend of colors, opening from plump buds to reveal tints of pink on an apricot base, and becoming pale crimson as they age. They are fairly full of broad, soft petals and do not retain their high centered form for long. There is a light fragrance. The flowers are produced on long stems and make good cut flowers if taken at an early stage. The free-branching plant grows a little taller than average, and is well furnished with leathery, dark green foliage.

AOTEAROA NEW ZEALAND
(New Zealand)
Large-flowered/Hybrid Tea
Bred by McGredy (New Zealand) in 1990 from 'Harmonie' × 'Auckland Metro', the bush is strong and healthy, moderately tall, growing to 5 feet (1.5 m), and has glossy foliage. The large, double blooms have a rich fragrance, with long, shapely buds in a soft, peach pink. It is a good, free-flowering garden variety. 'Aotearoa' was named by the breeder for New Zealand's sesquicentenary. Sam McGredy once said that new pink roses are very hard to sell, so his faith in 'Aotearoa' is quite inspiring.

APRICOT NECTAR
Cluster-flowered/Floribunda
'Apricot Nectar' was bred by Boerner (United States) in 1965 from seedling × 'Spartan'. The ovoid buds open into large, double, cupped flowers in shades of pink-apricot with a golden base. The fragrance is fruity. The flowers are borne in small trusses on a vigorous, medium, free-flowering, healthy, upright plant 4 feet (1.2 m) high, with dark, glossy foliage. It is a quality garden rose and is very popular around the world, winning many prizes at shows. 'Apricot Nectar' is a rose that can be safely planted by the beginner, winning an All-American Rose Selection award in the year of its introduction.

Rosa 'Aotearoa New Zealand'

Rosa 'Apricot Nectar'

ARTHUR BELL
Cluster-flowered/Floribunda

An easy yellow rose to grow, 'Arthur Bell' was bred by McGredy (Northern Ireland) in 1965 from 'Clare Grämmerstorf' × 'Piccadilly'. The yellow flowers fade to creamy yellow as they age. They are large, semi-double and very fragrant, repeating quickly. They are borne singly and in trusses on a vigorous, healthy, medium plant about 5 feet (1.5 m) high, with light green, semi-glossy foliage. It is another of the varieties named after alcoholic beverages, this one for a Scotch whisky. As a parent, it has been a source of the

Rosa 'Arthur Bell'

Kordes' sweet briar strain. 'Arthur Bell' is a good garden rose, although it seems to have lost ground to other varieties.

AUTUMN DELIGHT
Hybrid Musk

'Autumn Delight' was bred by Bentall (England) in 1933 from undisclosed parents. It grows very similarly to a Cluster-flowered and is only of medium height, compared with the other Hybrid Musks. The semi-double flowers are soft cream with maroon stamens, developing from shapely, deeper colored buds. They are borne in clusters on an upright, bushy plant with few thorns and dark green, leathery foliage. It makes a good bedding rose and is an asset in any garden.

BALLERINA
Hybrid Musk

'Ballerina' was bred by Bentall (England) in 1937. Bentall was a gardener for Reverend Joseph Hardwick Pemberton, a distinguished English rosarian, exhibitor, President of the Royal National Rose Society and rose breeder. He originated the Hybrid Musks and following his death, his two gardeners both entered the nursery

Rosa 'Autumn Delight'

business, Bentall following in the footsteps of the master rosarian and releasing his own Hybrid Musks. 'Ballerina' is more like a large polyantha, perhaps even warranting classification as a Modern Shrub. It bears its large clusters of small, soft pink to white flowers continuously throughout the season on a completely trouble-free shrub.

BANTRY BAY
Cluster-flowered Climber

'Bantry Bay' was bred by Sam McGredy in 1967, and gets its climbing habit from one of its parents 'New Dawn'. Flowers come in clusters, are semi-double pale pink on the inside and deep pink on the reverse. Foliage is adequate and disease free and production is continuous. Growth is shortish for a Climbing rose — to 10 feet (3 m). There is some fragrance. 'Bantry Bay' can be used on pillars, arches and fences and tripods and its unassuming semi-double flowers associate well with perennials and bulbs.

Rosa 'Bantry Bay'

Rosa 'Ballerina'

BARONNE E. DE ROTHSCHILD
Large-flowered/Hybrid Tea

This rose was bred by Meilland (France) in 1968 from ('Baccará' × 'Crimson King') × 'Peace', and is one of Peace's many offspring, introduced exactly 100 years after the Hybrid Perpetual 'Baroness Rothschild'. It is a medium grower to 4 feet (1.2 m) with glossy, dark green foliage. The large, double, very fragrant blooms are ruby red with a silvery reverse and are good cut flowers. It is named after the wife of Baron Edmund de Rothschild, famous for his Exbury Hybrid Rhododendrons and is a good garden variety, whose old fashioned color and fragrance belie its modern roots.

BELLE POITEVINE
Hybrid Rugosa

A typical Rugosa, this rose was bred by Bruant (France) in 1894. The bush is resistant to black spot, but is not as tall as some of its family. The long, pointed buds open to semi-double flowers in shades of rich magenta-pink, often with mauve tones, enhanced by its creamy stamens. It is not as fragrant as some of the Rugosas and its heavily veined leaves are quite dark. The foliage is disease resistant.

BELLE PORTUGAISE
(Belle of Portugal)
Large-flowered Climber

Bred by Cayeux (Portugal) in 1903 from *Rosa gigantea* × 'Reine Marie Henriette',

Rosa 'Belle Poitevine'

Rosa 'Baronne Edmund de Rothschild'

Rosa 'Belle Portugaise'

Rosa 'Belle Story'

this very vigorous rose has become almost naturalized in parts of California. In other parts of North America it will not grow at all, as its *R. gigantea* heritage means that it is not frost hardy. A mixture of light salmon, pink, peach and cream shades, the flowers open wide and rather loosely with reflexed petal rims, and hang down on pendulous stems. The olive green leaves droop elegantly, but are susceptible to mildew at times. There is only one flowering, but in climates that suit it, the sight of hundreds of blooms on a high wall or fence is one of spring's horticultural treats.

BELLE STORY
(AUSelle, AUSspry, Bienenweide)
English Rose

David Austin (England) bred this beautiful rose from ('Chaucer' × 'Parade') × ('The Prioress' × 'Iceberg'). The large flowers, borne in sprays, open to resemble peonies, with petals incurving towards the center and reflexing round the outer edges of the flower, revealing the red-gold stamens within. They are rose pink, the shade lightening towards the petal tips, full-petalled, fragrant and bloom in summer. Growth is bushy and vigorous, to average height. The dark semi-glossy foliage is rather small and does not fully clothe the plant, which needs well-drained, fertile soil to thrive. 'Belle Story' was named to honor one of the first nursing sisters to join Britain's Royal Navy in 1864.

BETTY PRIOR
Cluster-flowered/Floribunda

This rose was bred by Prior (England) in 1938 from 'Kirsten Poulsen' × seedling. The ovoid buds are carmine, opening to carmine-pink, single, cupped flowers borne in clusters on a vigorous, healthy, bushy plant with dull, mid-green foliage. It is not particularly brilliant in color, form or perfume, but appears to be one of those roses which grow for anyone, anywhere, flowering continuously throughout the season with a minimum of fuss. A popular 'nostalgia' rose in Australia and New Zealand, it has also enjoyed long popularity in the United States.

Rosa 'Betty Prior'

Rosa 'Bewitched'

Rosa 'Big Purple'

BEWITCHED
Large-flowered/Hybrid Tea

This rose was bred by Lammerts (United States) in 1967 from 'Queen Elizabeth' × 'Tawny Gold', and it is still a popular rose in warm climates. The fairly full-petalled flowers are an even shade of phlox pink and they hold their color even in hot weather. They open with high centers and take on a pleasing rounded outline as the petals reflex, yielding a sweet damask fragrance. The long stems make it an excellent rose for cutting, and it will provide a succession of blooms through summer and autumn. It is a vigorous upright plant and does best in warmer climates. In 1967, it won the All-American Rose Selection and the Portland Gold Medal.

BIG PURPLE
(Nuit d'Orient)
Large-flowered/Hybrid Tea

Bred by Stevens (New Zealand) in 1987 from 'Purple Splendour' × unnamed seedling, the big, well-formed, highly fragrant, classic blooms are deep beetroot purple and are produced on long, single stems. There is some color variation in hot weather, tending more to crimson. The bush has medium, upright growth and is strong, healthy and free-flowering. The breeder was a long serving secretary of the New Zealand Rose Society and he called it as he saw it. It is interesting how many roses have good perfume, belying the statement that 'roses do not have the perfume they used to have'. Perhaps the truth is more like, 'for the most part, only the fragrant roses have survived'.

BILL WARRINER
(JACsur)
Cluster-flowered/Floribunda

This rose was bred from the prize-winning roses 'Sun Flare' × 'Impatient' by Zary (United States) in 1996. It has salmon-orange-coral flowers which are produced in well-spaced, large clusters. The blooms are quite large and are cupped, with a rounded outline as the petals reflex. They have a light fragrance and appear freely through summer and autumn on a free-branching, upright plant with crisp, dark green foliage. It was named for Bill Warriner who is credited with raising over 150 roses during his 25 years with the Jackson & Perkins company.

BISHOP DARLINGTON
Hybrid Musk

Bred by Thomas (United States) in 1926 from 'Aviateur Blèriot' × 'Moonlight', 'Bishop Darlington' has large, loose, informal flowers which are creamy-white to pink with a yellow base to each petal. They are borne freely throughout the season in sprays on a vigorous arching bush with mid- to dark-green foliage, which has a bronze tinge. The blooms are lightly fragrant, typical of the Hybrid Musk roses in its quality.

BLANC DOUBLE DE COUBERT
Hybrid Rugosa

This rose was bred by Cochet-Cochet (France) in 1892 from *R. rugosa* × 'Sombreuil'. Coubert is the village in France where the breeder lived. Jack Harkness questions the listed parentage as well as the big reputation of the rose. As a breeder himself, he could see difficulties achieving such a cross and, although it is the only double, white flowered Rugosa, the blooms are not really all that spectacular compared with other varieties—they spoil in wet weather, the bush is not as well-foliaged as some of the other Rugosas and it is

reluctant to form hips. All this aside, it is still a handsome plant with a sweet perfume and very healthy, disease resistant foliage, typical of its background.

BLAZE
Large-flowered Climber

Kallay (United States) bred this rose in 1932 from 'Paul's Scarlet Climber' × 'Gruss an Teplitz', and it has been popular ever since. Its cheerful scarlet blooms form sheets of color in summer. They are carried in large clusters on strong stems, and open to fairly full-petalled blooms of neatly cupped form.

Rosa 'Bishop Darlington'

Rosa 'Blaze'

Rosa 'Blanc Double de Coubert'

There are often so many blooms that even though they are not large they become rather crowded and the stems may bow under the weight. There is a pleasant light fragrance. It is an easy plant to grow where an extensive, pliable, all-purpose climber is required, for it makes vigorous climbing shoots and covers itself with plentiful medium green leaves which are generally very healthy, though when introduced into Britain they proved prone to mildew.

BLUE GIRL
(KORgi, Cologne Carnival, Kölner Karneval)
Large-flowered/Hybrid Tea
This Kordes bred rose has large, full flowers with about 40 rather short petals, which open to display neatly formed centers before the petals reflex and the shape becomes loosely cupped. They are borne either singly or in clusters, in a pleasing shade of lilac-mauve, which shows bluish notes in periods of warm sunny weather. It flowers freely on its first flush, and

Rosa 'Blue Moon'

maintains a respectable show through summer and autumn. As a garden rose, it is one of the better performers in this color range, and is suitable for beds and borders. It has a bushy habit and dark, leathery, glossy leaves. It won the gold medal in Rome in 1964.

BLUE MOON
(Blue Monday, Mainzer Fastnacht, Sissi)
Large-flowered/Hybrid Tea
'Blue Moon' was bred by Tantau (Germany) in 1964 from undisclosed parents, probably 'Sterling Silver' × unnamed seedling. The name is a little misleading as the color is more a faded lilac, almost gray in dull weather, but brighter in sunlight under a blue sky. The medium sized, well-formed, double blooms are gloriously fragrant and are carried on a healthy, vigorous, upright, free-flowering plant of moderately tall growth, about 5 feet (1.5 m) with few thorns, making a good garden rose and a good cut flower. True blue is genetically impossible for roses, and unless nature takes a hand in converting the pigment through mutation, or genetic engineers can manufacture it or splice it in from another species, the blue rose will remain an elusive dream.

Rosa 'Bonica'

BONICA
(Bonica 82, Demon)
Shrub

The first Shrub rose to win an All-American Rose Selection award, 'Bonica' was bred by Meilland (France) in 1981 from (*R. sempervirens* × 'Mlle Marthe Carron') × 'Picasso'. The smallish flowers are borne continuously in small and large sprays on an arching shrub. They are double (about 40 petals) with an old fashioned look and are a pleasant, medium pink, which is lighter on the edges of the blooms. The foliage is small, dark and semi-glossy. It is a wonderful plant and because it has a lavish flower production, and is easy to care for, every garden should have one.

BONN
Shrub

This is one of Wilhelm Kordes 'park' roses, and was bred in 1950 from 'Hamburg' × 'Independence'. The 'park' roses are designed to be planted and left to their own devices to flower. They do not need to be pampered. The orange-scarlet, double (25 petals) flowers in clusters of ten have a musk perfume. This can be attributed to the Hybrid Musk, 'Eva', from which 'Hamburg' was developed.

Rosa 'Bonn'

The flowers age to purple, but it is not unattractive. 'Bonn' repeats better if the spent blooms are removed, but the later blooms can be allowed to form attractive hips in the autumn. The plant is upright and bushy with healthy, glossy foliage.

BRANDY
Large-flowered/Hybrid Tea

'Brandy' was bred by Swim and Christensen (United States) in 1981 from 'First Prize' × 'Dr A. J. Verhage'. The beautiful, rich apricot color of the well-formed, double blooms fades a little as they age. The flowers have a light, fruity fragrance and are borne freely on a medium sized 4 ½ foot (1.3 m) bush with large, dark green leaves. It needs some protection against black spot. 'Brandy' won the prestigious All-American Rose Selection award in 1982.

BRASS BAND
(JACcofl)
Cluster-flowered/Floribunda

This rose was bred by Christensen (United States) in 1993 from 'Gold

Rosa 'Brandy'

Rosa 'Breath of Life'

flowers age. The medium to large-sized blooms are full petalled. The young flowers have high centers; these become cupped with waved petals as they age. It is very good for flower arrangements as the blooms are long lasting and hold their color when cut; deadhead old flowers. The plant is stiff and upright; if it is to be trained sideways this needs to be done early while the long stems are still pliable. Britain's Royal College of Midwives chose the name, which signifies both the Creator Spirit in Genesis and everybody's first vital act on coming into the world.

BROWN VELVET
(MACcultra, Colorbreak)
Cluster-flowered/Floribunda
Sam McGredy has constantly surprised the rose world with his roses of extraordinary coloring, this one being an unusual blend of orange-red and brown. In cooler climates the brownish tones predominate; in sunnier climates the brown becomes overlaid with orange. Crowded clusters of round buds open into double flowers with quartered petals, which soon reflex to allow golden stamens to peek through and make a pretty contrast with the brownish color. The medium-sized flowers are lightly scented, and continue blooming through summer and autumn. It makes an upright bush of average height and has glossy dark green leaves. It was bred from 'Mary Sumner' × 'Kapai', and won Gold Star of the South Pacific, New Zealand in 1979.

Badge' × seedling. It carries clusters of very full-petalled flowers that open from plump, orange-yellow buds into medium-sized blooms with a rounded form. As they open, they display a fruit salad of colors—melon, peach, papaya and apricot. They have a fruity fragrance for added measure. The flowers appear through summer and autumn, and are especially good in cool weather, which brings out the apricot tones. They contrast nicely with the bright green leaves, which is an important factor to consider when choosing the most effective roses to plant. This rose has an upright, bushy habit. It won the All-American Rose Selection in 1995.

BREATH OF LIFE
(HARquanne)
Large-flowered Climber
This climber was bred by Harkness (England) from 'Red Dandy' × 'Alexander'. It is the color of apricot skin, becoming apricot-pink as the

BUFF BEAUTY
Hybrid Musk
This rose was bred by Bentall (England) in 1939 from 'William Allen Richardson' × unknown. There is some doubt about both the breeder and the parentage of

Rosa 'Buff Beauty'

Rosa 'Cardinal Hume'

Rosa 'Carefree Beauty'

this rose. Some attribute it to Pemberton, who died 12 years before its introduction, while others claim Ann Bentall, the widow of his gardener, is responsible. David Austin claims that the color, growth and scent are consistent with 'Lady Hillingdon' being one of the parents. Whatever the case, it is a glorious shrub, with sprays of small, rich, apricot-yellow blooms, fading to buff and with a sweet, Tea rose fragrance. The long, arching canes are covered in large, leathery, dark-green leaves and when grown closely, can be formed into a dense, lush hedge.

CARDINAL HUME
Shrub

This rose was bred by Harkness (England) in 1984 from (('Lilac Charm' × 'Sterling Silver') × ('Orangeade' × 'Lilac Charm') × ('Orange Sensation' × 'Allgold') × *R. californica*) × 'Frank Naylor'. Now there is a complicated pedigree for you! Significantly, this rose and 'International Herald Tribune' were the start of a new type of rose bred from *R. californica*. The small, almost double, purple blooms are borne in clusters close to the stems, amidst the dark green

foliage, showing off its yellow stamens. The flower color is similar to that of the Gallica 'Cardinal de Richelieu', and the breeder thought it appropriate to name it after a modern cardinal, Basil Hume, Archbishop of Westminster. It is, unfortunately, a little prone to black spot.

CAREFREE BEAUTY
Cluster-flowered/Floribunda

This rose was bred by Buck (United States) in 1977 from seedling × 'Prairie

Princess'. Listed as a shrub in *Modern Roses 10*, its habit of growth is more shrubby than bushy, but whether it is a Large-flowered Shrub or a Cluster-flowered Shrub is debatable. It does have clusters but not often more than four per stem, and the flowers are very big and blowzy. The buds are ovoid, long and pointed, opening to light-rose, lightly scented blooms with 15 to 20 petals on a vigorous, upright but spreading plant about 5 feet (1.5 m) high with olive green, smooth foliage. It is wonderfully healthy and always covered

Rosa 'Casino'

Rosa 'Carefree Delight'

in flowers, making an excellent, low-maintenance garden rose.

CAREFREE DELIGHT
(MEIpotal, Bingo Meidiland, Bingo Meillandecor)
Modern Shrub

Bred by Alain Meilland, 'Carefree Delight' gives a stunning display when planted *en masse*. The shrubs are literally covered with a haze of charming pink blooms continuously through the warmer months. Individually, the relatively small blooms are cup-shaped and semi-double with a hint of cream, and are carried in clusters of up to 15. The growth is vigorous, spreading and well-branched with an exceptional resistance to disease. The graceful, arching canes, covered with glossy green leaves during the growing season, are attractive even in winter and the pretty rosehips, which follow the flowers, bring hungry birds into the garden. It has won numerous awards, including the All-American Rose Selection in 1996.

CASINO
Large-flowered Climber

'Casino' was bred by Sam McGredy IV in 1963, and won a gold medal at The Royal National Rose Society Trials in 1963. Growth is vigorous to 10 feet (3 m), foliage is large, dark green and disease resistant. Flowers are large, and a pleasing clear soft yellow with very long stems. They repeat usually four or five times per year. The hips, if dead-heading is not completed, are large, round and attractive. The well-shaped buds open to very full quartered blooms that hold well. 'Casino' makes a good cut flower.

CATHERINE DENEUVE
Large-flowered/Hybrid Tea

Named for the French actress, 'Catherine Deneuve' was bred by Meilland

Rosa 'Cécile Brünner, Climbing'

Rosa 'Catherine Deneuve'

(France) in 1981 from undisclosed parents. This rose has long, elegant buds, opening to big, decorative, semi-double blooms of a rich salmon color, that give a lovely sweet fragrance. The flowers have long stems, are good for cutting and are set off by the dark green, thick foliage. This medium plant grows to 4 feet (1.2 m) high.

CÉCILE BRÜNNER
China

The breeding thought to be used by Ducher in 1881 was a double-flowered Multiflora × 'Souvenir d'un Ami'. It is popularly known as the 'Sweetheart Rose', and its classic Large-flowered shape, delicate pink color and miniature proportions make that a suitable name. The buds are long and pointed, opening to blush-pink blooms with a sweet, tea-rose fragrance on a compact plant to 32 in (80 cm), with small, pointed, soft, dark foliage. Because it has only 14 chromosomes, it is not easy for breeders to use. It should not be confused with the rampant-growing 'Bloomfield Abundance', with its huge heads of buds and elongated sepal on each bud, which is probably a sport of 'Cécile Brünner'. The photograph shows 'White Cécile Brünner'.

Rosa 'Cécile Brünner'

CÉCILE BRÜNNER, CLIMBING
Climbing Polyantha

This was discovered in 1894 by Hosp (United States), and went on to win the Royal Horticultural Society's Award of Merit. It is a very vigorous climber and a more successful form of plant than the bush version. Although technically a summer flowerer, a good plant on a warm wall will produce sporadic flowers until well into autumn. It is very popular and widely grown. Do not confuse it with 'Bloomfield Abundance'.

Rosa 'Champagne Cocktail'

Rosa 'Yellow Charles Austin'

CELEBRITY
Large-flowered/Hybrid Tea
This popular rose was bred by Weeks
(United States) in 1986 from
('Sunbonnet' × 'Mister Lincoln') ×
'Yellow Yo-Yo'. It has large, deep yellow
flowers which pale slightly as they age.
The well-formed, high centered blooms
have a delicious fruity fragrance and are
usually produced singly, making this a
very good rose for exhibition. It also
makes a wonderful cut-flower. 'Celebrity' is a very free flowering rose with
dark green, disease-resistant foliage. It
can be propagated by budding. This
really is a celebrity in the rose world!

CHAMPAGNE COCKTAIL
(HORflash)
Cluster-flowered/Floribunda
This rose won a gold medal in Glasgow
in 1990. It was bred by Horner (England) in 1983 from 'Old Master' ×
'Southampton'. It certainly lives up to its
name with its pale apricot-yellow,
medium-sized flowers, which are flecked
and splashed pink with a yellow reverse.
The double blooms have a delicate

fragrance and are repeat-flowering. The
foliage is medium green and glossy on a
bushy plant which is ideal both as a
bedding plant and as a standard.

CHARLES AUSTIN
(and Yellow Charles Austin)
English Shrub
Named for the breeder's father, this rose
was bred in 1973 from 'Aloha' ×
'Chaucer'. It is another of the varieties
suitable for use as a pillar rose when
supported and lightly pruned, with its
large, cupped, full-petalled flowers of
apricot-yellow, paling with age and
becoming tinged with pink. They have a
strong, fruity fragrance and are borne
singly or in clusters of two to seven, on
arching stems, on a vigorous plant with
dense, green foliage. The yellow sport,
'Yellow Charles Austin', with similar
characteristics was released in 1981, and
is shown in the photograph.

CHARLOTTE ARMSTRONG
Large-flowered/Hybrid Tea
This rose was bred by Lammerts
(United States) in 1940 from 'Soeur

Thérèse' × 'Crimson Glory'. It is a highly acclaimed rose and has won many awards, including the All-American Rose Selection in 1941 and the RNRS gold medal in 1950. It has large pointed buds which open to well-formed, deep pink double flowers containing 35 petals. They are fragrant. The foliage is dark and leathery and the plant is vigorous but compact.

CHAUCER
English Shrub

One of David Austin's early varieties, 'Chaucer' was bred in 1970 from 'Duchesse de Montebello' × 'Constance Spry'. Its repeat flowering is somewhat surprising, given that neither parent is remontant. One of the parents of 'Constance Spry' is certainly remontant, so one must conclude that the Gallica parent must also have had a remontant ancestor. The deeply cupped flowers, some showing stamens in the center, are a light pink color, paling towards the

edges, with a 'myrrh' fragrance, delicious to some, but not appreciated by all noses. The medium, upright bush has Gallica-like prickles with large, modern, medium green, matte leaves. 'Chaucer' features in the breeding of many good roses bred after 1970.

Rosa 'Charlotte Armstrong'

Rosa 'Chaucer'

CHERISH
(JACsal)
Cluster-flowered/Floribunda

This is one of a series of compact, slightly spreading roses bred by Warriner (United States) in 1980. Its parents were 'Bridal Pink' × 'Matador'. It has short flat buds which produce coral-pink flowers containing 28 petals. There is only a slight fragrance. The foliage is dark green and healthy on an attractive, compact plant with a slightly spreading habit. It can be propagated by budding. 'Cherish' won the All-American Rose Selection in 1980.

CHICAGO PEACE
Large-flowered/Hybrid Tea

This sport of the famous 'Peace' was discovered by a gardener named Johnston in Chicago, hence the name. It was introduced in 1962 by the Conard-Pyle Company. Some roses, like 'Peace', readily mutate. 'Chicago Peace' has, with 'Climbing Peace' and 'Climbing Chicago Peace', stood the test of time. 'Tony Peace', 'Narre Peace' or 'Kronenbourg' ('Flaming Peace') are not grown much nowadays. 'Chicago Peace' is identical to 'Peace' in all ways except the color, which is more intense and shaded variably with yellow, pink, copper and orange tones. Like its parent, it needs protection from black spot. The lightly perfumed flowers are well-formed and double on a glossy foliaged, spreading bush up to 4 feet (1.2 m) high.

CHRISTIAN DIOR
Large-flowered/Hybrid Tea

Named for the Parisian fashion designer, 'Christian Dior' was bred by Meilland (France) in 1959 from ('Independence' × 'Happiness') × ('Peace' × 'Happiness'). The large, well-formed blooms in a crimson red with lighter reverse are of exhibition standard. The flowers have a negligible scent. When protected from powdery mildew, the plant makes a good garden specimen about 3 feet (1 m) tall, bearing its flowers freely and singly on long stems that are excellent for cutting. It won the Geneva gold medal in 1958 and the All-American Rose Selection award in 1962.

Rosa 'Cherish'

Rosa 'Chicago Peace'

Rosa 'Circus'

Rosa 'Chrysler Imperial'

CHRYSLER IMPERIAL
Large-flowered/Hybrid Tea

This was bred by Lammerts (United States) in 1952 from 'Charlotte Armstrong' × 'Mirandy'. The large, double, well-formed blooms are a deep, velvety, rich crimson but turn bluish as they age. The flowers have a pleasant fragrance. The matte, medium green foliage enhances the appearance of the flowers on this compact (30 in (75 cm) high) plant, but it does suffer from die back after a few years and mildew in cold weather. It won an All-American Rose Selection award in 1952. There was some dispute raised by the car company over the name, as it was originally intended to be named simply 'Chrysler'.

CIRCUS
Cluster-flowered/Floribunda

'Circus' was bred by Swim (United States) in 1956 from 'Fandango' × 'Pinocchio'. The urn-shaped buds open to large, double (45–58 petals), high-centered flowers which are yellow marked with pink, salmon and scarlet. They have a spicy fragrance and are borne in large clusters on a medium, bushy plant to 3 feet (1 m), with semi-glossy, leathery foliage. It is a well-decorated rose, winning gold medals in Geneva and England and an All-American Rose Selection award.

Rosa 'Claire Rose'

CLAIRE ROSE
English Shrub

Austin named this rose for his daughter Claire Calvert in 1986. Its parents are 'Charles Austin' × (seedling × 'Iceberg'). The flowers are large and of perfect old-fashioned form, in a delicate blush pink shade, which fades almost to white with age. They are cupped at first, opening to flat, many-petalled rosettes with a lovely perfume on a strong, upright plant about 4 feet (1.2 m) high, which has an abundance of pale green leaves. It can become marked by rain, but this is a small fault and it makes an excellent companion plant in a border (it is sometimes, like its parent, 'Charles Austin', a little ungainly on its own), being one of the most exquisitely beautiful English roses.

Rosa 'Color Magic'

Rosa 'Cocktail'

Rosa 'Clair Matin'

CLAIR MATIN
Cluster-flowered Climber

The result of a complicated series of crosses, 'Clair Matin' was bred in France by Meilland in 1960. It flowers in huge panicles of 30 or 40 small flowers, which are soft salmon pink and open quickly to show stamens. There are only 15 petals. Fragrance is that of Sweet Briar. The rich green foliage is dark, leathery and disease-free. Very few hips are produced leading to continuous flowering. Growth is to 10–14 feet (3–4 m). 'Clair Matin' is an excellent Pillar rose, or can be grown on a tripod or used as a huge bush at the back of a border. The long arching panicles of flowers are ideal for large decorations. It won a thoroughly deserved gold medal at Bagatelle in 1960.

COCKTAIL
Cluster-flowered Shrub

This rose was introduced by Meilland in 1961. It was bred from 'Phyllis Bide' and two red roses, a double scarlet Cluster-flowered bush 'Independencs' and a semi-double Polyantha 'Orange Triumph'. 'Cocktail', however, has single flowers (five petals), which are geranium to yellow in color and borne in clusters on an upright semi-climbing shrub which reaches about 4 × 2 feet (2 m × 1.2 m). It is suitable for use either as a short climber, as pillar rose, as a shrub or as a standard. It is very spectacular because of the unusual intense color and the multitudinous flowers. 'Cocktail' is more or less continuous flowering and is said to tolerate poor soils.

COLOR MAGIC
(JACmag)
Large-flowered/Hybrid Tea

'Color Magic' was bred from seedling × 'Spellbinder' in 1978 by Warriner (United States). The apricot-pink buds open to large, double, 25-petalled blooms which turn as they open from ivory-pink to a rich deep rose. There is little scent, but this is made up for by the repeat-flowering. The blooms are borne on long stems making this a wonderful cut flower rose. It is a tall grower with dark, very healthy foliage. This is also a good bedding rose.

COMPASSION
(Belle de Londres)
Large-flowered Climber

The soft salmon apricot color with well-formed blooms of 36 petals borne on long stems is rare in Climbing roses. Bred by Harkness in 1973, it won gold medals in Baden-Baden, Orleans and Geneva, the Edland Fragrance Medal at The Royal National Rose Society in 1973 and was a winner in the German Rose Selection Trials too—quite an achievement. 'Compassion' grows to 10 feet (3 m) and is excellent as a Pillar rose or a large free-standing shrub. Foliage is large, dark green and tough and flowers are very durable. Good color, wonderful perfume, well-shaped buds and plenty of flowers over a long period make 'Compassion' very popular. It won't grow too big and can be controlled by pruning, with no loss of flower production.

CONSTANCE SPRY
English Shrub

The first of the English Roses, 'Constance Spry' was bred from 'Belle Isis' × 'Dainty Maid' in 1961. Being a cross between a Cluster-flowered and a Spring-flowering Gallica, it only flowers

Rosa 'Compassion'

once. It was the ancestor of most of the English Roses (the reds excluded, being mainly developed from the Chianti/ Tuscany line). It can be a large, sprawling shrub, but is better trained as a climber to attain its best. The extremely large, cupped, old-world flowers are a lovely soft pink. They have a strong myrrh fragrance, suggesting that 'Splendens' must have been in the ancestry of 'Belle Isis'. 'Constance Spry' has passed this fragrance on with remarkable persistence to its progeny. This graceful rose was named for the famous flower arranger.

CORNELIA
Hybrid Musk
Raised by the Reverend Pemberton of Essex, 'Cornelia' was released in 1925,

from unknown parents. It has been popular ever since. The color of the flowers ranges from a pale apricot to a salmon pink, and they are borne in clusters. True to its background, the fragrance is distinctly musky. An almost thornless plant, it can look very effective cascading down a wall or veranda, or trained around a pillar. It can grow up to 10 feet (3 m), and prefers a sunny spot out of the wind.

DAINTY BESS
Large-flowered/Hybrid Tea
This unusual rose was bred by Archer (England) in 1925 from 'Ophelia' × 'Kitchener of Khartoum'. It is unusual among the roses in this collection because it is a single rose, having only five petals. The blooms, which are borne in clusters, are a soft, rose pink with very distinct, maroon stamens and a fresh, light perfume. The upright bush is free-flowering and grows to about 3 feet (1 m) with dark green, semi-glossy foliage and was named for the breeder's wife. 'Dainty Bess' is a lovely decorative and garden rose.

DAPPLE DAWN
English Shrub
'Dapple Dawn' is a sport of 'Red Coat' introduced in 1983, and is one of the single roses belonging to this class. The breeder believes they should be placed

Rosa 'Constance Spry'

Rosa 'Dapple Dawn'

Rosa 'Dainty Bess'

Rosa 'Delicata'

with the Modern Shrubs, as they do not quite fit his intention for the English Roses, most of which have the large, many-petalled, flat, cupped or quartered blooms. The flowers are large, and are colored a delicate pink with stronger pink veins and long, yellow stamens. They are borne continuously and freely in well-spaced clusters on a shrub with mid-green foliage, which may be pruned in keeping with a bush rose, or grown to head-height with only light trimming.

DEEP SECRET
(Mildred Scheel)
Large-flowered/Hybrid Tea

'Deep Secret' was raised by Tantau (Germany) in 1977 from undisclosed parents. The large, well-formed, semi-double blooms are a very deep, velvety crimson and very fragrant. The strong stems make them suitable for cutting. The free-flowering plant is upright, to about 3 feet (1 m), and has glossy foliage. It is particularly healthy for a rose in this coloring. It is very popular in Britain, but not widely available elsewhere.

DELICATA
Hybrid Rugosa

This well-named rose was bred by Cooling (United States) in 1898. No

Rosa 'Deep Secret'

parents are listed. Because of the difficulties Rugosas present to breeders by shedding their pollen very early, many are probably self-pollinated or chance seedlings. 'Delicata' is a smaller plant than many Rugosas. Its sweetly fragrant, semi-double flowers are a soft, lilac-pink, similar to the species, showing attractive, creamy-yellow stamens. They are borne in clusters on a compact, dense plant with mid-green, rugose foliage, but only intermittently set hips.

DIAMOND JUBILEE
Large-flowered/Hybrid Tea

This rose was bred by Boerner in 1947 ('Maréchel Niel' × 'Feu Pernet-Ducher') to commemorate Jackson and Perkins' 75 years as rose growers and hybridizers. The bud is ovoid; the blooms are large (5–6 in (12–15 cm)), double (28 petals), of reasonable exhibition form, a gorgeous buff yellow color and sweetly perfumed. Being averse to spring rain, they're so

Rosa 'Don Juan'

Rosa, 'Diamond Jubilee'

much better in the autumn. Dark green leathery foliage covers a compact upright bush to 5 feet (1.6 m), often taller. It won the All-American Rose Selection in 1948.

DON JUAN
Large-flowered Climber
This is a dark velvety red climber with large double blooms (35 petals). The flowers have a good repeat cycle and are very fragrant. The foliage is dark, leathery and glossy on a plant which grows to medium height. This rose looks wonderful growing up a pillar or over a wall. It was bred by Malandrone (United States) in 1958 from 'New Dawn' seedling × 'New Yorker'.

DORTMUND
Shrub
Named after the city of Dortmund, this rose was bred by Kordes (Germany) in 1955 from seedling × *R. kordesii*. It can be treated as a small climber, a weeping standard or as a somewhat large and lax shrub. It has pointed buds, which open

to big, single flowers of crimson with a white eye. They are borne freely in clusters throughout the season, making quite an impact en masse. The attractive foliage is dark and glossy.

DOUBLE DELIGHT
Large-flowered/Hybrid Tea

Bred by Swim and Ellis (United States) in 1977 from 'Granada' × 'Garden Party', the name suggests two things to be excited about. The perfume is heavenly and the color unique. The usually well-formed, fairly full blooms are a rich cream color, splashed with pink to cherry red on the outside of the petals, depending on the aspect. The free-flowering, spreading bush grows to 3 feet (1 m). It prefers full sun. It won the All-American Rose Selection award in 1977 and was the fifth rose chosen for the World Federation of Rose Societies' Hall of Fame.

DOVE
English Shrub

'Dove' was bred by David Austin (England) in 1984 from 'Wife of Bath'

× 'Iceberg' seedling. The buds are pointed, but the flowers are rosette-shaped when they open, with a fresh, apple fragrance and are white, tinged with dusky blush. They are borne freely on a low, spreading, graceful plant with an abundance of dark, pointed foliage.

Rosa 'Dortmund'

Rosa 'Dove'

Rosa 'Double Delight'

DUBLIN BAY
Cluster-flowered Climber

'Dublin Bay' was bred by McGredy in 1974 from 'Bantry Bay' and 'Altissimo'. It gets its color and texture from 'Altissimo' and its freedom of flower from 'Bantry Bay'. 'Dublin Bay' is extremely popular in New Zealand, and gaining popularity elsewhere for its rich red, long lasting flowers and its ability to clothe itself with blooms from ground level to its summit. Flowers are largish

Rosa 'Duet'

and fragrance is quite strong. It makes a perfect Pillar rose to 10 feet (3 m) and is just as good on a tripod. Flowering is continuous if spent blooms are removed, and 'Dublin Bay' stands up well in both hot and cold conditions. Foliage is plentiful and disease resistant. It is a thoroughly reliable Climbing rose.

DUET
Large-flowered/Hybrid Tea

'Duet' was bred by Swim (United States) in 1960 from 'Fandango' × 'Roundelay'. This rose has stood the test of time and appears to be making a comeback. The semi-double blooms, often borne in clusters, are not especially big, particularly well-formed or fragrant, but the number of them and the quick repeating make 'Duet' an excellent garden variety. The color is salmon pink with a deeper reverse on its slightly ruffled petals. The plant is healthy, disease resistant, up to 5 feet (1.5 m) tall, with bronze-green, glossy foliage. It won the coveted All-American Rose Selection award in 1961 and remains a trouble-free rose for the beginner, even if the color is a little harsh for some eyes.

Rosa 'Echo'

Rosa 'Dublin Bay'

Rosa 'Edelweiss'

Rosa 'Electron'

ECHO
(Baby Tausendschön)
Polyantha

'Echo' is a Polyantha rose (Multiflora ×
China), introduced by Peter Lambert of
Trier in Germany in 1914. It is dwarf,
growing to about 24 in (60 cm) high,
carrying blooms in bouquets which are
about 12 in (30 cm) wide. The flowers
are full and pink, mottled with white.
It flowers repeatedly throughout the
season from spring to late autumn.
Interestingly, it is a sport of a Multiflora
Rambler, 'Tausendschön' ('Thousand
Beauties') of 1906. When such sports
occur from a once blooming rose, the
dwarf aberration, instead of putting its
energies to raising canes for the next
season, puts them into making more
flowers.

EDELWEISS
(Snowline)
Cluster-flowered/Floribunda

A rose that really should be better
known, 'Edelweiss' was bred by Poulsen
(Denmark) in 1970. The parentage is
not listed. The creamy-white flowers are
large and double (31 petals), and are
borne freely on a low plant about 24 in
(60 cm). It is a good bedding rose with a
pleasing fragrance.

ELECTRON
(Mullard Jubilee)
Large-flowered/Hybrid Tea

Sam McGredy (New Zealand) bred this
fine rose in 1970 from 'Paddy McGredy'
× 'Prima Ballerina'. It is a dual purpose
rose—it is good on the show bench as
well as being an excellent garden rose.
The very double flowers are deep rose
pink. They are slow to open but have
perfect form and a strong fragrance. The
bush is moderately tall and is well-
foliaged to ground level. It inherits its
magnificent foliage from 'Prima Ballerina'. This is a great bedding rose as the
flowers hold their color very well. It has
been awarded many gold medals, and
won the prestigious All-American Rose
Selection in 1973.

Rosa 'Elizabeth of Glamis'

Rosa 'Elina'

Rosa 'Elizabeth Harkness'

ELINA
(Peaudouce)
Large-flowered/Hybrid Tea
'Elina' was bred by Dickson (Northern Ireland) in 1983 from 'Nana Mouskouri' × 'Lolita'. The long-stemmed flowers are large, well-formed and double in a rich cream color, and are good for cutting. They are borne prolifically on a strong, healthy plant up to 6 feet (1.8 m) tall that is another easy-to-grow variety for the beginner. It is not a particularly fragrant rose. The name 'Elina' is the preferred one these days, as its synonym 'Peaudouce' is a perfect example of how an excellent variety can be spoiled by blatant commercialism, this being the name of a brand of babies' diapers.

ELIZABETH HARKNESS
Large-flowered/Hybrid Tea
Jack Harkness (England) bred this rose in 1969 from 'Red Dandy' × 'Piccadilly'. It is a perfect example of how unpredictable crosses can turn out, as the red and garish yellow and red parents would seem more likely to produce dazzling offspring. Not so! The large, well-formed, double blooms are the most

delicate of pastel shades in creamy buff with a hint of apricot deep in the center and a light fragrance. The bush, covered in mid green, semi-glossy foliage, is healthy, although not too tall, and is unlikely to exceed 3 feet (1 m). It was named for the breeder's daughter as a wedding present and performs better in a cooler climate.

ELIZABETH OF GLAMIS
(Irish Beauty)
Cluster-flowered/Hybrid Tea

Named for Britain's Queen Mother, 'Elizabeth of Glamis' was bred by McGredy (Northern Ireland) in 1964 from 'Spartan' × 'Highlight'. The large, flat, double (35 petals) blooms are a light orange-salmon and are borne in clusters on a vigorous, compact bushy plant, which grows to 3 feet (1 m). The bush is handsome, and the flowers have the most magnificent perfume. It won a gold medal in England. It is free-flowering,

but a little susceptible to disease, and requires good cultivation to achieve the best results.

ELLEN
(AUScup)
English Rose

'Ellen' was bred by Austin (England) in 1984 using 'Charles Austin' × seedling. The flowers are a rich but soft apricot tinged with brown. They are beautifully cupped in the bud stage and open to a loose quartered formation. The scent is very strong. There are about 40 petals in cool weather but fewer in summer heat. The leaves are large and rather coarse and there are quite a few thorns. It has a bushy but rather ungainly habit, with long shoots towering above the shorter growth. After an excellent performance in the spring, flowering is continuous but sparse in the summer and more profuse in the autumn. Individual blooms can be very beautiful.

Rosa 'Ellen'

Rosa 'Ena Harkness'

Rosa 'Ellen Willmott'

ELLEN WILLMOTT
Large-flowered/Hybrid Tea
Bred by Archer (England) in 1936 from 'Dainty Bess' × 'Lady Hillingdon', the cross is an unlikely one, since 'Lady Hillingdon', like many of the Tea roses,

is a triploid (21 chromosomes) and is difficult to breed with. The result has been, however, a charming, single variety with pronounced golden stamens surrounded by wavy, cream petals with a pink blush. The flowers are borne freely on a vigorous bush up to 5 feet (1.5 m), with glossy, dark green foliage and was named after the legendary gardener and author of *The Genus Rosa*, who was said to have ordered 400 plants of the variety bearing her name.

ENA HARKNESS
Large-flowered/Hybrid Tea
'Ena Harkness' was bred by an amateur breeder, Norman (England) in 1946 from 'Crimson Glory' × 'Southport'. It must have been frustrating for the professionals when, with limited re-sources and only a few seeds — perhaps only one hip — an amateur was able to produce three commercially viable plants, the most famous being the one named after the wife of his friend, William Harkness. The other two were 'Red Ensign' and 'William Harvey'. 'Ena Harkness' has shapely blooms of bright, velvety crimson, freely produced on a rather low bush, about 27 in (70 cm) with somewhat sparse, mid-green foliage. The necks of the blooms are weak and there are many better varieties to grow for the home gardener these days.

ERFURT
Hybrid Musk
'Erfurt' was bred by Kordes (Germany) in 1939 from 'Eva' × 'Réveil Dijonnais'. This rose could easily be included with the Modern Shrubs, but its seed-parent, 'Eva', a Hybrid Musk, justifies its place among the Hybrid Musks. The flowers are semi-single, open and colored bright pink, paling to white in the center, which

displays prominent brown anthers. They are about the same size as the average Cluster-flowered Rose and have a distinct musk perfume. The are borne throughout the season on a bushy, arching shrub, on which the new bronze growth, maturing to dark green, forms an attractive background for its flowers.

ESCAPADE
Cluster-flowered/Floribunda
An excellent garden specimen, 'Escapade' was bred by Harkness (England)

Rosa 'Escapade'

in 1967 from 'Pink Parfait' × 'Baby Faurax'. The large semi-double (12 petals) blooms are soft pink with a white center and are borne freely in trusses. They are well-spaced and never give the impression they are cluttered. The shrub-like plant is a medium height, about 4 feet (1.2 m), with light green, glossy foliage. The flowers have a light, spicy fragrance, with the pink becoming almost lilac as they age, making it a good companion with heritage roses. It lasts well when cut, but needs to be cut before the flowers actually open. 'Escapade' won gold medals in Baden Baden, Belfast and Erfurt, and a prize in Copenhagen, and deserves to be more widely grown.

ETOILE DE HOLLANDE
Large-flowered Climber
This rose was a climbing sport of the bush variety that occurred in Holland at Leenders Nursery in 1931. Flowers are bright red, of 35 to 40 petals that open to show golden stamens. The scent is very strong and of true damask perfume. This probably accounts for its continual

Rosa 'Etoile de Hollande'

Rosa 'Erfurt'

Rosa 'Europeana'

Rosa 'Eva'

popularity. Growth is vigorous to 14–16 feet (4–5 m), making 'Etoile de Hollande' a fine rose for training on a wall or fence. Repeat flowering is good and disease resistance is excellent for a red rose. Foliage is soft green and plentiful. Buds are pretty but open very quickly especially in warm weather. It is a good choice for planting near the house where its delicious perfume can be appreciated.

EUROPEANA
Cluster-flowered/Floribunda

'Europeana' was bred by de Ruiter (Netherlands) in 1963 from 'Ruth Leuwerik' × 'Rosemary Rose'. The large, dark crimson, slightly fragrant flowers are rosette-shaped and are borne in large, heavy clusters on a 3 feet (1 m) high bushy, vigorous plant. It has large, bronze-green foliage with dark red tones when new. It won gold medals at The Hague and Portland as well as an All-American Rose Selection award. Although there are many red Cluster-flowered Roses, this one has maintained its popularity because of its excellent health, continuous flowering and the fact that it is a good all-around garden variety.

EVA
Hybrid Musk

Another Kordes rose, 'Eva' was bred in 1938 from 'Robin Hood' × 'J. C. Thornton'. It does not possess the elegance or popularity of some of the Hybrid Musks, but it achieved the goals of vigor and hardiness set by its breeder. It passed these characteristics on to the Cluster-flowered 'Pinocchio', and through it, to its many excellent progeny. Through another of its off-spring, 'Baby Château', came 'Queen Elizabeth' and the modern geranium-scarlet roses. It is a somewhat stiff plant with dark green, matte foliage, covered with trusses of almost single, carmine to red flowers.

EVELYN
(AUSsaucer)
English Rose

'Evelyn' is one of David Austin's most beautiful roses. It gets its color from 'Tamora' and its vigor from 'Graham Thomas'. The huge, very full blooms of

Rosa 'Evelyn'

Rosa 'Evelyn Fison'

over 40 petals open from a very broad shallow cup to become rosette form at maturity. The color is usually rich apricot with a yellow base but it can be much more pink in hot weather. It makes a strong, upright shrub of medium growth, and flowering is continuous and profuse. This rose has one of the most delicious perfumes of all the Austin roses. The firm of Crabtree & Evelyn chose 'Evelyn' to advertise their perfume company.

EVELYN FISON
(Irish Wonder)
Cluster-flowered/Floribunda
Named for the wife of a friend of the breeder Sam McGredy, 'Evelyn Fison' was bred in 1962 from 'Moulin Rouge' × 'Korona'. The double, scarlet blooms with light fragrance are borne in broad clusters on a medium, spreading plant about 4 feet (1.2 m) high, with dark, glossy foliage. Like many other roses in this coloring, the mites love its foliage.

Being one of the earliest to be attacked, it may be planted in the garden as an indicator, to let you know when measures to deal with spider mites need to be implemented. It is an excellent garden and exhibition rose, and is generally healthy and free-flowering.

EYE PAINT
Cluster-flowered/Floribunda
Another McGredy rose, 'Eye Paint' was bred in 1975 from seedling × 'Picasso'. It is one of the early 'hand-painted' roses McGredy pioneered through the introduction of 'Fruhlingsmorgen', a hybrid *pimpinellifolia*, to his breeding program. The ovoid buds open to medium-sized, single flowers, which are bright red with a whitish eye enhanced by prominent, yellow stamens. The

plants are spreading and shrubby with medium green, glossy foliage. It can become very tall almost behaving like a pillar rose, with its free-flowering, big clusters making quite an impact. It may need some protection from black spot. Apparently 'Eye Paint' was only intended as a nickname, but it stuck.

FAIR BIANCA
(AUSca)
English Rose

'Fair Bianca', the first of David Austin's white roses, was bred in 1982, and has

Rosa 'Eye Paint'

medium-sized, flat and quartered flowers that form full rosettes. The very double blooms have 60 or more petals and appear in clusters. The color is variable, being quite pink in the center of the bloom in hot weather and buff in autumn, but they are always beautiful. The perfume is very strong and flowering is continuous. An average-sized upright plant, it is excellent for small gardens and looks charming with perennial plants and bulbs in borders. Clumps of 3, 5 or 7 plants look far more pleasing than single specimens.

FELICIA
Hybrid Musk

This rose was bred by Pemberton (England) in 1928 from 'Trier' × 'Ophelia'. It is one of the best of the class and if pruned harder, makes an elegant Cluster-flowered Rose; light pruning allows it to develop into a graceful shrub, but this takes time, so be patient. The coral-apricot buds open to rather loose, semi-double blooms, which are blush-peach-pink, paling as they age. The pleasing, moderate fragrance enhances its appeal as a fine, free-flowering garden rose.

Rosa 'Felicia'

Rosa 'Fair Bianca'

Rosa 'First Kiss'

'Fimbriata' are reminiscent of a dian-thus. Perhaps the fimbriation is caused by the breakdown in the genetic make up of the plant as a result of crossing two widely separated parents, neither of which displays this attractive character-istic. The fragrant blooms are white, blushed pale pink, and are borne in clusters on a compact, bushy, upright shrub with light green foliage. Like many of the Rugosas, it is an excellent hedging rose, which, when grown en masse, forms a dense, impermeable barrier. Some of the more robust Rugosas are also used effectively as crash barriers along roadways.

Rosa 'Fimbriata'

FIMBRIATA
(Phoebe's Frilled Pink, Dianthiflora)
Hybrid Rugosa
Bred by Morlet (France) in 1891 from
R. rugosa × 'Madame Alfred Carrière',
the small, frilly, double flowers of

FIRST KISS
(JACling)
Cluster-flowered/Floribunda
Warriner (United States) bred this rose in 1991 from 'Sun Flare' × 'Simplicity'. It bears small clusters of pale pink, moderately full flowers with 25 petals

Rosa 'First Love'

Rosa 'First Prize'

that shade to yellow at the base. They are slightly fragrant and have an appealing simple charm. The medium green foliage is bushy to ground level and the plant is compact and has good disease resistance. It is suitable for bedding.

FIRST LOVE
(Premier Amour)
Large-flowered/Hybrid Tea

The parents of 'First Love' are 'Charlotte Armstrong' × 'Show Girl', and it was bred by Swim (United States) in 1951. It has long, elegant buds which open to semi-double blooms of soft, blush pink with deeper shadings. There is some fragrance in the blooms, which are borne on long stems suitable for cutting. It is a medium bush, growing to about 3 feet (1 m) tall, with light green, leathery foliage. It is a parent of the better known 'Eiffel Tower', which is more popular because of its perfume.

FIRST PRIZE
Large-flowered/Hybrid Tea

This lovely rose was bred by Boerner (United States) in 1970 from 'Enchant-ment' seedling × 'Golden Masterpiece' seedling. The huge, well-formed, fragrant blooms in a blend of soft pinks, with a hint of cream at the center, are borne singly on long, straight stems that make it a very good cutting rose. A free-flowering, vigorous and upright plant, growing to 4 feet (1.2 m), it has dark green, leathery foliage. It is a good garden rose. As the name suggests, it has won many prizes, especially in the United States, where it won an All-American Rose Selection award as well as the American Rose Society's gold medal. In addition to its value as a bedding plant, it has been used extensively in breeding programs with some very successful progeny.

F. J. GROOTENDORST
Hybrid Rugosa

Named after a Dutch nurseryman, this rose was bred by de Goey (Holland) from *R. rugosa rubra* × 'Madame Norbert Levavasseur', and was introduced in 1918. Like 'Fimbriata', the blooms of 'F. J. Grootendorst' are small with fringed petals. The clusters are tighter, lacking in fragrance and are a rather dull crimson. It is, however, more robust and flushes are repeated more freely than on most of the Rugosa hybrids. Although the leaves are typically rugose, they also show signs of their Polyantha heritage. It is not inclined to set hips, which might be a reason for its free-flowering nature.

FLAMINGO
(Margaret Thatcher, Porcelain, Veronica)
Large-flowered/Hybrid Tea

Kordes (Germany) bred this rose in 1979 from an unnamed seedling × 'Ladylike'. The medium sized, shapely blooms of a delicate porcelain pink have a slight fragrance and are borne singly on long, straight stems that make it an excellent cutting rose. The plant is of medium height, about 4 feet (1.2 m), and is healthy and vigorous, with plenty of dark green, matte foliage. 'Flamingo', like many other pale varieties, spots after rain, and the centers are a little too flat for it to be a very successful exhibition rose but it is, nevertheless, an excellent garden rose, and performs well under glass as a quality cut flower variety.

FLOWER CARPET
Ground Cover

'Flower Carpet' was bred by Noack (Germany) in 1989 from 'Imensee' × 'Amanda'. The small, globular, semi-double (15 petals) flowers are deep pink with a lighter reverse to the petals. They are lightly fragrant and are borne profusely and in sprays of up to 25 throughout the season. The plant has small dark green, glossy foliage and small, dark, hooked prickles. It is vigorous and hardy with low spreading

Rosa 'F. J. Grootendorst'

Rosa 'Flower Carpet'

Rosa 'Flamingo'

growth, showing its *R. wichuraiana* heritage. The flowers fall cleanly and repeat quickly, as one would expect on such a variety. There have been rather extravagant claims made suggesting that it is disease resistant (it is not quite disease proof) and requires less maintenance than grass. Time will judge such claims.

FRAGRANT CLOUD
(Duftwolke, Nuage Parfume)
Large-flowered/Hybrid Tea

Tantau (Germany) bred this rose in 1963 from an unnamed seedling × 'Prima Ballerina'. The coral red, well-formed blooms do not age well, but the perfume is unparalleled. The free-flowering plant is a fairly low grower (about 30 in (75 cm)), and is well-covered in deep green, leathery foliage. At one time it was the most popular rose in England, according to the number sold. It can only be assumed that the perfume was the reason, as the flower color is not all that remarkable, even when the blooms are fresh, but it remains a popular bedding rose, and has some potential for breeding. 'Fragrant

Rosa 'Fragrant Cloud'

Cloud' was the third rose chosen in the World Federation of Rose Societies' Hall of Fame.

FRANCIS E. LESTER
Hybrid Musk

This rose was bred by Lester Rose Gardens (United States) in 1946 from 'Kathleen' × unnamed seeding. It is usually classified as a rambler, although its parent 'Kathleen' is a Hybrid Musk. It is certainly more vigorous, perhaps rampant, in comparison with others, making a wide, lax shrub about 14 feet (4 m) high, if allowed to develop naturally. It is not remontant, indicating

Rosa 'Frau Dagmar Hastrup'

Rosa 'Francis E. Lester'

Rosa 'French Lace'

the other parent must have been spring-flowering. It is a magnificent sight when in full bloom, smothered with trusses of beautifully fragrant, single flowers, which are predominantly white, with pink markings on the edges of the petals. The pointed leaves are coppery tinted and glossy, enhanced by decorative clusters of small red hips in autumn.

FRAU DAGMAR HASTRUP
(Frau Dagmar Hartopp)
Hybrid Rugosa
Bred by Hastrup (Germany) in 1914, this rose is thought to be a seedling of *R. rugosa*, because it is very similar in many respects to the species. The rich pink, long, pointed buds open to form large, single, fragrant blooms, which are a delicate pink, showing prominent creamy white stamens. The plant is lower-growing and more spreading than the species, carrying its large, deep red,

tomato-like hips with the repeat flushes. This makes an attractive and decorative display. It deserves its reputation as one of the most popular Rugosas and can be propagated readily from seed, although it does not always come true to type. It suits a small garden.

FRENCH LACE
Cluster-flowered/Floribunda
The very appropriately named 'French Lace' was bred by Warriner (United States) in 1980 from 'Dr A. J. Verhage' × 'Bridal Pink'. The buds are pointed, opening to double (30 petals), ivory blooms tinted with pastel apricot to white in clusters of between one and 12. The color and form make it quite unique, although the bush is somewhat indifferent. The name certainly reflects the mood set by the flowers. This rose does not seem to be as vigorous or as tall in warmer climates as in other places.

Rosa 'Friesia'

Rosa 'Fritz Nobis'

Rosa 'Georg Arends'

FRIESIA
(Sunsprite, KORresia)
Cluster-flowered/Floribunda

Kordes (Germany) introduced this rose in 1977 from seedling × 'Spanish Sun'. The ovoid buds develop into large, flat, double (28 petals), deep yellow blooms with a glorious perfume. The color is unfading, enhanced by the light green, glossy foliage on an upright, healthy plant which is low growing to about 30 in (75 cm). It won a gold medal in Baden Baden. 'Friesia' was named for a province of the Low Countries which is one of Germany's dairy regions. Its free-flowering nature makes it a good bedding rose, where its height is appropriate for a border. It has a good fragrance for a yellow rose.

FRITZ NOBIS
Shrub

Bred by Kordes (Germany) in 1940 from 'Joanna Hill' × 'Magnifica', it is unfortunate that this rose is non-recurrent, because it is such a beautiful and rewarding plant to grow. It inherited its strong, bushy growth from its Sweet Briar parent, forming a vigorous shrub about 6 feet (2 m) high and wide, while it inherited the more delicate flowers of the Large-flowered parent. The flowers start as pointed buds, which open to shapely, semi-double blooms in a pale, soft pink color with salmon shadings and a delicious fragrance of cloves. It is a dense shrub in both its dark foliage and the flowers when in bloom. To compensate for the lack of blooms later in the season, there is an attractive crop of hips to bring color to this beautiful shrub.

GEORG ARENDS
Hybrid Perpetual

Bred by Hinner (Germany) in 1910 from 'Frau Karl Druschki' × 'La

France', there are two unusual aspects about its breeding. It is sometimes classified as a Large-flowered Rose, although one of its parents is 'Frau Karl Druschki', a Hybrid Perpetual. Secondly, its Large-flowered parent, 'La France', has an odd number of chromosomes, making it a reluctant parent. Whatever its type, it is a useful plant, flowering freely, with clear, rose pink, fragrant blooms, which are big, initially high-centered and somewhat blowzy in the end. The vigorous, shrubby growth to 5 feet (1.5 m) has plenty of gray-green foliage. In spite of its age, 'Georg Arends' is a worthy addition to any garden.

GERTRUDE JEKYLL
English Shrub

This rose was bred in 1987 from 'Wife of Bath' × 'Comte de Chambord'. The buds are small, like those of an Alba, opening into surprisingly large, rich pink, rosette-shaped blooms in the style of the Portland pollen parent. It also inherited from this parent a strong fragrance in the Old Rose style, so much so that they were tested and found to

contain more essential oil for extraction than any other variety. The plant is tall and vigorous with grayish-green, pointed foliage and is named for the well known gardener and writer, among whose writings is the classic *Roses for English Gardens* first published in 1902.

GLAMIS CASTLE
(AUSlevel)
English Rose

The large flowers on 'Glamis Castle' are carried in small clusters, and open out into wide shallow cups, showing the pointed petal edges to endearing effect. The basic color is creamy white, with buff tints in the heart of the blooms. They have a sharp myrrh scent. They are not spoiled by wet weather, and the plant continues to produce flowers through summer and autumn. It grows to average height. The leaves are semi-glossy and medium green, and are rather prone to seasonal mildew. David Austin (England) introduced this rose in 1992 and named it for the Scots seat of the Bowes Lyon family, where Queen Elizabeth the Queen Mother spent part of her childhood.

Rosa 'Gertrude Jekyll'

Rosa 'Glamis Castle'

GOLD MEDAL
Large-flowered/Hybrid Tea

'Gold Medal' was bred by Christensen (United States) in 1982 from 'Yellow Pages' × ('Granada'× 'Garden Party'). The golden yellow, flushed copper orange blooms are medium sized, well-formed and open. It has been described as both highly and lightly fragrant, evidence that sense of smell is very individual. The blooms fade to buff, but not until they have been around for some time. They are carried at times in clusters on a vigorous, healthy bush with medium green, leathery foliage, about 5 feet (1.5 m) tall, but if lightly pruned, can go even higher. This free-flowering rose with few thorns is highly recommended for easy care in the garden or for cutting.

GOLDEN CELEBRATION
(AUSgold)
Modern Shrub

This David Austin (England) English Rose was bred from 'Charles Austin' ×

'Abraham Darby' in 1992. The round buds open into large flowers with a cupped form, recessed in the center. They are fully double and intricately formed, with the larger petals forming a ring and overlapping each other around the outside, while the base of the cup is filled with smaller, creased and folded petals. The deep yellow color is more golden than most roses with that word in their name. There is a strong scent and it

Rosa 'Gold Medal'

Rosa 'Golden Celebration'

Rosa 'Golden Wings'

Rosa 'Golden Showers'

continues to bloom through summer and autumn. In wet weather the arching stems may be bowed down by the heavy flowers. 'Golden Celebration' is a very suitable rose for a border, making a rounded shrub of average height with dark glossy leaves.

GOLDEN SHOWERS
Cluster-flowered Climber

'Golden Showers' was bred by Lammerts (United States) in 1956, from 'Charlotte Armstrong' × 'Captain Thomas'. It is still probably the most popular yellow Climbing rose in the world, because of its excellent repeat flowering, long almost thornless stems, rich green, abundant, disease-free foliage and a growth to 10–14 feet (3–4 m). Flowers are rich yellow in bud, but fade to creamy yellow in the full blooms in hot weather. The buds are long, pointed and most attractive. 'Golden Showers' can be used as a pillar, on a tripod or a fence or against buildings where its abundant foliage shows off the flowers to good effect. 'Golden Showers' was one of the few climbing roses ever to win the coveted All-American Rose Selection in 1957.

GOLDEN WINGS
Shrub

This lovely rose was bred by Shepherd (United States) in 1956 from 'Soeur Thérèse' × (*R. pimpinellifolia* 'Altaica' × 'Ormiston Roy'). There are few good remontant shrubs with single blooms. This is surprising, given that the original wild roses had this form, but 'Golden Wings' is undoubtedly one of them. The pointed buds, which are sometimes borne in clusters, open to large, single, sulphur-yellow flowers, which fade with age. They have a light but very pleasant perfume, occurring throughout the season on a plant covered with rich, light green foliage. It is a hardy and upright plant, but may occasionally need some judicious pruning to induce it to branch a little better.

Rosa 'Graham Thomas'

Rosa 'Granada'

Rosa 'Grüss an Aachen'

GRAHAM THOMAS
English Shrub
Bred in 1983 from 'Charles Austin' × ('Iceberg' × seedling), 'Graham Thomas' is deservedly one of the most popular English Roses, with its tea-scented, pure, rich yellow blooms. They are cupped, opening to wide Edwardian-style roses, carried freely and at times in clusters, on a very vigorous, healthy, branching shrub. It can even produce climbing type canes and makes an excellent pillar rose when allowed to develop inside a cylindrical support. It was chosen by Graham Thomas to be named after him and it is appropriate that this popular variety should bear the name of one who was a prime mover for the reintroduction of Old Garden roses, without which the English Roses may not have been developed.

GRANADA
(Donatella)
Large-flowered/Hybrid Tea
Bred by Lindquist (United States) in 1963 from 'Tiffany' × 'Cavalcade', this rose won, on its release, an All-American Rose Selection award in 1964 and a Gamble medal for fragrance. The medium sized, semi-double blooms are sweetly fragrant and are an attractive blend of yellow, pink and red, flowering early and repeating quickly. The flowers are carried mainly in clusters on a bush about 4 feet (1.2 m) high with dark, olive green foliage. It is an excellent garden and cutting variety in spite of the tendency to mildew in cooler climates. It boasts, in its progeny, such roses as 'Double Delight' and 'Gold Medal'.

GRÜSS AN AACHEN
(Salut d'Aix la Chapelle)
Cluster-flowered/Floribunda
This rose has something of an old fashioned look. It was bred by Geduldig (Germany) in 1909 from 'Frau Karl

Druschki' × 'Franz Deegen' and bears clusters of medium-sized blooms which are soft apricot with yellow in the bud stage, opening to a soothing blend of pearly blush and cream. Before becoming cupped, they display well-formed centers, with many petals folding in on one another in a charmingly random fashion. There is a pleasing fragrance, and the flowers continue to appear through summer and autumn. It is normally short, making it useful to edge a border, or for a small bed. The name means 'greetings to Aachen', the breeder's home city, famous as the burial place of Charlemagne.

GUINÉE
Large-flowered Climber
Mallerin (France) raised this rose in 1938 using 'Souvenir de Claudius Denoyel' × 'Ami Quinard' as parents. It is perhaps the best of the blackish red climbing roses, combining great beauty with ease of cultivation. The intensely dark flowers have a velvety sheen on the young petals, which open to reveal lovely golden stamens. The fragrance is noticeable on warm days, but becomes hard to detect in windy or cool weather. It is a lovely cut flower and is best grown on a fairly sunny wall or strong fence. The leathery, dark green foliage may form mildew if the roots do not get enough moisture. It was named after the former French colony in West Africa.

HANDEL
Cluster-flowered Climber
Another McGredy rose, 'Handel' was bred in 1965. It could be classed as either a Large-flowered Climber or a Cluster-flowered Climber. Flowers are smallish, occur in clusters of three or more on long stems and are a pleasing soft cream color edged with deepest pink

on petal edges. Buds are well-shaped, and full blooms open to show stamens, giving a pleasing fresh effect. Repeat is continuous with an excellent autumn flush. Growth is strong to 14–16 feet (4–5 m) which makes 'Handel' good for tall fences, arches and pergolas and screens. It can be kept to size by hard pruning in winter with little loss in flowering. Perfume is very slight. 'Handel' deservedly won a gold medal in Portland in 1975.

Rosa 'Handel'

Rosa 'Guinée'

HARRY WHEATCROFT
(Caribia)
Large-flowered/Hybrid Tea

Discovered by Harry Wheatcroft (England), and chosen by him to perpetuate his name, this rose is a sport of 'Piccadilly'. It was released in 1972. It contains all the red and yellow colors of the parent, but splashed and striped in a flamboyant manner in keeping with its discoverer. 'Harry Wheatcroft' is a suitable tribute to one of England's greatest rose entrepreneurs, who was well-known during his lifetime as a pop star, and was also a very shrewd, kind-hearted and successful nurseryman. The lightly-scented blooms are carried freely on a compact plant about 30 in (75 cm) high with coppery-green, semi-glossy foliage.

HAWKEYE BELLE
Modern Shrub

This rose was bred by Buck (United States) in 1975 from ('Queen Elizabeth' × 'Pizzicato') × 'Prairie Princess'. The large, beautiful flowers are borne in clusters on strong stems. The plump, pointed buds open to show high centers

at first, then, as they expand, the many petals resemble a coiled spring at the heart of the bloom. The petals gradually part to create overlapping layers, which give a charming effect at the fully open stage. The color is ivory white, lightly suffused with azalea pink as the flowers mature. There is a sweet scent, and flowering continues through summer and autumn, which makes this a good subject for mixed borders where a vigorous shrub of average growth is required.

HELEN TRAUBEL
Large-flowered/Hybrid Tea

This rose was bred from 'Charlotte Armstrong' × 'Glowing Sunset' by Swim (United States) in 1951. The flowers are a fetching combination of warm pink-peach with flushes of yellow at the base, fading slightly as they age. Borne sometimes singly, but quite often

Rosa 'Harry Wheatcroft'

Rosa 'Helen Traubel'

in threes, these elegant blooms have 24 high centered petals which later become cupped. They have a sweet scent and appear continuously through summer and autumn. Weak flower stems cause the blooms to nod, which detracts from its value as a bedding rose, but in a border among other plants it fits in well. It was named in honor of the American soprano (1899–1972), and won a gold medal in Rome in 1951 and the All-American Rose Selection in 1952.

HELMUT SCHMIDT
(Simba)
Large-flowered/Hybrid Tea
Named for the German statesman, 'Helmut Schmidt' was bred by Kordes (Germany) in 1979 from 'New Day' × an unnamed seedling. The medium sized, yellow, well-formed, lightly fragrant blooms are held erect on firm stems suitable for cutting. The healthy, free-flowering, vigorous bush grows to 4 feet (1.2 m), and has matte, dark green foliage. There are few good yellows, but this is one for the beginner, making an excellent garden specimen. Its value was recognized in both Switzerland and Belgium, where it won gold medals.

HENRY KELSEY
Modern Shrub
This exceptionally hardy rose for cold climates was bred by Svejda (Canada) from *Rosa kordesii* × seedling. The flowers are borne in heavy clusters of up to 18 medium to large-sized flowers. They are full-petalled, and a warm, bright shade of red. As the petals reflex, the blooms become cupped to reveal prominent golden stamens. There is a sharp, spicy fragrance. The flowers age to rose red before dropping their petals cleanly, and they repeat-bloom through summer and autumn. It makes an arching, pendulous shrub of lower than

Rosa 'Helmut Schmidt'

average height, but spreading in habit, with trailing stems. It has glossy foliage that withstands mildew, but may be affected by black spot.

HERITAGE
English Shrub
If you only grew one English Rose, this one would be a good choice. 'Heritage' was bred in 1984 from seedling × ('Iceberg' × 'Wife of Bath'). It is one of the most popular English roses and deservedly so. The medium-sized, cupped blooms with many clear, shell pink petals in the center and near-white outer petals have a beautiful Old rose fragrance with a hint of lemon. They are borne very freely and continuously in small clusters on a medium to tall, vigorous, bushy plant, which grows 4–6 feet (1.2–2m) high, with pointed (like 'Iceberg'), dark, semi-glossy leaves and very few thorns.

HONOR
(JAColite, Honour, Michele Torr)
Large-flowered/Hybrid Tea
This rose was bred by Warriner (United States) from undisclosed parents. It has

Rosa 'Iceberg'

delicate soft white flowers which show golden stamens when they are fully open. The large, long lasting blooms are borne on long stems, making it a lovely cut flower. It was released in 1980 as part of a series of three roses. 'Honor' completed the 'Honor', 'Love' and 'Cherish' group and was easily the best of the three. It is a tall, vigorous, upright plant which is resistant to black spot and mildew. It won a gold medal at Portland in 1978, and the All-American Rose Selection in 1980.

ICEBERG
Cluster-flowered/Floribunda

A very popular rose, 'Iceberg' was bred by Kordes (Germany) in 1958 from 'Robin Hood' × 'Virgo'. The long, pointed buds open to large, semi-double, pure white blooms, borne in small and large clusters. There may be a hint of pink in cooler weather, and in wet weather, pink rain spots appear. It is only lightly perfumed. The tall, shrubby plant grows to about 5 feet (1.5 m) and

is almost continuously free-flowering, repeat-growth beginning before the old flowers have finished. It makes a wonderful garden rose and the blooms (picked before the flowers are fully open) last well when cut. It won gold medals in England and Baden Baden, and was selected by the World Federation of Rose Societies as the fourth World's Favorite Rose to be placed in the Hall of Fame.

ICEBERG, CLIMBING
Cluster-flowered Climber

This rose sported from the bush form in Colchester, England in 1968. The flower buds are well-shaped, of pure white in warm weather, slightly more pink in winter cold, and come in small and large clusters among plentiful pale green foliage. There is a strong fragrance. The growth is robust to 14–16 feet (4–5 m) and flowering is continuous. The climbing canes have very close nodes and are easy to train. 'Climbing Iceberg' makes a perfect pillar rose and, because there are few thorns, it is ideal for pergolas, arches and veranda posts. Black spot and mildew can occur in damp climates. 'Climbing Iceberg' is one of the best climbers available. Unfortunately, it sometimes reverts to the bush form when transplanted. When this occurs, transplant the bush somewhere else and plant another climbing form.

ICED GINGER
Cluster-flowered/Floribunda

'Iced Ginger' was bred by Pat Dickson (Northern Ireland) in 1971 from 'Anne Watkins' × seedling. The large, well-formed, double (45 petals), sweetly fragrant blooms are the palest pink and have a coppery reverse to the petals. It is very large flowered for a rose classified as Cluster-flowered, but the blooms are borne in clusters, justifying this description. They make excellent cut flowers. The bush, unfortunately, is a little lanky and open and has red-veined foliage, so it is advisable to plant something shorter in front of it to disguise this shortcoming.

INGRID BERGMAN
Large-flowered/Hybrid Tea

'Ingrid Bergman' was bred by Poulsen (Denmark) in 1986 from 'Precious Platinum' × an unnamed seedling. The blooms are an excellent shade of deep red that do not 'blue' with age. The form is not always good, depending on the time of year but the long stems make it a good cut flower. The free flowering bush is healthy and upright, growing to about 27 in (70 cm) tall, with dark green, leathery foliage. Named after the beautiful Swedish actress, it has won awards at Belfast, Madrid and The Hague.

INTRIGUE
(Lavaglow, Lavaglut)
Cluster-flowered/Floribunda

This Kordes hybrid was bred in 1978 from 'Gruss an Bayern' × seedling. It carries its medium-sized, dark red, globular, double (24 petals) flowers in clusters on a vigorous, upright, bushy plant with glossy foliage. It may need protection in areas where black spot is common, but otherwise is a good

Rosa 'Iced Ginger'

Rosa 'Ingrid Bergman'

Rosa 'Irish Elegance'

Rosa 'Intrigue'

bedding plant with all the attributes one would expect of a Floribunda. It is not as readily available as the next rose which bears the same name.

INTRIGUE
Cluster-flowered/Floribunda

This 'Intrigue' was bred by Warriner (United States) in 1982 from 'White Masterpiece' × 'Heirloom'. The large, double (20 petals), very fragrant flowers are a reddish purple color. The plant is of average height with dark, semi-glossy leaves, tinted plum. It is an intriguing color and the small clusters and large flowers put it into the in-between category of a decorative Large-flowered or Hybrid Tea. It is confusing when two roses apparently have the same name, even when those names are not used in the same country. It would appear that the earlier Kordes rose was not listed in *Modern Roses* primarily under that name, which made it available for this Warriner-bred one.

IRISH ELEGANCE
Large-flowered/Hybrid Tea

This delicate rose was bred by Dickson (Northern Ireland) in 1901 from

undisclosed parents. Alex (Grandpa) Dickson was certainly better known for his large, many-petalled, exhibition roses, but this one is a soft, bronze-yellow, single bloom with a hint of pink. Singles were very popular in the early years of the twentieth century, and they are probably the easiest form of rose to breed, but since single roses are not as popular today, they have to be good and novel to succeed. The bush is quite tall and the semi-glossy foliage complements the flower beautifully.

JACQUELINE DU PRÉ
Cluster-flowered/Floribunda

Harkness (England) bred this rose in 1988 from 'Radox Bouquet' × 'Maigold'. The flowers are creamy-blush to white, semi-double (15 petals with scalloped edges) with red-gold, prominent stamens. The cupped, fairly loose blooms, with a moderate musk fragrance, are carried in clusters of three to five and are borne freely on a vigorous, spreading shrub with dark, glossy foliage. It is a rose with character, and the breeding would suggest Jack Harkness was looking for something unusual with two such contrasting parents. Several months before her death from multiple sclerosis, the cellist Jacqueline du Pré chose this rose to bear her name and initial sales gave some support to the MS Society.

JOHN F. KENNEDY
Large-flowered/Hybrid Tea
This lovely rose was bred by Boerner in 1965 from an unnamed seedling × 'White Queen'. The huge (nearly 6 in (14 cm) across), very fragrant, well-formed blooms are white with a hint of lime green in the center and are borne on a vigorous, upright bush growing up to 3 feet (1 m), with leathery, mid-green foliage. It grows well under glass and is good for cutting, but it can be a little susceptible to mildew. Following the assassination of President Kennedy, Jackson and Perkins offered to name a rose after him. His widow, Jacqueline, requested that the rose be white.

JOSEPH'S COAT
Large-flowered Climber
This rose was bred in the US by Armstrong and Swim in 1964. Its parents were 'Buccaneer' a very tall yellow Grandiflora rose and 'Circus', a coppery yellow Cluster-flowered. Although classed as a Large-flowered Climber it could equally be classed as a tall growing Cluster-flowered. As its

Rosa 'John F. Kennedy'

Rosa 'Jacqueline du Pré'

Rosa, 'Joyfulness'

Rosa 'Joseph's Coat'

name suggests it is a combination of red, yellow and gold. Blooms are semi-double, and come in heads of up to seven. Fragrance is slight, foliage is dark and growth rarely exceeds 6 feet (2 m). Blooms are very recurrent and the combination of colors very attractive. It won a gold medal in Bagatelle in 1964.

JOYFULNESS
Cluster-flowered/Floribunda
This is a tall, somewhat reluctant rose bred in 1961 by Matthias Tantau, which he named 'Frohsinn'. The blooms are a blend of pale apricot, cream and shell pink, and have a slight perfume. They can be high-centered, exhibition style and cupped with a bull nose. They are large and have 25 petals and are freely produced, usually on solitary long stems. The attractive bush is upright and open and grows to about 5 feet (6 m).

JUDY GARLAND
(HARking)
Cluster-flowered/Floribunda
This rose certainly has a complicated parentage. It was bred by Harkness

(England) in 1978 from (('Tropicana' × 'Circus') × ('Sabine' × 'Circus')) × 'Pineapple Poll'. The flowers are yellow with the outer petals edged a light red or orange. They are medium-sized and fully double, better looking as shapely buds than as a loose fully blown flower when they become as little washed out. The bush is of average height with a spreading habit and good healthy foliage. This is more of a novelty rose and is not always to the liking of purists. It is best suited to mass planting. It was named for the fabulous American actor and singer.

JULIA'S ROSE
Large-flowered/Hybrid Tea
Named for the renowned floral artist, Julia Clements, 'Julia's Rose' was bred by Tysterman (England) in 1976 from 'Blue Moon' × 'Dr A. J. Verhage'. Its most attractive feature is the unusual color which could be described as a sepia and lavender blend. The flowers are slightly fragrant, lightly petalled, frilled and are borne singly or in small clusters on an unfortunately indifferent plant, which could only be recommended for the rose enthusiast or floral artist. The bush grows to a medium height of some 30 in (75 cm), and has

Rosa 'Julia's Rose'

Rosa 'Just Joey'

dark foliage with reddish tones, but it is neither quick to repeat nor a vigorous grower and does best in warm weather or under glass.

JUST JOEY
Large-flowered/Hybrid Tea

'Just Joey' was bred by Pawsey (England) in 1972 from 'Fragrant Cloud' × 'Dr. A. J. Verhage'. The blooms, with ragged edges on the petals, are in coppery tones and delightfully perfumed. The bush is moderately tall (about 30 in (75 cm)) and spreading, but in temperate climates can grow up to 5 feet (1.5 m). It has dark green foliage. The rose was affectionately named after the raiser's wife and makes a good garden rose. 'Just Joey' was the eighth rose in the Hall of Fame chosen by the World Federation of Rose Societies at its 1994 conference in Christchurch, New Zealand.

KARDINAL
Large-flowered/Hybrid Tea

This beautiful rose was bred by Kordes (Germany) in 1985 from an unnamed

Rosa 'Kardinal'

seedling × 'Flamingo'. The cardinal red blooms are perfectly formed, very double and carried on long, strong stems. Its lasting qualities make it one of the best cut flowers available. It is also an excellent garden and exhibition variety, with an upright, healthy, free-

Rosa 'Kathleen'

Rosa 'Kathryn Morley'

Rosa 'King's Ransom'

flowering bush growing up to 5 feet (1.5 m) high. The dark green, matte foliage complements the flowers, being one of the first varieties to come into bloom each year. Its only fault, if you can call it that, is its lack of perfume. It is a good grower and is highly recommended. 'Kardinal' was rated No. 1 in Australia by those exhibiting on the show bench.

KATHLEEN
Hybrid Musk
'Kathleen' was bred by Pemberton (England) in 1913 from 'Daphne' × 'Perle des Jeannes'. The former is an earlier Pemberton Hybrid Musk, but perhaps the latter should read 'Perle des Jardins'. 'Kathleen' has clusters of small, single flowers, opening from pink buds to almost white blooms. They have a sweet, musk fragrance and are borne on somewhat sprawling shrub up to 10 feet (3 m) high, having dark green foliage on grayish green stems.

KATHRYN MORLEY
(AUSclub, AUSvariety)
English Rose
Austin (England) bred 'Kathryn Morley' in 1990, using 'Mary Rose' × 'Chaucer'. The flowers are medium to large in size and very full, with over 40 petals. They are borne singly or in small clusters and open into pale pink flowers of a charming old-fashioned appearance, the outer

petals reflexing while the remainder are enfolded and slightly incurved, giving what has been described as a 'cup and saucer' effect. There is a pleasant scent, and flowering continues through summer and autumn. It is a somewhat uneven, rangy grower with long canes as well as shorter stems, and is best grown in a border where the beauty and scent of the flowers can be appreciated, but with lower growing plants in front.

KING'S RANSOM
Large-flowered/Hybrid Tea
'King's Ransom' was bred by Morey (United States) in 1961 from 'Golden Masterpiece' × 'Lydia'. The well-formed, moderately fragrant blooms are high-centered and luminous yellow, which do not fade much in the sun as they open. The stems are firm, good for cutting and covered with light green, leathery leaves with good black spot resistance. An upright and free-flowering cultivar growing up to 32 in (80 cm) high, it was for many years the best yellow garden rose available, winning an All-American Rose Selection award in 1962, but there are others which have since surpassed it.

KRONENBOURG
(Flaming Peace)
Large-flowered/Hybrid Tea
Discovered on Sam McGredy's nursery (Northern Ireland), 'Kronenbourg' is a

Rosa 'Kronenbourg'

Rosa 'La France'

Rosa 'La Sevillana'

sport of 'Peace' and was introduced in 1965. The bush is, in all respects, similar to 'Peace'. The mutation was in the color. 'Kronenbourg' is a bicolor rose, crimson on the inside of the petals, the outside the same light yellow as 'Peace', although this quickly changes to a dull purple with cream reverse. The color appears to be a reversion to the color of 'Queen Alexandra', an ancestor of 'Peace'. The Kronenbourg brewery overlooked the office of his French agent, yet interestingly, McGredy describes the color as claret and traminer! The staff members who discovered the rose were given £50 each, and one used the money to buy a motor bike, affectionately known as 'Kronenbourg'.

LA FRANCE
Large-flowered/Hybrid Tea
'La France' was bred by Guillot (France) in 1867 from a seedling thought to have come from the Tea Rose 'Madame Falcot'. This all seems rather indefinite for the rose considered to be the first Large-flowered Rose, but it displayed the vigor of a Hybrid Perpetual with the refinement of a Hybrid Tea. The blooms are a silvery pink,

with a rose-pink reverse, globular but with a high center and richly fragrant. It was not vigorous by today's standards nor all that healthy these days, so it really is a rose grown only by specialist heritage and nostalgia rose nurseries.

LA SEVILLANA
Cluster-flowered/Floribunda
'La Sevillana' was bred by Meilland (France) in 1978 from (MEIbrim × 'Jolie Madam') × ('Zambra' × 'Zambra') × ('Tropicana' × 'Tropicana') × ('Poppy Flash' × 'Rusticana'). It is an unusual parentage listed in *Modern Roses 10*, as 'Poppy Flash' and 'Rusticana' are alternative names for the same rose. From these parents, one would expect a cluster flowered rose in orange or vermilion shades and it is just that. The conical buds and semi-double (13 petals), vermilion flowers are borne in clusters on a vigorous, bushy plant with bronze foliage.

LADY OF THE DAWN
(INTerlada)
Shrub
This rose is variously described as a Cluster-flowered or Floribunda Rose

and as a shrub. It was bred by Ilsink (The Netherlands) in 1984 from INTerdress × 'Stadt an Helder'. It produces long stiff shoots that become bowed under the weight of the blooms, which can easily number 20 or more in the cluster. The lightly scented flowers are creamy blush and rimmed pink around the petal edges. They open like saucers to reveal red and gold stamens. Blooming continues through summer and autumn. It is suitable as a hedge, in a border or for planting in a bed where a sizeable grower is required. It has dark green leathery leaves and grows vigorously with an upright, arching habit.

LAGERFELD
Large-flowered/Hybrid Tea

Named for the French couturier, 'Lagerfeld' was bred by Christensen (United States) in 1986 from 'Blue Nile' × ('Ivory Tower' × 'Angel Face'). The medium-sized blooms are well-formed and double in a silvery lavender shade with a magnificent fragrance. The single to small sprays are carried on a healthy,

Rosa 'Lagerfeld'

vigorous, upright bush well-clothed in medium green, matte foliage. 'Lagerfeld' is free-flowering and tall (about 6 feet (1.8 m) high). The color is rather pale and can look washed out, especially in hot weather. Such colors attract thrips and hibiscus beetle, which leave their untidy, dirty marks all over the petals, so it does need some protection. In spite of this, it makes a good garden and cut rose.

LAS VEGAS
(KORgane)
Large-flowered/Hybrid Tea

This prize-winning rose is another from the Kordes nursery. It was bred in 1981 from 'Ludwigshafen am Rhein' ×

Rosa 'Lady of the Dawn'

Rosa 'Las Vegas'

Rosa 'Lavender Pinnochio'

'Feuerzauber', and is an attractive confection of orange and yellow. The inside of the petals is orange-vermilion and the reverse is chrome yellow with red veining. Both colors are seen together as the flowers unfold. The effect is gaudy but more restrained than the lights of the city whose name it bears. The foliage is dark green and semi-glossy on an upright, vigorous plant. It is a rewarding performer in the garden and makes a good hedge.

LAVENDER LASSIE
Hybrid Musk

'Lavender Lassie' was bred by Kordes (Germany) in 1960 from 'Hamburg' × 'Madame Norbert Levavasseur'. The seed parent was bred from 'Eva', a Hybrid Musk, and 'Daily Mail Scented', a dark red Large-flowered with maroon shades, while the pollen parent was one of the early Polyanthas. Although classified as a Hybrid Musk, it behaves more like a large Cluster-flowered Shrub. It is one of the few repeat-flowering shrubs in this color and is

Rosa 'Lavender Lassie'

therefore valued. All parents were red, which means the lavender color must go back more than two generations. The flowers, sometimes more lilac-pink than lavender, are old fashioned and fragrant. It makes a delightful, disease resistant garden rose with its dark green foliage.

LAVENDER PINOCCHIO
Cluster-flowered/Floribunda

This rose was bred by Boerner (United States) in 1948 from 'Pinocchio' × 'Grey

Pearl'. The light chocolate-olive-brown buds open to pink-lavender flowers, which are large, double, fragrant and are borne in clusters on a vigorous, bushy, compact plant with matte-green leaves. The name reflects the intention of the breeder, who was known as 'the father of Floribundas' for his successful work developing and making popular this class of rose, as he intended this rose as a lavender version of 'Pinocchio', but the flowers are not a simple lavender. They are mixed with milk coffee colors. It was the first of the lavender shaded Cluster-flowered Roses, and is still a good variety.

Rosa 'Leander'

LEANDER
English Shrub

'Leander' was bred in 1982 from 'Charles Austin' × seedling. In warm climates, it grows extremely tall for a bush rose, and is more suitably treated as a pillar rose. It occasionally repeat flowers. The flowers are only medium-sized, smaller than the parent, 'Charles Austin', but are of perfect rosette form in an unusual, deep apricot shade with a sweet, fruity fragrance. The are borne in clusters, mainly in spring, on a tall, arching shrub up to 6 feet (2 m), with shiny, dark, disease-resistant, modern-looking foliage.

L. D. BRAITHWAITE
(AUScrim, Braithwaite, Leonard Dudley Braithwaite)
Modern Shrub

David Austin (England) bred this rose in 1988 from 'The Squire' × 'Mary Rose'. The fairly large flowers are attractively formed; they open to show a rounded form, with many petals infolded one against another in the center. The color, an even tone of dark crimson, is well held through the life of the flowers, which are borne singly and in wide-spaced clusters on firm upright stems. They have a pleasing fragrance. The blooms continue to appear through summer and autumn and withstand wet weather well. This is a good rose to group in a border, the flower color consorting particularly well with older roses and a wide range of garden plants.

Rosa 'L. D. Braithwaite'

LILAC ROSE
(AUSlilac, Old Lilac)
English Rose

This rose bears large flowers of lilac-pink, with over 40 petals. The blooms are borne in small clusters and open out wide like big rosettes, though they may ball and fail to open in wet conditions. There is a strong fragrance, and it maintains a continuity of bloom through summer and autumn. In a garden rose it adds interest towards the front of a shrub border, the color according well with old garden roses and many other garden plants. 'Lilac Rose' grows with a bushy, upright habit to a little below average size and has attractive, olive green, semi-glossy leaves. It was bred in 1990 by Austin (England) from seedling × 'Hero'.

Rosa 'Lilian Austin'

Rosa 'Lilac Rose'

Rosa 'Lili Marlene'

LILIAN AUSTIN
English Shrub

Named for the breeder's mother, who had a love of roses, 'Lilian Austin' was bred in 1973 from 'Aloha' × 'The Yeoman'. The semi-double to double blooms open to rather informal, ruffled blooms in shades of salmon-pink, tinged apricot, deepening towards the center. They are borne freely and continuously in clusters of one to five on a low growing, spreading, modern-looking shrub that can almost be used as a ground cover. The foliage is dark and glossy. 'Lilian Austin' became an important parent to pass on the 'Aloha' characteristics to future generations of English roses.

LILI MARLENE
Cluster-flowered/Floribunda

Named for the song, 'Lili Marlene' was bred by Kordes (Germany) in 1959 from ('Our Princess' × 'Rudolph Timm') × 'Ama'. The ovoid buds develop into medium red, double (25 petals), cupped flowers, carried in trusses on a bush of medium height. It is a vigorous plant with dark, leathery foliage. It is extremely free-flowering and makes an excellent bedding rose. It can be seen all over Europe, making a vivid splash of red in parks and gardens. The name was suggested by Sam McGredy following an evening with Reimer Kordes after much drink, merriment and song, an appropriate christening for his new variety.

Rosa 'Livin' Easy'

Rosa 'Lucetta'

LIVIN' EASY
(HARwelcome, Fellowship)
Cluster-flowered/Floribunda

'Livin' Easy' is an excellent rose bred in 1992 by Harkness (England) using 'Southampton' × 'Remember Me'. The flowers are a particularly glowing salmon-orange color. The well-formed buds open to cupped-shaped blooms that reveal a central boss of stamens. This is a vigorous and spreading bush with dark green, glossy, disease-resistant foliage. It makes an excellent bedding rose, as the flowers retain their color well. There are good beds of this rose in Regents Park in London that are very popular with the public. It won the Royal National Rose Society Gold Medal in 1990 and the All-American Rose Selection in 1996.

LUCETTA
English Shrub

'Lucetta' was bred in 1983, from unknown parents. The breeder indicates that one of the early English Roses and 'Iceberg' are somewhere involved in its breeding. It is a delightful rose to grow and is another of those best treated as a pillar, being tall to 10 feet (3 m), and arching if not supported. The flowers are semi-double, open and flat, showing a cluster of stamens in the center, in shades of soft, blush pink, fading to almost white. They are fragrant and freely borne in small clusters on long stems with medium green, semi-glossy foliage and few thorns. They can be planted in groups of three to form a tall, elegant shrub.

MADAME BUTTERFLY
Large-flowered/Hybrid Tea

This rose is a sport of 'Ophelia' and was released by Hill (United States) in 1918. 'Ophelia' was unique for the number of sports it produced, with no less than 23 being introduced; and the sports themselves sported, including 'Sylvia', a famous sport of 'Madame Butterfly', bringing the total to an incredible thirty

Rosa 'Madame Butterfly'

six. 'Joanna Hill', one of the parents of 'Peace', was bred from 'Madame Butterfly'. The well-formed, very fragrant blooms are blush pink with a darker center and some yellow at the base, and, at times, are borne in clusters. The free-flowering bush, about 27 in (70 cm) high, has only a sparse covering of medium green foliage. It is mainly grown these days by those interested in the nostalgia roses.

MADAME CAROLINE TESTOUT
Large-flowered/Hybrid Tea
Another of the nostalgia roses, this was bred by Pernet-Ducher (France) in 1890 from 'Madame de Tartas' × 'Lady Mary Fitzwilliam'. It has pointed buds with bright satiny rose flowers, which have darker centers and are edged with soft, carmine pink. The large, double, fragrant flowers are borne on vigorous,

bushy plants with soft, rich green foliage. This rose established Large-flowered Roses as the leading bedding rose, and was once planted by the thousands along the streets of Portland, Oregon. Caroline Testout was engaged in selling Parisian fashions through a London showroom when she bought the naming rights to this rose as an adver-tisement, an astute and forward-thinking action, as the rose was an outstanding success.

MADAME GREGOIRE STAECHELIN
(Spanish Beauty)
Large-flowered Climber
Pedro Dot bred this rose in 1927 in Spain. Flowers are loosely formed of a very pale pink stained with crimson on the reverse. The full blooms are semi-double, large and fragrant. Foliage is dark green, plentiful and disease

Rosa 'Madame Caroline Testout'

Rosa 'Madame Gregoire Staechelin'

Rosa 'Margaret Merrill'

Rosa 'Maigold'

resistant. Growth is extremely vigorous to 14–16 feet (4–5 m) and there is no repeat bloom. If spent blooms are not removed, an enormous crop of very large, decorative pear-shaped hips are produced that turn slowly from green to yellow to orange. It makes a very good espaliered plant and is strong enough to grow into small trees where its pale nodding flowers show up well against dark foliage.

MAIGOLD
Large-flowered Climber
Another Kordes rose, 'Maigold' was bred in 1953, a cross between a Cluster-flowered and a Shrub Rose. Flowers are bronzy-yellow, have only 14 petals and fade quickly in hot climates. Fragrance is very strong. Growth is very thorny and upright to 6 feet (2 m) or more. Its chief virtue is that it heralds the rose season as it flowers very early. There is no repeat. Flowering period is short in warm areas which makes 'Maigold' more suitable for cold climates. It will withstand very frosty winters with no harm to the canes of the plant.

MARGARET MERRILL
Cluster-flowered/Floribunda
Harkness (England) bred this rose in 1977 from ('Rudolph Timm' × 'Dedication') × 'Pascali'. The large, full flowers are blush white and double (28 petals) with wavy petals, having a satin sheen. They are very fragrant and are borne on a healthy, upright plant about 3 feet (1 m) high with dark, leathery foliage. The rose was named after a fictional beauty adviser to the makers of Oil of Ulan and Peter Harkness tells of three real life

Margaret Merrills who have come forward to plant one and claim it as their own. It has won awards at Monza, Geneva, The Hague, Rome and in England and New Zealand. 'Margaret Merrill' prefers cooler climates.

Rosa 'Margo Koster'

MARGO KOSTER
Polyantha

This rose was attributed to Koster (Holland) in 1931. The small, cupped flowers are deep salmon pink, born in large clusters, as is customary for Polyanthas, on a compact, almost dwarf, bushy plant of attractive proportions and about 16 in (40 cm) tall. The flowers are larger than some Polyanthas and are lightly fragrant. 'Margo Koster' was a sport of the pink 'Dick Koster', which was a sport of the red 'Anneke Koster', which was in turn a sport of the red 'Greta Kluis', itself a sport of Peter Lambert's 'Echo', which was a dwarf, remontant sport of the climber, 'Tausendschon'.

MARGUERITE HILLING
(Pink Nevada)
Shrub

A pink sport of 'Nevada', this rose was released by Hilling (England) in 1959. It

Rosa 'Marguerite Hilling'

Rosa 'Majorie Fair'

Rosa 'Maria Callas'

is one of at least three pink sports from 'Nevada'. It is identical in all respects, except color, to its creamy white parent and, although it has not enjoyed the same popularity as 'Nevada', some believe that 'Marguerite Hilling' is better, as the color suits the bush more. Like many sports, there is a tendency to revert, and if a branch of the creamy 'Nevada' blooms appears, it is easy to prune it away. It produces large, semi-double blooms in soft rose-pink, paling towards the center, mainly at the beginning of the season, but with intermittent flowering throughout the remainder. It is sometimes classified as Hybrid moyesii.

MARIA CALLAS
(Miss All-American Beauty)
Large-flowered/Hybrid Tea

'Maria Callas' was bred by Meilland (France) in 1965 from 'Chrysler Imperial' × 'Karl Herbst'. The bud is ovoid, opening to large, dark pink, double, cupped, very fragrant flowers. The vigorous, bushy plant grows to about 4 feet (1.2 m) high, and has dark green, leathery foliage. It has won gold medals at Portland and in England. It was named for the tragic Greek opera singer.

MARJORIE FAIR
(Red Ballerina, Red Yesterday)
Modern Shrub

Harkness (England) bred this rose in 1978 from 'Ballerina' × 'Baby Faurax'. Having been bred from 'Ballerina', 'Marjorie Fair' deserves to be classified the same way, but that could be as a Polyantha, a Hybrid Musk or Modern Shrub, depending on which book you read. What is really important, however, is what kind of plant it is and whether it is what you are looking for in the garden. Named for a friend of the breeder, it flowers continuously in large clusters of small, lightly fragrant single blooms, which are a medium red with a white eye. The plant is dense and bushy with light green, semi-glossy foliage and is a no-nonsense, easy-care bedding variety.

Rosa 'Mary Rose'

Rosa 'Matangi'

MARY ROSE
English Shrub

This rose was bred in 1983 from 'Wife of Bath' × 'The Miller'. The strong, rose-pink flowers are cupped to start with and open to loose-petalled, old-fashioned looking blooms without the strong perfume one would expect. They are freely and continuously borne through-

Rosa 'Masquerade'

out the season. It is about 4 feet (1.2 m) tall, but can grow taller, and has fine, prickly stems. It makes an excellent all-around shrub. It was named for the Mary Rose Trust, to mark the recovery of Henry VIII's flagship from the Solent after more than 400 years. It has been used successfully in David Austin's breeding and has produced two success-ful sports ('Redouté' and 'Winchester Cathedral'). It is usually the first Austin rose to flower every season.

MASQUERADE
Cluster-flowered/Floribunda
'Masquerade' was bred by Boerner (United States) in 1949 from 'Goldilocks' × 'Holiday'. The buds are small, ovoid and yellow, but when they open, the flowers, which start bright yellow, turn salmon-pink and then red. They are slightly fragrant, medium-sized and semi-double (17 petals) and may be borne in clusters of as many as 25. The medium, upright, vigorous and free-flowering bush is about 4 feet (1.2 m) high and covered in dark, leathery foliage. It won a gold medal in England and makes a fine bedding plant, with the multicolored flowers adding a very decorative touch to the garden.

MATANGI
Cluster-flowered/Floribunda
This 'hand-painted' rose was bred by McGredy (Northern Ireland) in 1974 from seedling × 'Picasso'. The ovoid buds open to large, double (30 petals) flowers, which are orange-red with a silver eye and reverse. They are freely borne in clusters on an upright, bushy plant about 3 feet (1 m) high with mid-green, glossy foliage. Like many of the 'hand-painted' roses, the color is more spectacular in cooler weather or in cooler climates, when the color recedes

Rosa 'Medallion'

from the petal edges, leaving them fringed with silver. It makes a good bedding rose, but not a particularly good cut flower, as the stems droop quite quickly. Also characteristic of the class are the long, pointed thorns and the need for protection from black spot.

MEDALLION
Large-flowered/Hybrid Tea
This rose was bred by Warriner (United States) in 1973 from two excellent garden roses — 'South Seas' × 'King's Ransom'. It produces long, pointed buds of soft apricot that are double, large and full. The buds open slowly to well-shaped, full blooms. There is a pleasant fragrance. The foliage is dark, leathery and abundant and growth is vigorous, upright and very healthy. It won a gold medal in Portland in 1972 and the All-American Rose Selection in 1973.

MEG
Large-flowered Climber

'Meg' gets its climbing growth from 'Paul's Lemon Pillar' and its lovely soft salmon-apricot color and red stamens from 'Madame Butterfly'. The flowers have 10 petals, which are very large for a single rose. They come in small and large clusters. The foliage is dark and glossy on a strong and upright plant.

The repeat-flowering is fair in summer and slightly more profuse in autumn. It is a great rose for a pillar, a tripod or an arch and looks stunning growing against a brick house. It is a popular rose in all climates. If spent blooms are not removed, a good crop of large round hips can be produced in autumn. It won a gold medal at the National Rose Society in 1954.

Rosa 'Meg'

MERMAID
Large-flowered Climber

So impenetrable and vicious are its thorns that 'Mermaid' could have been used to hedge Sleeping Beauty's Castle, had it been available at the time! Introduced by William Paul of Waltham Cross in 1918, it is derived from a cross between *R. bracteata*, a wild Chinese rose and an unnamed yellow Tea Rose. The flowers are single, a soft subtle yellow, big and fragrant. The stamens are prominent. It is remontant and climbs to 33 feet (10 m) or more. It must be grown on its own roots and takes some time to get going. It doesn't care to be pruned much, and is not hardy in cold climates. It is not immune to black spot.

Rosa 'Mermaid'

Rosa 'Michèle Meilland'

MICHÈLE MEILLAND
Large-flowered/Hybrid Tea

Bred by Meilland (France) in 1945 from 'Joanna Hill' × 'Peace', the semi-double blooms of this rose are light pink, shaded lilac, with salmon centers and a light perfume. The dark green-foliaged bush (about 4 feet (1.2 m) tall) is vigorous and healthy, with near thornless, plum-colored stems on the flowers, which are excellent for cutting. 'Michèle Meilland' is one of the evergreen varieties that continue to perform after so many years. Michèle is the daughter of the original principal breeder of the family, Francis, whose untimely death from cancer cut short a career that had already achieved so much, having bred 'Peace' and successfully campaigned for plant variety rights in Europe.

MISCHIEF
Large-flowered/Hybrid Tea

McGredy (Northern Ireland) bred this rose in 1961 from 'Peace' × 'Spartan'. The large, double, salmon pink blooms are fragrant, showing more intense colors in the autumn. The free-flowering plant, up to 3 feet (1 m) high, is upright and vigorous with light green foliage and won gold medals in England and Portland. When Sam McGredy first staged it at a show, the story is told that Major-General Frank Naylor asked what it was to be called. Sam indicated that it had not been named yet, so Frank suggested 'Mischief', to which Sam agreed. It was only later that he found out he had named his rose after the Major-General's dog.

MISTER LINCOLN
Large-flowered/Hybrid Tea

'Mister Lincoln' was bred by Swim and Weeks (United States) in 1964 from 'Chrysler Imperial' × 'Charles Mallerin'. The bud is urn-shaped, followed double, well-formed, dark, velvety red, cupped flowers on very long stems that are excellent to cut. It is intoxicatingly fragrant. A favorite red for some 30 years, this 6 feet (2 m) tall healthy, vigorous, free-flowering plant with its matte, dark green foliage is a must in every garden, although, because of its height, it should be planted at the back. It won an All-American Rose Selection award in 1965. Although the flowers do not age very gracefully and it is said to be prone to mildew in some cooler climates, its positives far out weigh any negatives.

Rosa 'Mischief'

Rosa 'Montezuma'

Rosa 'Moonsprite'

MONTEZUMA
Large-flowered/Hybrid Tea
This rose was bred by Swim (United States) in 1955 from 'Fandango' × 'Floradora'. The buds are urn-shaped and the large, high-centered blooms are orange pink and double (36 petals). They are slightly fragrant and are borne on a vigorous, tallish (5 feet (1.5 m)) bush with leathery, semi-glossy foliage. It won gold medals at Geneva, Portland and in England. It was somewhat overshadowed by 'Super Star', and some people find the color a little harsh, but it is nevertheless a good garden rose in spite of its intolerance to extreme conditions and its susceptibility to mildew. Montezuma, the great Aztec emperor who died at the hands of his own people after the Spanish invasion, was reputedly a gardener.

MOONSPRITE
Cluster-flowered/Floribunda
The aptly named 'Moonsprite' was bred by Swim (United States) in 1956 from

Rosa 'Mrs. Herbert Stevens'

Rosa 'Mount Hood'

'Sutter's Gold' × 'Ondine'. The ovoid buds open to creamy white, medium-sized flowers with pale gold centers. They are cupped and double with up to 80 petals arranged in an old-fashioned way, and have a delightful fragrance. They grow freely in clusters on a dwarf, bushy plant with semi-glossy, leathery foliage. In spite of winning gold medals in Baden Baden and Rome, it did not gain the recognition it deserved from the rose-buying public when first released, but with today's fashion for old-fashioned and dwarf plants, it could be due for a revival.

MOUNT HOOD
(MACmouhoo, Foster's Melbourne Cup)
Large-flowered/Hybrid Tea
This rose was bred by McGredy in 1996 from 'Sexy Rexy' × 'Pot O' Gold'. The fragrant flowers are ivory white. They

are very double, containing 40–45 petals, with good high symmetrical centers, and occur mainly in clusters, giving the bush a snow-capped appearance. The foliage is glossy, deep green on a full branching, tall, upright plant which has excellent vigor and disease-resistance. It has an amazing capacity for bloom production, but the flowers usually require a little heat to open fully. It was named after the majestic snow-capped Mount Hood which rises above the Columbia Gorge on the Oregon Trail. It won the All-American Rose Selection in 1996.

MRS. HERBERT STEVENS
Large-flowered/Hybrid Tea
Bred by McGredy (Northern Ireland) in 1910 from 'Frau Karl Druschki' × 'Niphetos', the buds are long and pointed. The double, high-centered, fragrant flowers are white and are carried on a bushy, vigorous plant with light foliage. While the cross indicates this rose is a Large-flowered Rose, it looks more like a Tea rose and is most often placed in the company of Tea roses

by rosarians, although it does have fairly firm flower stems, which are the result of its German mother. 'Mrs. Herbert Stevens' won a gold medal in England.

MRS. OAKLEY FISHER
Large-flowered/Hybrid Tea
'Mrs. Oakley Fisher' was bred by Cant (England) in 1921 from unknown or unlisted parents. The moderately fragrant, single flowers with amber stamens are deep, orange yellow and are carried freely in clusters on a vigorous, medium bush growing to 30 in (75 cm) with bronze green, glossy foliage and purple stems. It is one of the most charming of the single roses and enjoyed considerable popularity in the 1920s.

Rosa 'Mrs. Oakley Fisher'

MRS. SAM MCGREDY
Large-flowered/Hybrid Tea

This rose was bred by McGredy (Northern Ireland) in 1929 from ('Donald McDonald' × 'Golden Emblem') × (seedling × 'The Queen Alexandra Rose'). The buds are pointed, opening to double flowers in shades of scarlet-copper-orange with the reverse heavily flushed red. The large, high-centered blooms are borne on a somewhat indifferent bush with reddish bronze, glossy foliage. It fades a little on opening but the color is unique. It was a favorite rose prior to World War II. Chosen by Ruth McGredy, wife of Sam III, against the advice of the men, it became a favorite in spite of the thin stems, sparse foliage and magnetic attraction to black spot. The climbing version is a better option for those who would like to grow this old favorite.

Rosa 'Nevada'

MOONLIGHT
Hybrid Musk

'Moonlight' was bred by Pemberton (England) in 1913 from 'Trier' × 'Sulphurea'. It was one of the first Hybrid Musks introduced by Pemberton. It is so vigorous, it is better treated as a Climber rather than a Shrub. The cluster of creamy white, almost single flowers with prominent stamens are quite stark against the dark green foliage. They are moderately fragrant with the typical musk rose scent, held on stems tinted with mahogany. It has the distinction of being one of the few climbing roses in this color that repeat flower and is a wonderful adornment for any home.

Rosa 'Moonlight'

NEVADA
Shrub

This popular rose was bred by Dot (Spain) in 1927 from 'La Giralda' × a form of *R. moyesii*. Some experts surmise that this is probably 'Fargesii', others doubt the *R. moyesii* influence at all, suggesting that *R. pimpinellifolia* is more likely (Harkness and Beales). It is a dense shrub with long arching canes, having few thorns, along which the large, loosely-formed creamy blooms are carried. These would be consistent with the *moyesii* breeding. Repeat flowering occurs along the branches, not in big clusters on the ends of water shoots, which is the habit of the Hybrid Musks. There is plenty of light green foliage to dress the plant with its chocolate brown stems.

NEW DAWN
Large-flowered Climber

In 1910, a hybrid seedling from a *wichuraiana*/safrano cross itself crossed with a Large-flowered Rose, 'Souvenir du President Carnot' (of 'Lady Mary Fitzwilliam' lineage) and gave rise to a vigorous Large-flowered Climber, with fine cupped, well-scented pale flesh pink semi-double non-repeating blooms. It was created in the United States by Dr. William van Fleet, a medical man turned plant breeder, regarded by some as the greatest of them all. In the 1920s this rose sported to a repeat flowering form which was introduced in 1930 as 'The New Dawn'. It was the first in America to be patented and is one of the 'greats'. Van Fleet also created 'American Pillar' and 'Silver Moon'.

Rosa 'New Dawn'

Rosa 'Oklahoma'

OKLAHOMA
Large-flowered/Hybrid Tea

Swim and Weeks (United States) bred 'Oklahoma' in 1964 from 'Chrysler Imperial' × 'Charles Mallerin'. The bud is ovoid, long and pointed, opening to very dark red, double (48 petals) flowers with the most intoxicating perfume. They are carried mainly singly on a medium sized, vigorous, bushy plant about 4 feet (1.2 m) high with dark, leathery foliage. 'Oklahoma' is one of three popular roses with the same parentage, the others being 'Mister Lincoln' and 'Papa Meilland'. 'Oklahoma' is about as close as you can get to a black rose.

OLD MASTER
Cluster-flowered/Floribunda

A good bedding variety, this rose was bred by McGredy (Northern Ireland) in 1974 from ('Maxi' × 'Evelyn Fison') × ('Orange Sweetheart' × 'Frühlingsmorgen'). The flowers are carmine with a white eye and reverse to the petals, and have a light fragrance. They are large, semi-double and borne in clusters on a medium-sized plant, growing to about 3 feet (1 m) tall, with dark, semi-glossy foliage. It shares the long thorns, susceptibility to black spot and variation in color in cooler weather of the other early 'hand-painted' roses.

OTHELLO
English Shrub

'Othello' is one of many English Roses named for Shakespearian characters. It was bred in 1986 from 'Lilian Austin' × 'The Squire'. The large, cupped, very full blooms are a dark, dusky crimson, but can also have purple, cerise and mauve tints. Usually, they are a mixture of colors and, in spite of their size and apparent coarseness, the strongly fragrant flowers (characteristic of the dark reds) are most attractive, growing on a tall, upright plant about 5 feet (1.6 m) high, with stiff stems and thick, rough-textured, dark green leaves.

Rosa 'Othello'

Rosa 'Old Master'

OLYMPIAD
Large-flowered/Hybrid Tea
Named for the 1984 Los Angeles Olympics, 'Olympiad' was bred by McGredy (New Zealand) in 1982 from 'Red Planet' × 'Pharaoh'. The large, double, exhibition flowers are a brilliant, medium red, but with only a slight fragrance. The flowers are borne mainly singly on long, stiff stems, suitable for cutting, on a medium sized, upright, bushy plant of about 4 feet (1.2 m) with medium green, matte foliage. It is a good garden rose, and won an All-American Rose Selection award as well as a gold medal at Portland.

OPHELIA
Large-flowered/Hybrid Tea
'Ophelia' was introduced by Paul (England) in 1912, perhaps a chance seedling of 'Antoine Rivoire'. The buds are long and pointed, with light salmon-flesh blooms, tinted light yellow at the

Rosa 'Olympiad'

Rosa 'Ophelia'

center. The flowers are double (28 petals) and fragrant, and are borne on a vigorous plant with leathery foliage. A nostalgia rose, its willingness to sport has already been mentioned ('Madame Butterfly' being one of the better known ones), but it is interesting to add that with its own sports, their sports and sports of all their offspring, a Miss Wylie wrote in the Royal Horticultural Society's Journal for January 1955, that the 206, for which she could account, represented just over half the Large-flowered (Hybrid Tea) sports in a 25-year period.

OPHELIA, CLIMBING
Large-flowered Climber

This rose is a climbing sport of the bush variety introduced by Paul in 1912. It occurred in Dickson's Nursery in Northern Ireland in 1920. The buds of 'Ophelia' are small, pointed and elegant of a soft salmon-flesh color with tints of yellow at the center. They open to a strongly fragrant flower of 28 petals.

Foliage is pale green and leathery. Growth is close-jointed and very strong to over 20 feet (6 m). When trained horizontally, the canes of 'Climbing Ophelia' produce shoots at every node, giving an amazing display of spring flowers. Repeat flowering is good with another display in autumn. It can be used on fences, pergolas, arches and walls to great advantage. Spring blooms can be damaged by thrips, but disease resistance is excellent.

ORANGES AND LEMONS
Cluster-flowered/Floribunda

Another McGredy rose, 'Oranges and Lemons' was produced in 1994 from 'New Year' × ('Freude' × seedling). The lightly fragrant flowers are large and full in a striking mixture of orange and yellow stripes. They are borne in small clusters on a tall, spreading, very vigorous plant with dark green, glossy foliage. When young, the leaves are a dark red color, which adds to the attraction of this plant.

PAPA MEILLAND
Large-flowered/Hybrid Tea

Bred by Meilland (France) in 1963 from
'Chrysler Imperial' × 'Charles Mallerin',
the buds are pointed, followed by large,
dark, velvety crimson blooms of excellent form and heavenly perfume. They
are double (35 petals) and are borne on
a vigorous, upright plant growing to 5
feet (1.5 m) with leathery, glossy, olive
green foliage. It won a gold medal at
Baden Baden and a Gamble Fragrance
Medal. Four generations of Francis
Meilland's family were honored with
roses—this one and 'Madame A.
Meilland' ('Peace') after his parents,
'Grand'mère Jenny' after his grandmother, 'Manou Meilland' after his wife,
Marie-Louisette, 'Michèle Meilland' and
'Alain' after his children—three genera-
tions of breeders included. 'Papa
Meilland' became the sixth rose placed
in the Hall of Fame (World's Favorite
Rose) by the World Federation of Rose
Societies in 1988.

Rosa 'Papa Meilland'

Rosa 'Paradise'

PARADISE
Large-flowered/Hybrid Tea

'Paradise' was bred by Weeks (United
States) in 1978 from 'Swarthmore' ×
seedling. The buds are long and pointed,
developing into large, well-formed,
double (28 petals) flowers of silvery
lavender, with ruby red shading on the
edges. The medium, healthy, upright
bush of 3 feet (1 m) is well-clothed in
dark green, glossy foliage. It is good for
both garden display and cut flowers,
winning an All-American Rose Selection
award and a gold medal at Portland. The
color combination is unusual and, even if
the contrasting red fades as the flower
ages, it remains a worthy beginner's
rose.

PARFUM DE L'HAŸ
(Rose a Parfum de l'Haÿ)
Hybrid Rugosa

'Parfum de l'Haÿ' was bred by
Gravereaux (France) in 1901 from (*R.
damascena* × 'General Jacqueminot'). It
is not an easy rose to classify, because of
its mixed parentage, but since it displays
many characteristics of the Rugosas, it is

Rosa 'Parkdirektor Riggers'

probably better with this group than any other. Its large, globular buds open to flat, bright red flowers, which become darker in hot sun. The flowers are fragrant and look beautiful against the dark green foliage on its bushy plant with ample thorns. The Rugosas perform equally well in shade and this one is no exception.

PARKDIREKTOR RIGGERS
Cluster-flowered Climber
Bred by Kordes in 1957, this rose can be classed as a Shrub-Climber. Growth is very strong to 10 feet (3 m) or more, canes are very prickly and growth is gaunt and upright. Flowers come in spring in enormous clusters of up to 50, and are rich velvety crimson, opening to semi-double full blooms. Fragrance is slight. Large round hips are produced if spent blooms are not removed and these are most attractive. 'Parkdirektor Riggers' can be relied upon for a splash of rich color particularly in the spring. It is best planted at the back of the border where its gaunt base can be covered by other plants. A reliable rose for large country gardens, it is not recommended for small gardens.

Rosa 'Rose à Parfum de l'Haÿ'

PASCALI
Large-flowered/Hybrid Tea
A wonderful choice as a garden rose, 'Pascali' was bred by Lens (Belgium) in 1963 from 'Queen Elizabeth' × 'White Butterfly'. The medium-sized, well-formed flowers are creamy white and double (30 petals). The bush grows to about 6 feet (2 m) high, and has mainly single blooms carried on long, strong stems that made it, for years, the best white rose for cut flowers. It has little perfume. 'Pascali' is vigorous and healthy with dark, leathery foliage and won an All-American Rose Selection award, gold medals at The Hague and Portland, as well as being the World Federation of Rose Societies' seventh choice for World's Favorite Rose in 1991.

Rosa 'Paul Shirville'

PAUL SHIRVILLE
(Heart Throb)
Large-flowered/Hybrid Tea
This beautiful rose was bred by Harkness (England) in 1981 from 'Compassion' × 'Mischief'. The medium-large, high-centered double blooms are light salmon pink and are borne singly or in small clusters of three. The fragrance is sweet and strong. Its color, form and fragrance are captivating. The medium-sized (about 4 feet (1.2 m)) plants are somewhat spreading and are covered in dark, shiny foliage. It was named for a design engineer as a surprise retirement present.

PAX
Hybrid Musk
Pemberton (England) bred 'Pax' in 1918 from 'Trier' × 'Sunburst'. The plant is tall and spreading with arching, brown stems and dark green leaves. The long, pointed buds open to large, loose, semi-double blooms in shades of creamy white to pure white, displaying yellow stamens when fully open. They are borne throughout the season in large, well-spaced clusters on this elegant, useful garden plant.

PEACE
(Madame A. Meilland, Gioia, Gloria Dei)
Large-flowered/Hybrid Tea
The story of 'Peace', bred by Francis Meilland (France) in 1945 from

Rosa 'Pascali'

('George Dickson' × 'Souvenir de Claudius Pernet') × ('Joanna Hill' × 'Charles P. Kilham') × 'Margaret McGredy' is legendary. The large, perfectly-formed flowers are soft yellow, edged rose pink, with the cream fading as the blooms age, and having a light fragrance. They are borne on firm stems, good for cutting, with large, leathery, glossy foliage, on a mainly healthy (it may need protection from black spot), fairly spreading plant whose height depends on when it is planted. Older bushes are taller and more vigorous, seeming to indicate that the variety has deteriorated. 'Peace' has won all the major awards and was the first rose selected for the Hall of Fame (World's Favorite Rose) by the World Federation of Rose Societies. It was named for the breeder's mother, but he was unable to communicate this when the bud wood was dispatched in the last diplomatic bags to leave France before the German invasion in World War II, so it was given other names, the most affectionate being 'Peace', given by the Americans to celebrate the end of the war. It is the most significant parent rose of the twentieth century and may be found in the ancestry of most of good, modern, bush roses.

Rosa 'Peace'

Rosa 'Pax'

Rosa 'Perdita'

Rosa 'Penelope'

PEACE, CLIMBING
(Climbing Madame A. Meilland, Climbing Gioia)
Large-flowered Climber

'Climbing Peace' was introduced in 1950 and is a very strong climber to 14–16 feet (4–5 m) with the ability to flower over a very long period in hot climates. Its very long, thick climbing shoots need to be carefully bent down into an horizontal position to induce flowering shoots at every node in spring. It is best used on post and wire fences as its shoots are too strong for pillars and pergolas. Color is soft yellow with each petal heavily edged with soft pink, and the suffusion of the two colors in the huge full blooms of over 40 petals is most appealing. This is a Climbing rose that reaches its peak performance in Southern Australia, Southern California, Spain and Italy.

PENELOPE
Hybrid Musk

An exquisitely beautiful shrub rose, 'Penelope' was bred by Pemberton (England) in 1924 from 'Ophelia' × 'Trier'. It can almost behave like a Cluster-flowered if pruned hard, but when treated lightly and allowed to develop more naturally, it forms a graceful, spreading shrub. The coppery-salmon tinted buds open to medium sized flowers that are almost white with a hint of pink, having some darker tones, especially on the frilled edges of the petals. They are sweetly fragrant, and enhanced by the dark foliage with its bronze tints, which also show on the stems. It helps to accelerate the second flush if the plant is dead-headed, but if allowed to develop, the autumn hips are an attractive coral-pink.

PERDITA
English Shrub

Bred in 1983 from 'The Friar' × (seedling × 'Iceberg'), 'Perdita' is a neat, medium-sized, bushy plant about 5 feet (1.5 m) tall with dark green, healthy foliage. It is freely covered with medium-sized, fully double, quartered blooms of apricot-blush. The buds are Tea-like at first and so is the fragrance, which is one of the rose's attractions, winning it the Edland Medal for fragrance in the United Kingdom. It is a highly regarded rose and makes a good bedding plant, modern in appearance, with new, slightly arching growth springing from the base regularly. It was named after the Shakespearian heroine from *The Winter's Tale*.

PERLE D'OR
(Yellow Cécile Brunner)
Polyantha

'Perle d'Or' was bred by Rambaud (France) 1884 from a polyantha × 'Madame Falcot'. At that time in rose history, yellow would have been an acceptable description, because that was about as yellow as roses were before Pernet-Ducher's Persiana hybrids. It is more a buff-apricot shade with deeper tones in the center, becoming more pink as it opens, finally fading to cream. It is in nearly all respects like 'Cécile Brunner', with more loosely formed flowers and a slightly taller bush (about 4 feet (1.2 m) high). It has also been classified, with 'Cécile Brunner', as a Hybrid China, but there is little justification for this, except perhaps from its Tea parent.

PICCADILLY
Large-flowered/Hybrid Tea

'Piccadilly' was bred by McGredy (Northern Ireland) in 1960 from 'McGredy's Yellow' × 'Karl Herbst'. The large, double (28 petals), high centered, slightly fragrant blooms have a scarlet base with a gold reverse. The vigorous, upright, branching bush is of medium height (about 4 feet (1.2 m)), clothed in dark, glossy foliage, tinted red on the new growth. It won awards in Rome and Madrid. There is a large bed of these roses, not far from Piccadilly Circus in London, the inspiration behind the name of the rose being its bright lights.

Rosa 'Perle d'Or'

Rosa 'Piccadilly'

PIERRE DE RONSARD
(MEIviolin, Eden, Eden Rose 88, Grimpant Pierre de Ronsard)
Large-flowered Climber

This vigorous rose was bred from ('Danse des Sylphes' × 'Handel') × 'Pink Wonder, Climbing' and bears large, full flowers which are creamy white, heavily suffused with lavender-pink and carmine. The shape is like a round cabbage, and the blooms open to disclose a charming muddle of infolded petals. They repeat-flower through summer and autumn, and have a light fragrance. It is suitable to grow on a wall or fence where the strong branching shoots can spread out, or it can be trained up a tall pillar, or grown with support as a shrub. Pierre de Ronsard (1524-1585) was a court poet in Scotland and France, and also a keen gardener.

Rosa 'Pierre de Ronsard'

Rosa 'Pink Grootendorst'

PINK GROOTENDORST
Hybrid Rugosa

This rose is a sport of 'F. J. Grootendorst' and has soft pink flowers. In all other respects it is like its parent. The color is complementary to the foliage, being neither harsh nor clashing as with the parent. 'Pink Grootendorst', as is the custom with some sports, can revert to the original red, and has on occasions shown both colors on the one head of blooms. It is generally a handsome and easy-to-grow shrub, as well as bearing flowers suitable for cutting.

PINK LA SEVILLANA
Cluster-flowered/Floribunda

A sport of 'La Sevillana', this rose was released by Meilland (France) in 1984. It is in all ways similar to its parent, except for the color of the blooms, which are a clear, rose pink. The single blooms are borne in clusters on a tall, spreading bush which grows up to 5 feet (1.5 m). It has a light fragrance and makes an excellent landscaping rose.

PINK PARFAIT
Cluster-flowered/Floribunda

This lovely rose was bred by Swim (United States) in 1960 from 'First

Rosa 'Pink Parfait'

Love' × 'Pinocchio'. The buds are ovoid to urn-shaped, opening to flowers, the outer petals of which are medium pink blending to a creamy pink in the center. They are lightly perfumed, high-centered to open, and are borne continuously in clusters. 'Pink Parfait' is a medium-sized, bushy, upright, vigorous plant about 4 feet (1.2 m) high, with leathery, semi-glossy foliage. As a bedding rose, it has few peers for health, flower production and repeating. In spite of the fleeting nature of the flowers, 'Pink Parfait' is recommended to the beginning rose grower. The lack of thorns make it a little easier to handle.

Rosa 'Pink Peace'

PINK PEACE
Large-flowered/Hybrid Tea
This warm climate rose was bred by Meilland (France) in 1959 from ('Peace' × 'Monique') × ('Peace' × 'Mrs John Laing'). The large flowers are dusty, deep pink and double (58 petals), having an exquisite perfume. It is a vigorous, medium plant (about 3 feet (1 m) high) with bushy growth and leathery foliage. The name suggests a sport of 'Peace' or a similar rose, but neither is the case, so it is reasonable to assume it was a name designed to cash in on the success of its grandparent, 'Peace'. It won gold medals in Geneva and Rome, and is more popular in the United States than elsewhere.

Rosa 'Playboy'

Rosa 'Playgirl'

Rosa 'Polar Star'

PLAYBOY
(Cheerio)
Cluster-flowered/Floribunda

This rose was bred by Cocker (Scotland) in 1976 from 'City of Leeds' × ('Chanelle' × 'Piccadilly'). The large, almost single flowers, with wavy petals, are an attractive blend of red and yellow, with the yellow eye giving way to the red as the flowers age. They are lightly fragrant and are borne in free-flowering clusters on a medium-sized upright, bushy plant about 3 feet (1 m) high with dark, glossy foliage. The impact of the plant is quite brilliant, and it makes a good bedding rose suitable for a spot in the garden which needs to be brightened. It is very popular in the United States.

PLAYGIRL
(MORplag)
Cluster-flowered/Floribunda

This lovely rose was bred by Ralph Moore (United States) in 1986 from 'Playboy' × 'Angel Face'. The flowers of 'Playgirl' are pink and open out like saucers emphasizing the contrast with the yellow stamens. They are freely borne through summer and autumn and serve almost limitless purposes in the garden, in beds, border, as hedges, in tubs, and for exhibition. There is not much scent, so it must be the color that attracts bees to the flowers. The foliage is semi-glossy on a plant with a dense and bushy habit. It will grow to average height.

POLAR STAR
(Polarstern)
Large-flowered/Hybrid Tea

'Polar Star' was bred by Tantau (Germany) in 1982 from undeclared parents. The flowers are a rich creamy white color with just a hint of lime in the buds. They are medium-sized, exhibition type (good form), double blooms (35 petals), with only a little perfume. The plant is bushy and tallish, growing to 5 feet (1.5 m) in height, and has matte, light green foliage. The stiff stems are good for cutting and its general health and vigor make it a rose to grow for beginners as well as the more serious and experienced rosarian.

Rosa 'Polka'

Rosa 'Precious Platinum'

POLKA
(MEltosier, Lord Byron, Polka 91, Scented Dawn, Twilight Glow)
Large-flowered Climber

This rose from the famous Meilland nursery has an old-fashioned air—it opens wide and flat, with the short petals reflexing one layer upon another. The double, medium-sized blooms are carried singly or in small clusters on stiff stems. The color is coppery salmon, fading to salmon-pink as the petals expand, but retaining copper tones in the depths of the flower. There is only a light fragrance. It is ideal for pillars, walls and fences where a shorter than average climber is required. The growth is vigorous and rather shrubby, not rampant, and the plant has a good coverage of glossy foliage.

PRECIOUS PLATINUM
(Opa Potschke, Red Star)
Large-flowered/Hybrid Tea

Dickson (Northern Ireland) bred
'Precious Platinum' in 1974 from 'Red
Planet' × 'Franklin Englemann'. The
medium to large flowers are cardinal-
red and high-centered. The free flowering, healthy, vigorous plant, about 3 feet
(1 m) high, is well-clothed in glossy
foliage. Altogether, it is an attractive
package, in spite of a lack of perfume.
The name is a little strange for a red
rose—hardly platinum—but what
breeder in his right mind would turn
down a sponsor, in this case a firm of
refiners of precious metals?

PRETTY JESSICA
(AUSjess)
English Rose

Austin (England) bred 'Pretty Jessica'
in 1983 from 'Wife of Bath' × seedling.
It produces rosettes of medium-sized,
pink flowers with 41 petals. They have a
strong, old fashioned fragrance. This is a
bushy plant with a low-growing habit
and is very suitable for a small garden.
The foliage is mid-green and is not
overly disease-resistant.

Rosa 'Pretty Jessica'

Rosa 'Princesse De Monaco'

Rosa 'Priscilla Burton'

PRINCESSE DE MONACO
Large-flowered/Hybrid Tea
This is the second rose named for
Princess Grace by the Meilland firm, the
first, 'Grace de Monaco', by Francis
Meilland in 1955 and this one by his
widow, Marie-Louisette. 'Princesse de
Monaco' was bred 1982 from 'Ambassa-
dor' × 'Peace'. The high-centered, large,
double, fragrant blooms have cream
petals edged with pink. The plant has
bushy, upright growth to about 5 feet
(1.5 m) with an abundance of large,
dark, glossy leaves. It is an outstanding
multi-purpose rose, useful for garden
display, exhibition and cutting and, like
its namesake, would be at home in any
setting.

PRISCILLA BURTON
Cluster-flowered/Floribunda
The wife of the chairman of Fison's, the
English garden products company, gave
her name to this rose, which was bred by
McGredy (Northern Ireland) in 1978
from 'Old Master' × seedling. The semi-
double (10 petals) blooms make an eye-
catching display of deep carmine, pink
and white in varying combinations, but
always with the distinct, 'hand-painted'
look. They are borne freely in clusters
on a vigorous, upright, bushy plant of
medium height with dark, glossy foliage.
It may need protection from black spot.
It won a gold medal and President's
International Trophy in the UK.

Rosa 'Pristine'

PRISTINE
Large-flowered/Hybrid Tea

Bred by Warriner (United States) in 1978 from 'White Masterpiece' × 'First Prize', the long buds develop into near white flowers, with shadings of light pink. They are very large, double, lightly perfumed and have exquisite form. They are borne mainly singly on an upright bush about 3 feet (1 m) high with a background of dense, dark green foliage. The perfume presents a paradox. The breeder described this rose as 'lightly perfumed', but some people can detect no scent, although it won a fragrance award in England. It also won a gold medal at Portland, and has won lots of hearts. It is certainly worthy of a place in the garden for display or cut flowers.

PROSPERITY
Hybrid Musk

The wonderfully named 'Prosperity' was bred by Pemberton (England) in 1919 from 'Marie-Jeanne' × 'Perle des

Rosa 'Prosperity'

Jardins'. This is a Polyantha × Tea and both parents are evident, the clusters of small flowers inherited from the Polyantha and the graceful bush showing the Tea influence. The small, white, rosette-shaped flowers are borne in clusters, which weigh down the long stems, giving an arching effect. The foliage is dark green and contributes to the value of this excellent garden rose.

PROSPERO
English Shrub

'Prospero' was bred in 1982 from 'The Knight' × 'Château de Clos Vougeot'. 'Prospero', another of the Shakespearian characters, is not a very vigorous rose and needs to be pampered a bit to do its best. It is only low growing (about 3 feet (90 cm) high, but, if it is in good soil, in a good location, well-fed and protected from disease, the flowers are all the reward you need. They are medium-sized and are of perfect old-rose form, very full, highly perfumed, opening rich crimson and aging to purple and mauve. In many roses, this characteristic is quite ugly, but in 'Prospero' it is an asset.

PURPLE TIGER
Cluster-flowered/Floribunda

'Purple Tiger' was bred by Christensen (United States) in 1991 from 'Intrigue' × 'Pinstripe'. The large, double (26–40 petals) blooms are an eye-catching combination of very deep purple with stripes and flecks of white and mauve-pink. They are slightly fragrant and are borne in small clusters on a bushy plant about 32 in (80 cm) high with mid-green, glossy foliage and few thorns. The name evokes the color and the stripes of the tiger, and it is quite a stunning rose.

Rosa 'Prospero'

Rosa 'Purple Tiger'

QUEEN ADELAIDE
(Yves Piaget)
Large-flowered/Hybrid Tea

'Queen Adelaide' was bred by Meilland (France) in 1983 from ('Pharaoh' × 'Peace') × ('Chrysler Imperial' × 'Charles Mallerin'). The large, deep pink, double (40+ petals) blooms look quite old fashioned, and are very fragrant. They are borne, however, on a thoroughly modern bush, up to about 30 in (80 cm) high, with dark green, glossy foliage. It is sometimes classified as a shrub, but it is doubtful whether this classification is valid, 'Queen Adelaide' having been bred from Large-flowered Roses and having large-flowered growth, in spite of its old world appearance.

QUEEN ELIZABETH
Large-flowered/Hybrid Tea

Bred by Lammerts (United States) in 1954 from 'Charlotte Armstrong' × 'Floradora', the buds are pointed with

Rosa 'Queen Elizabeth'

Rosa 'Queen Adelaide'

the ensuing flowers of a medium pink. They are large, double and high-centered to cupped, with light fragrance. The flowers are borne singly and in clusters on a very tall (to 6 feet (2 m)) plant with very vigorous, bushy, upright growth. The foliage is dark and leathery. This is one of the best roses ever grown for all-around garden performance. It is difficult to classify, having been bred from a Large-flowered and a Cluster-flowered. In America, it is classified a Grandiflora; in Europe, a Floribunda; in Australia, a Hybrid Tea. 'Queen Eliza-beth' was chosen as the second rose to be placed in the Hall of Fame by the World Federation of Rose Societies.

QUEEN MARGRETHE
(POUlskov, POUskul, Dronning Margrethé, Enchant-ment, Königin Margrethe, Queen Margarethe)
Shrub
This rose was introduced by Poulsen (Denmark) in 1994. The flowers are

Rosa 'Queen Nefertiti'

light pink. It won a gold medal in New Zealand the year before it was released commercially.

QUEEN NEFERTITI
English Shrub
'Queen Nefertiti' was bred in 1988 from 'Lilian Austin' × 'Tamora'. The medium-sized, rosette-shaped, fragrant blooms are a soft yellow, tinged with pink as the flowers age. They are borne freely and continuously on a compact, hardy, bushy plant, that branches freely, and grows to 3 feet (1 m) tall. The breeder is not keen on the tendency for the flowers to become tinged with pink in hot sunlight, like 'Peace', but for most people, this is not a problem, as the rose is so lovely.

Rosa 'Queen Margrethe'

Rosa 'Raspberry Ice'

Rosa 'Raubritter'

RASPBERRY ICE
(Hannah Gordon, Tabris)
Cluster-flowered/Floribunda

'Raspberry Ice' was bred by Kordes (Germany) in 1983 from seedling × 'Bordure'. The flowers are a raspberry color with the petals edged deep pink, more contrasting than its parent, 'Bordure', or 'Strawberry Ice'. They are large and double (35 petals) with a light fragrance on a bush that can become very tall, with medium green, semi-glossy foliage. When in full flower, the blooms are so thick, the bush is hardly visible. It makes a huge impact in its first year, but in the second year, the flowers mainly bloom above head height. It does require protection from black spot and is not all that generous with its repeating. Its synonym is in honor of the celebrated English actress Hannah Gordon.

RAUBRITTER
Shrub

Another Kordes rose, 'Raubritter' was bred in 1936 from 'Daisy Hill' × 'Solarium'. The small, cupped, clear pink flowers are borne in clusters along the stems of this delightful, spreading shrub.

It can be as wide as 6 feet (2 m) but not usually higher than 3 feet (1 m), making a wide mound of color. While it has the appearance of an old fashioned rose, the globular, almost bell-like flowers are like little else. The stems are rather thorny, with their grayish-green, matte foliage and there is little perfume. In spite of the occasional bouts of mildew and black spot, it is a rose worthy of a place in the garden.

RED CEDAR
(Loving Memory, Burgund '81)
Large-flowered/Hybrid Tea

Also known as 'Loving Memory', this rose was bred by Kordes (Germany) in 1983 from an unnamed seedling × 'Red Planet' seedling. The large, high-centered exhibition type blooms are very double and are medium red in color but unfortunately they have very little fragrance, which seems a shame in a red rose. The 4 feet (1.2 m) high plant is upright and bushy with medium green, glossy foliage. When the variety was first brought to Australia, it was named 'Burgund '81' by the breeder. However, Roy and Heather Rumsey (the Australian

Rosa 'Red Cedar'

agents for Kordes), still grew the earlier variety, 'Burgund', and felt it would be confusing to have two similar names. They were invited to name it something else and chose 'Red Cedar'. It is popular in Europe and Australia.

REGENSBERG
Cluster-flowered/Floribunda
'Regensberg' was bred by McGredy (New Zealand) in 1979 from 'Geoff Boycott' × 'Old Master'. The flower petals are hot pink, edged white with a white reverse and the 'hand-painted' flowers have a white eye and yellow stamens. They are large, semi-double (21 petals), cupped to flat and have a light fragrance. The plants are low (about 15 in (40 cm)) and bushy, almost like a patio rose in stature, with medium green, glossy foliage. It was the first rose

Rosa 'Regensberg'

bred by Sam McGredy after moving to New Zealand, winning a gold medal in Baden Baden in 1970. The rose is named after the home town of the Swiss flower painter, Lotte Gunthardt who already had a rose named after her.

REMEMBER ME
Large-flowered/Hybrid Tea

Named for the 'Not Forgotten Associa-
tion', this rose was bred by Cocker
(Scotland) in 1984 from 'Ann Letts' ×
('Dainty Maid' × 'Pink Favorite'). The
large, semi-double (20 petals) blooms
are a blend of orange, yellow and
copper, with a light fragrance. They are
borne singly or in clusters, with long
stems suitable for cutting, on a vigorous,
bushy, upright plant about 3 feet (1 m)

Rosa 'Robusta'

Rosa 'Remember Me'

high with coppery green, leathery
foliage. The color becomes a little
washed out in hot climates. The parentage given here is from *Modern Roses 10*,
but it is elsewhere listed as 'Alexander'
× 'Silver Jubilee', which seems more
consistent with the rose, in both growth
and color.

ROBUSTA
Shrub

This rose was bred by Kordes (Germany) in 1979 from *R. rugosa* 'Regeliana'
× unnamed seedling. It could have been
classified with the Hybrid Rugosas,
which it is, but it is not entirely characteristic. It has inherited thorniness and
dark, rough, leathery foliage, but not
quite to the usual extent of the typical
Rugosa. 'Robusta' is a head-high,
upright plant, topped by sprays of
brilliant red, single flowers throughout
the season. It is not always easy to breed
the immunity of the Rugosas to fungus
diseases into hybrids, and this one does
suffer a little from black spot.

Rosa 'Rock 'N' Roll'

Rosa 'Roseraie de l'Haÿ'

ROCK 'N' ROLL
(Tango)
Cluster-flowered/Floribunda

This rose, bred by McGredy (New Zealand) in 1989, appears to be one of the 'hand-painted' roses developed by McGredy from the 'Picasso' line. Beales indicates it is a 'Sexy Rexy' seedling. The petals are an orange-red color with yellow margins and a yellow eye in the center of the bloom. The semi-double blooms are borne in large clusters on a medium-sized, healthy, upright bush which grows to about 3 feet (1 m) tall. The name suggests a lively rose, which, like most of the other 'hand-painted' roses, makes a good bedding plant.

ROSERAIE DE L'HAŸ
Hybrid Rugosa

Named for the famed rose garden, this rose was released by Cochet-Cochet (France) in 1901, a sport from an unknown Hybrid Rugosa. A number of experts have expressed doubt about the listed origin of this rose. It is one of the most beautiful Rugosas, having large, double blooms of rich, crimson-purple, with a strong but sweet fragrance. They open flat from pointed buds and are borne freely throughout the season, in clusters at times. The dark green foliage seems an unlikely combination with the dark colored rose, but somehow it works. Unfortunately, it rarely sets hips, contrary to the habit of many of the Rugosas.

ROYAL DANE
(Troika)
Large-flowered/Hybrid Tea

'Royal Dane' was bred by Poulsen (Denmark) in 1971 from ('Super Star' × ('Baccará' × 'Princesse Astrid')) × 'Hanne'. The large, classically formed, very fragrant flowers are a blend of orange, copper and red. They are borne on long stems, suitable for cutting, on a tallish vigorous, upright, bushy plant growing to 5 feet (1.5 m), with dark, glossy foliage, which has red tones on the immature growth. The Royal Family of Denmark had not given permission for their name to be used, so it was changed to 'Troika', a threesome or a coach drawn by three horses. This rose is a good garden variety, but seems to appeal more in cooler climates where the coloring is more intense. 'Royal Dane' repeat flowers.

ROYAL HIGHNESS
(Konigliche Hoheit)
Large-flowered/Hybrid Tea

Bred by Swim and Weeks (United States) in 1962 from 'Virgo' × 'Peace', the buds of 'Royal Highness' are long and pointed. The large, double (43 petals), exhibition type blooms are the palest of pinks. The very fragrant, long stemmed roses, which are almost thornless and good for cutting, are borne on a vigorous, upright, bushy plant about 4 feet (1.2 m) tall with dark green, glossy foliage. It won an All-American Rose Selection award as well as gold medals at Portland and Madrid. 'Royal Highness' is a beautiful and functional rose, but does not like being rained on, with blemishes and disease the likely consequences.

SADLER'S WELLS
Shrub

'Sadler's Wells' was bred by Beales (England) in 1983 from 'Penelope' × 'Rose Gaujard'. It probably qualifies as a Hybrid Musk, having been bred from one. It is a vigorous but neat shrub, about 4 feet (1.2 m) high, and flowers freely and continuously throughout the season. The well-spaced sprays of lightly-scented, semi-double flowers are particularly weather resistant and last well when cut. The blooms are silvery pink shading to cherry red on the outer petals and the color is even more intense in autumn. The plant is covered with dark green, shiny foliage and is tolerant of most conditions—low light, poor soil and inclement weather.

Rosa 'Sadler's Wells'

Rosa 'Royal Dane'

Rosa 'Royal Highness'

Rosa 'Savoy Hotel'

Rosa 'Sally Holmes'

Rosa 'Sarah van Fleet'

SALLY HOLMES
Hybrid Musk

This rose was bred by Holmes (England) in 1976 from 'Ivory Fashion' × 'Ballerina'. Like many of the Hybrid Musks, this rose can be kept smaller with harder pruning, but is best left to develop into the graceful arching shrub it can be. In warmer climates, it can be treated as a climber. The clusters may need some disbudding to allow the flowers to display their true beauty. The pointed buds are a buff-peach color and open to large, single buff-white flowers with prominent stamens. It is well covered with healthy, pointed leaves that are medium green and semi-glossy.

SARABANDE
Cluster-flowered/Floribunda

Named after a popular Spanish dance, 'Sarabande' was bred by Meilland (France) in 1957 from 'Cocorico' × 'Moulin Rouge'. The medium, semi-double (13 petals), cupped to flat blooms are light orange-red with yellow stamens. They have a light fragrance and are borne in large trusses on a low, bushy, healthy plant with semi-glossy foliage. It won an All-American Rose Selection award as well as gold medals at Bagatelle (Paris), Geneva, Rome and Portland. In spite of its good credentials, 'Sarabande' lost some popularity with the rise of the exhibition-worthy Cluster-flowered Roses.

SARAH VAN FLEET
Hybrid Rugosa

Flowering throughout the season, 'Sarah van Fleet' was bred by Van Fleet (United States) in 1926 from *R. rugosa* × 'My Maryland'. Doubt is again expressed about the parents, this time on the basis of a chromosome count. The pointed buds open to semi-double, slightly cupped, fragrant blooms of china pink, showing yellow stamens at the center. They are borne in small clusters on a tall, vigorous, upright, bushy shrub. The dark green foliage and myriad of vicious thorns are typically Rugosa.

SAVOY HOTEL
(Integrity)
Large-flowered/Hybrid Tea
Named to mark the centenary of
London's Savoy Hotel, this rose was
bred by Harkness (England) in 1987
from 'Silver Jubilee' × 'Amber Queen'.
The high-centered, well-formed, double
(40 petals) blooms are a delicate shade
of phlox-pink with a deeper shade on the
reverse side of the petals. They are borne
usually singly and have a sweet fragrance. The plant is of medium height,
about 4 feet (1.2 m), with dark green,
semi-glossy foliage on bushy, upright
growth. It won a gold medal in Dublin.
It is an excellent bedding rose and the
flowers are long lasting when cut.

SCABROSA
Hybrid Rugosa
Introduced by Harkness (England) in
1960, the origin of this rose is unknown,
as it was found at a nursery among a
batch of plants called 'rose apples'.

'Scabrosa' was subsequently introduced.
It means 'rough to the touch', not 'rose
apples'. It could be a selection from *R.
rugosa* or a hybrid. Whichever, it is a very
pleasing plant, being almost continuously
in bloom, with large, single, fragrant
flowers on an almost rampant plant,
which carries large, red hips after the
first flush. The color has been described
as mauve red, violaceous crimson,
mauve pink and rosy magenta. The buds
are pointed and somewhat darker,
occurring singly and in small clusters.

SCARLET QUEEN ELIZABETH
Large-flowered/Hybrid Tea
This rose was bred by Dickson (Northern Ireland) in 1963 from ('Korona' ×
seedling) × 'Queen Elizabeth'. Another
of the in-between varieties with different
classifications in different countries,
'Scarlet Queen Elizabeth' has the
vigorous, upright, tall growth (up to 6
feet (2 m)) of its more popular parent,
but with rather harsh colored, large,

Rosa 'Scarlet Meidiland'

cupped, flame-scarlet flowers, borne in medium sized clusters. It won a gold medal at The Hague, but it does not live up to the initial claims its name suggests.

SCARLET MEIDILAND
Shrub

This rose was bred by Meilland (France) in 1987. The parentage is not listed. It is one of the landscaping roses developed specifically to be healthy and maintenance free. The plant produces heavy clusters of small, clear scarlet flowers on a dense, spreading bush with dark green, glossy foliage. It is free-flowering and the stems arch up to 3 feet

(1 m) before spilling onto the ground, making a wide mound of color.

SCENTIMENTAL
(WEKplapep)
Cluster-flowered/Floribunda

This is a charming Cluster-flowered Rose, which is striped red and pink, creating a startling visual impact. It is a vigorous, bushy, free-flowering plant with healthy, large, luxurious foliage. It is a very modern looking bedding rose which also makes a good standard. 'Scentimental' deservedly won the prestigious All-American Rose Selection in 1997.

Rosa 'Scentimental'

Rosa 'Sea Foam'

SCHNEEZWERG
(Snow Dwarf)
Hybrid Rugosa

This beautiful rose was bred by Lambert (Germany) in 1912 from *R. rugosa* × a Polyantha rose. It is not too short, in spite of its name, but is smaller than many of this class. It has also been claimed to be a hybrid of *R. bracteata*, which could account for the dark, shiny foliage, not typical of a Rugosa. Its attributes are the compact, neat plant with its continuous supply of small, semi-double, pure white flowers, having an attractive ring of pale yellow stamens in the center. The hips are small and orange-red.

SEA FOAM
Ground Cover

'Sea Foam' was bred by Schwartz (United States) in 1964 from (('White Dawn' × 'Pinocchio') × ('White Dawn' × 'Pinocchio')) × ('White Dawn' × 'Pinocchio'). 'Sea Foam' is basically a rambler, but its canes are not as long as those of most ramblers, being only about

Rosa 'Schneezwerg'

10 feet (3 m). This makes it more suitable for a ground cover or weeping standard rose. It was one of the few recurrent flowering ramblers, until recently, when a German breeder introduced a new series fitting this description. The medium-sized, double flowers are white with a pink blush and are borne in lightly fragrant (fruity) clusters. It has small, glossy, medium green foliage.

Rosa 'Sharifa Asma'

Rosa 'Sexy Rexy'

Rosa 'Sheer Bliss'

SEXY REXY
Cluster-flowered/Floribunda

McGredy (New Zealand) bred this rose in 1984 from 'Seaspray' × 'Dreaming'. The medium-sized, double (40 petals) blooms are a medium to light pink blend and are borne in large clusters on a medium, free-flowering plant about 3 feet (1 m) tall, with light green, glossy foliage. The flowers are rather flat and camellia-like, but it is proving to be a good parent as well as a very satisfactory bedding rose. One wonders whether Sam McGredy was honoring one of his friends in the name, or referring to the prowess of the rose, having such roses as 'Auckland Metro' and therefore 'Aotearoa', 'Miriam', 'Spek's Centennial', 'Moody Blues', 'Whiteout' and 'Kapiti' among its progeny.

SHARIFA ASMA
English Shrub

Bred in 1989 from 'Mary Rose' × 'Admired Miranda', the extremely fragrant flowers are cupped and open, forming a very double rosette of delicate blush-pink with a touch of gold at the base of the petals and fading with age to almost white on the outer petals. They grow on a vigorous, bushy plant about

3 feet (1 m) tall, with arching canes and mid-green foliage. 'Admired Miranda' bore beautiful flowers, on a somewhat indifferent plant. 'Mary Rose' lacks the delicacy of 'Admired Miranda', but is a vigorous plant. 'Sharifa Asma' combines the best qualities of both parents. This does not always happen in breeding, as depending on dominance, it is possible to get the worst of both.

SHEER BLISS
Large-flowered/Hybrid Tea
'Sheer Bliss' was bred by Warriner (United States) in 1985 from 'White Masterpiece' × 'Grand Masterpiece'. The large, well-formed, double (35 petals) blooms are white with blush pink centers and a spicy fragrance. They are carried singly or in small clusters on a medium sized, upright, bushy plant adorned with medium green, matte foliage. It won an All-American Rose Selection award and a gold medal in Japan. It was bred by the same team who bred 'Pristine', Bill Warriner and

Jackson and Perkins, and in many ways is a similar rose. Only time will tell which is better, but in the meantime, it will tantalise the senses of those who plant this excellent rose.

SHOCKING BLUE
Cluster-flowered/Floribunda
This rose was bred by Kordes (Germany) in 1974 from an unnamed seedling × 'Silver Star'. The large, double, high-centered flowers are a rich lilac-mauve and are borne in wide sprays on a medium-sized plant growing to 4 feet (1.2 m) high, with dark, glossy foliage. It has a strong but sweet fragrance, and, being healthy and free-flowering, deserves to be more widely grown. However, the color has not in general been one the public has flocked to buy, and there does not seem to be a great deal of contrast between the flowers and the foliage, making it a little less spectacular as a bedding rose. It is quite popular, however, with flower arrangers.

Rosa 'Shocking Blue'

SHOT SILK
Large-flowered/Hybrid Tea

Dickson (Northern Ireland) bred this rose in 1924 from 'Hugh Dickson' seedling × 'Sunstar'. The double (28 petals), high-centered, very fragrant flowers are cherry-cerise, shading to golden yellow at the base. The light green, glossy foliage enhances the blooms on this once very popular and vigorous rose, which won a gold medal in England in 1923. In spite of the pride of place it took in the gardens of England for over 20 years, it did not live up to the promise many thought it offered the breeder. Its name is indicative of the flower.

Rosa 'Climbing Shot Silk'

SHOT SILK, CLIMBING
Large-flowered Climber

This rose was introduced in 1931 and is still popular around the world. The color of the flowers—a rich coppery salmon with cerise undertones was a new color in roses and this, combined with excellent disease free glossy foliage and a strong habit of growth, has ensured its popularity ever since. Flowers are large, double, well-formed and very fragrant. Spring production of flowers is very good and continuity through summer fair with an excellent autumnal flush. 'Climbing Shot Silk' is suitable for pillars, tripods, fences and pergolas and looks well against mellow brick walls.

SHOWBIZ
(Ingrid Weibull)
Cluster-flowered/Floribunda

Tantau gave this rose a rather flashy name when he bred 'Showbiz' in 1983 from 'Dream Waltz' × 'Marlena'. The medium-sized, double (28 petals) flowers are a bright, medium red. They are borne continuously in large clusters on a lowish, healthy, bushy plant with dark, semi-glossy foliage. It won an All-

Rosa 'Shot Silk'

American Rose Selection award in 1985, an indication of its all-around performance under a variety of conditions, being valuable as a bedding rose or as a cut flower. Unlike many of the red Cluster-flowered Roses, 'Showbiz' seems to be resistant to mildew.

SILVER JUBILEE
Large-flowered/Hybrid Tea

'Silver Jubilee' was bred by Cocker (Scotland) in 1978 from (('Highlight' × 'Color Wonder') × ('Parkdirektor Riggers' × 'Piccadilly')) × 'Mischief'. The large, double (33 petals), high-centered blooms are silvery pink with a darker reverse to the petals and with a pleasing, light perfume. It is very disease resistant and vigorous in the United Kingdom, where the medium plant (to about 4 feet (1.2 m)) is covered in dark, glossy foliage, but seems susceptible to black spot in humid conditions. Occasionally, new blood is needed to re-invigorate the Large-flowered line and the introduction of *R. kordesii*, with *R. rugosa* and *R. wichuraiana* in its background, through 'Parkdirektor Riggers', did just that. Jack Harkness predicted in his 1978 book, *Roses*, that it would be a forerunner for the future, but he could not have anticipated the extent of the influence 'Silver Jubilee' has had on roses bred in the past 20 years.

Rosa 'Showbiz'

Rosa 'Silver Jubilee'

Rosa 'Silver Moon'

Rosa 'Simplicity'

SILVER MOON
Large-flowered Climber

Another rose from Dr. Walter Van Fleet (see 'New Dawn') this rose was introduced in 1910, and said to be from *R. wichuraiana* × *R. laevigata*. There is also some 'Devoniensis' in 'Silver Moon'. The foliage is handsome, large, dark and glossy, the growth vigorous to 16 feet (5 m) or more and the big flowers are pure white and open with about 20 petals. They are also fragrant and show prominent yellow stamens. It flowers once only. *R. laevigata*, the Cherokee Rose, is one of the earliest roses to flower in the spring, displaying big white single flowers and light green healthy foliage. Although Chinese in origin it has become naturalized through parts of North America, hence its common name.

SIMPLICITY
Shrub

Warriner (United States) bred this quietly unassuming rose in 1978 from 'Pink Parfait' × unnamed seedling, and it certainly lives up to its name. The long pointed buds open to medium pink, semi-double (18 petals) flowers. They are quite large and flat when fully open, borne freely in clusters and have a refreshing light fragrance. The plant is bushy and upright with light green foliage. Planted close together, bushes of 'Simplicity' make a most attractive hedge, or as nurserymen Jackson and Perkins advertised it, a 'blooming fence'. It fulfills the expectation of being an easy rose to grow especially for those who feel that they cannot grow roses.

SINGIN' IN THE RAIN
(MACivy, Spek's Centennial, Love's Spring)
Cluster-flowered/Floribunda

McGredy (New Zealand) bred this rose in 1994 from 'Sexy Rexy' × 'Pot o' Gold'. The flowers are a neon apricot-copper that just lights up any garden. The moderately full blooms have 25–30 petals and a light fragrance, and are borne in large clusters. The foliage is dark glossy green on a medium, upright, free-branching plant. It is always in bloom, providing a colorful display all year long. 'Singin' in the Rain' is easy to grow, and is resistant to mildew and black spot. Floral arrangers and exhibitors both admire this rose for its vibrant color and wonderful inflorescence. It won the All-American Rose Selection in 1994.

Rosa 'Singin' in the Rain'

SONIA
(Sonia Meilland, Sweet Promise)
Large-flowered/Hybrid Tea

Bred by Meilland (France) in 1974 from 'Zambra' × ('Baccará' × 'White Knight'), 'Sonia' has long buds, opening to double (30 petals), high-pointed flowers in a shade of pink, suffused with coral and yellow. The fragrance is fruity. The plants are of low to medium height, about 30 in (75 cm) and have dark, glossy, leathery foliage. It is probably the most commonly grown glasshouse rose but it also makes a good garden rose, needing protection from fungus diseases.

SPARRIESHOOP
Shrub

Named for the village where Kordes' nursery is located, 'Sparrieshoop' was bred by Kordes (Germany) in 1953 from ('Baby Château' × 'Else Poulsen') × 'Magnifica'. 'Magnifica' is one of the Sweet Briar (Eglanteria) Hybrids and 'Sparrieshoop' inherited its somewhat rampant growth. It can be trained as a shortish climber or allowed to develop naturally into a large, spreading shrub. Its almost single, sweetly perfumed flowers are borne in large trusses of apple-blossom pink on stems, whose young growth has bronze tints and whose mature foliage is dark green and glossy.

Rosa 'St. Cecilia'

Rosa 'Sonia'

Rosa 'Sparrieshoop'

Rosa 'Sundowner'

ST. CECILIA
English Shrub

'St. Cecilia' was bred in 1987 from 'Wife of Bath' × seedling. The medium-sized flowers are pale buff-apricot in color, with a strong myrrh fragrance. They are cupped at first, but then open to flat blooms with muddled centers in the typical old rose fashion. They are borne in well-spaced sprays on a compact, bushy plant about 4 feet (1.2 m) tall with arching growth, which is adequately covered with soft green foliage, tinted bronze. It makes an excellent bedding rose and is one of the best for limited space.

SUNDOWNER
(MACcheup, MACche)
Large-flowered/Hybrid Tea

McGredy (New Zealand) bred 'Sundowner' in 1978 from 'Bond Street' × 'Peer Gynt'. This is an enormous grower producing very long stemmed flowers that are apricot-orange with a yellow base to the petals. They are double, have excellent form, and are very fragrant. The foliage is healthy and mid-green but a little prone to mildew in the autumn. It has an upright growth habit. This is excellent for picking when very long stemmed roses of a bright

Rosa 'Sunflare'

color are required. It looks wonderful with fruit and berries for interior decoration in the autumn. 'Sundowner' won the All-American Rose Selection in 1979.

SUNFLARE
(JACjem, Sun Flare)
Cluster-flowered/Floribunda
This rose was bred by Warriner (United States) in 1983 from 'Sunsprite' ×

seedling. The slightly fragrant, medium yellow flowers are borne in very well-spaced clusters of 3–15. They open flat and show attractive stamens. The abundant foliage is small, glossy and disease-free. This is a superb rose for a low hedge or for bedding and makes an ideal standard. If spent blooms are not removed, a large crop of round red hips are produced which can look very attractive. It won a Gold Medal in Japan in 1981, the All-American Rose Selection in 1983 and a Gold Medal in Portland in 1985.

SUNNY SOUTH
Large-flowered/Hybrid Tea
'Sunny South' was bred by Clark (Australia) in 1918 from 'Gustav Grunerwald' × 'Betty Berkeley'. The large, semi-double, cupped flowers are pink, flushed carmine, with a yellow base and are sweetly fragrant. The plant is vigorous and tall, up to 6 feet (2 m), and the stems can be up to 3 feet (1 m) long. In spite of its age, this variety is still valued, somewhat in the mold of 'Queen Elizabeth' with regard to its vigor and size, but the blooms are a softer blend of pink and cream and are delightfully informal.

SUPER STAR
(Tropicana)
Large-flowered/Hybrid Tea
This rose was bred by Tantau (Germany) in 1960 from (seedling × 'Peace') × (seedling × 'Alpine Glow'). The pointed buds are followed by large, well-formed, double (33 petals) blooms of coral-orange with a strong, fruity fragrance. The vigorous, upright plant has dark green, glossy and leathery foliage. When this previously unknown color was first introduced, it became very popular. However, 'Super Star' developed a tendency to mildew, which affected its vigor. In America, it is known as 'Tropicana', because Jackson and Perkins, who released it, felt there would be a conflict of interests with the Conard-Pyle company, who called their plants 'Star Roses'. This represented two changes from the original intention of the breeder to call it 'Ilse Tantau' after his wife.

Rosa 'Sunny South'

Rosa 'Super Star'

SUSAN LOUISE
Shrub

'Susan Louise' was bred by Adams (United States) in 1929. It was a seedling of 'Belle Portugaise', a *R. gigantea* hybrid. Alister Clark in Australia had extensively used *R. gigantea* to breed vigorous, hardy plants that thrive in warmer climates. In climates where winters are mild, as they are in Australia, they even seem to continue flowering into winter. Very few other breeders have made much use of this rather interesting native of China, but Adams in California had similar conditions to work with. The deep pink buds of 'Susan Louise' are long and pointed, opening into flesh pink, semi-double flowers. They have only a light fragrance. The blooms are borne freely on a vigorous, bushy plant about 5 feet (1.5 m) tall.

Rosa 'Sutter's Gold'

SUTTER'S GOLD
Large-flowered/Hybrid Tea

Named to mark the centenary of the discovery of gold at Sutter's Creek, this rose was bred by Swim (United States) in 1950 from 'Charlotte Armstrong' × 'Signora'. The buds are orange, overlaid with Indian red, opening to golden orange, often with red on the outer petals and fading to a creamy yellow. The blooms are double (33 petals), large and deliciously perfumed. It is a shame they are so fleeting. The plant is very free-flowering early in the season with dark green, leathery foliage. It won an All-American Rose Selection award, gold medals at Portland, Bagatelle and Geneva, as well as the Gamble Medal for fragrance. The miners were 'forty-niners', which was the name of another rose of Herb Swim's, released in 1949.

SWAN
English Shrub

'Swan' is like a white version of 'Claire Rose', and was bred in 1987 from 'Charles Austin' × (seedling × 'Iceberg'). The large, fragrant, perfectly formed rosette-shaped blooms are white with at times, a hint of buff. In wet weather, the blooms, like many other light varieties, develop spots, but it is truly magnificent in warm, dry conditions. It repeats satisfactorily and, to prevent it from becoming too tall and leggy, it can be cut back to half its height. The plant is vigorous, upright and shrubby with soft, mid-green foliage. It grows to about 4 feet (1.2 m).

SYMPHONY
English Shrub

This lovely rose was bred in 1986 from 'The Knight' × 'Yellow Cushion'. The formation of 'Symphony' is like 'The Knight', which is red, but the color came from 'Yellow Cushion'. There are splashes of red on the outside of the buds, which remain on the outer petals, with fragrant, predominantly soft, pure yellow blooms. The rosette-shaped flowers are freely produced on a modern-looking plant with bushy, upright growth 3–6 feet (1–2 m) tall, and light green foliage. Although it develops red spots in wet weather, this is not a major problem.

TABOO
(TANelorak, Barkarole, Grand Château)
Large-flowered/Hybrid Tea

The delicately scented flowers of this rose are long and slender, and made up of broad petals which form classic high centers. They are among the darkest red roses to be found, and as they are carried on long stems, they provide plenty of blooms for cutting. The succession of bloom is well maintained through summer and autumn. The foliage is large, dark and glossy on a vigorous and somewhat uneven bush which grows to above average height. It is not really suitable for a border, and is best grown for cut flowers.

Rosa 'Symphony'

TALISMAN
Large-flowered/Hybrid Tea

'Talisman' was bred by Montgomery (United States) in 1929 from 'Ophelia' × 'Souvenir de Claudius Pernet'. The pointed buds develop into double, flat medium sized, fragrant blooms in golden yellow and copper-red tones. The plant has vigorous, bushy growth with light green, semi-glossy leaves. It used to be a very useful cut flower rose for many years and, when it was first introduced, the breeders charged six times the amount for other roses, and people were prepared to pay. Like 'Ophelia', 'Talisman' was prone to sport, producing 39 of these, the best of which was probably the red 'Mary Hart'. It has been replaced mainly by its descendant, 'Granada'.

Rosa 'Talisman'

TAMORA
(AUStamora)
English Rose

David Austin (England) crossed 'Chaucer' × 'Conrad Ferdinand Meyer' to produce this exquisite rose. The

Rosa 'Tamora'

reddish orange buds open into fairly large flowers of apricot-yellow, deeper in their hearts, and paling towards the margins. They are made up of over 40 silky-textured petals that are arranged layer upon layer in old-fashioned style, and finally part to form a deep cup in the center of the blooms. There is a sharp fragrance, and flowers continue to appear through summer and autumn. This whole effect is quite charming. 'Tamora' is suitable for a group in a shrub border and is especially recommended for warmer climates. It is a vigorous plant, rather spreading in habit and grows to below the average height of a shrub rose. The foliage is small, dark and semi-glossy. This really makes a wonderful addition to the garden.

TEQUILA
Cluster-flowered/Floribunda

'Tequila' is another Meilland rose, bred in 1982 from 'Rusticana' × ('Rumba' × (MEIkim × 'Fire King')). The large, semi-double (20 petals) flowers are light yellow, overlaid with orange and stained carmine on the outer petals. The lightly fragrant blooms are borne freely in clusters on a tall plant with dark green, bronze-tipped, matte foliage. It is not just another of the yellow-opening Cluster-flowered Roses, which turn red with age, although it does exhibit some of these color mutations. However, it does retain some of the lighter color and does not hang on to the older flowers like its parent 'Rumba'. It is a useful addition to the range of roses suitable for bedding.

Rosa 'Tequila'

Rosa 'Tequila Sunrise'

TEQUILA SUNRISE
Large-flowered/Hybrid Tea

A beautiful rose, 'Tequila Sunrise' was bred by Dickson (Northern Ireland) in 1988 from 'Bonfire Night' × 'Freedom'. The double (40 petals) blooms are bright yellow with bright orange-red splashed on the outer edges of the petals. The slightly fragrant blooms are borne freely and mainly singly on a medium bushy plant up to 3 feet (1 m), clothed in medium-green, glossy foliage. The flowers last well when cut. 'Tequila Sunrise' won gold medals in England, Rome and The Hague and a prize in Baden Baden. It is aptly named, creating the impression of a bright sunrise especially when planted en masse.

THE FAIRY
Polyantha

'The Fairy' was bred by Bentall (England) in 1932 from 'Paul Crampel' × 'Lady Gay'. Most modern authorities, including Peter Beales and *Modern Roses 10*, give this as the parentage, rather

Rosa 'The Miller'

Rosa 'The Fairy'

than classify it as a sport of 'Lady Godiva'. Either way, there is *Wichuraiana* in its heritage, and it seems to have the typical growth one would expect of such a parent, the lax stems, thorns and shiny foliage as well as the late blooming, small, cupped flowers in pale pink clusters. It has a spreading growth that would suggest a ground cover. There is little polyantha in it, but it certainly deserves the high regard in which it is held, and the new wave of popularity it is enjoying, being an excellent landscaping rose.

THE MILLER
English Shrub

Named after one of the characters in Chaucer's *Canterbury Tales*, 'The Miller' was bred in 1970 from 'Baroness Rothschild' × 'Constance Spry'. This is one of the early English Roses. The flowers are medium sized, rosette-form and clear, rose-pink in color. They are borne in small, open clusters on a tall, extremely healthy plant, which can become as tall as 6 feet (2 m) if not pruned heavily. It will grow under the most adverse conditions, its mid-green, matte foliage seemingly impervious to whatever may come its way.

Rosa 'The Pilgrim'

Rosa 'The Prince'

THE PILGRIM
(AUSwalker, Gartenarchitekt Günther Schulze, Pilgrim)
English Rose

Bred by Austin (England) from 'Graham Thomas' × 'Yellow Button', the
softly textured blooms of this rose are
beautifully formed, made up of scores of
small, infolded petals which together
create an intricately constructed flat
flower with rich hints of yellow in their
young centers, paling to creamy buff.
They are carried in clusters on strong
stems, have a pleasing fragrance and
continue to appear through summer and
autumn. This is an excellent rose to
plant in the border, either as a specimen
plant or in a group, where it will prove a
useful resource for cutting for small
arrangements. It grows vigorously with
a compact and graceful habit to above
average height, and may be trained as a
small climber. It is amply furnished with
polished-looking mid-green foliage.

THE PRINCE
(AUSvelvet)
English Rose

The flower is everything in this rose. It
was bred in 1990 by Austin (England)

using 'Lilian Austin' × 'The Squire'. The
inky buds are hard and round and open
into rich deep crimson blooms which
soon change to royal purple. There is
lovely fragrance. 'The Prince' is best
sited where the unusual character of the
blooms can be enjoyed but where the
plant is not readily in view, for the weak
flower stems and poor constitution are
serious visual drawbacks in its overall
performance. Given a warm climate and
good cultivation it can thrive, but it
needs the dedication of a connoisseur. It
grows to about half the height of an
average shrub rose and has a skimpy
provision of dark leaves.

THISBE
Hybrid Musk

Another of Pemberton's roses, 'Thisbe'
was released in 1918. It was a sport of
'Daphne'. The sulphur-straw colored
flowers of semi-double, rosette form, are
borne in large clusters on an upright,
bushy shrub with arching canes. It
grows as wide as it grows tall with ample
mid-green glossy foliage. The flowers
are moderately fragrant. It is recommended as a good garden specimen.

Rosa 'Thisbe'

Rosa 'Timeless'

Rosa 'Tineke'

perfectly formed high centers and are borne on strong, upright stems. They open slowly, keeping their symmetrical shape thanks to the firm texture of the 30 or so petals. They are very popular with florists. The continuity of blooms through summer and autumn is excellent, and as a colorful garden rose for a bed, border or hedge, this is a dependable choice. It is an upright, sturdy bush which grows to average height, and has dark, semi-glossy foliage. It won the All-American Rose Selection in 1997.

TINEKE
Large-flowered/Hybrid Tea
Bred by Select Roses BV of Holland in 1989 from two unnamed seedlings, 'Tineke' is a cut flower rose that has successfully made the transition to a garden/exhibition rose, and is especially good in warmer climates. The almost pure white, large, double blooms, (53 petals), are scentless, but possess excellent exhibition form. It is a prolific prize winner at Australian Rose Shows. It is tall, upright bush with dark green, semi-glossy foliage and grows to 6 feet (1.8 m) high.

TIMELESS
(JACecond)
Large-flowered/Hybrid Tea
As the blooms unfold, the colors presented to the eye veer between deep pink and medium red, with the inside surface of the petal deeper than the outside. The sizeable flowers have

TITIAN
Cluster-flowered/Floribunda

'Titian' was bred by Riethmuller (Australia) in 1950. Its parentage is not listed, but it was reputedly developed from the Kordes Shrub rose strain. It can be grown as a pillar rose or a rather bushy Cluster-flowered Shrub. The blooms, borne in clusters, are a deep, vibrant pink with a light fragrance. Their color intensifies with age. 'Titian' has soft green foliage, is very healthy and easy to grow, but it does need plenty of space.

TOURNAMENT OF ROSES
(JACient, Berkeley, Poesie)
Large-flowered/Hybrid Tea

Warriner (United States) bred this rose in 1988 from 'Impatient' × seedling. It carries big clusters of sizeable flowers on firm stems. The blooms are symmetrical, and show contrasting tones of pink as the petals unfold—deep pink on the outer surfaces and creamy pink within.

There is a light spicy fragrance, and an excellent continuity of blooms through summer and autumn. The color is particularly fine in warmer weather. This is a good rose for a hedge, in a group or a bed. It is a very vigorous, upright grower with glossy green leaves. Its name refers to the annual rose parade held in Pasadena, and this rose was launched to mark the centenary of that event. It won the All-American Rose Selection in 1989.

TROILUS
English Shrub

'Troilus' was bred in 1983 from ('Duchesse de Montebello' × 'Chaucer') × 'Charles Austin'. The large, honey-buff flowers are cupped, the outer petals incurving to form a container for the many inner petals. They have a strong, sweet fragrance that is reminiscent of honey, to match the color of the flowers. They are borne on a sturdy, upright plant, about 4 feet (1.2 m) high with

Rosa 'Titian'

Rosa 'Tournament of Roses'

Rosa 'Troilus'

Rosa 'Trumpeter'

mid-green, modern-looking foliage.
'Troilus' is a good bedding plant,
compact enough for the small garden
and preferring a warm dry climate to do
its best. It is named for the hero of
Shakespeare's *Troilus and Cressida*.

TRUMPETER
Cluster-flowered/Floribunda

Named after the great jazz trumpeter,
Louis 'Satchmo' Armstrong, as was its
parent, this rose was bred by McGredy
(New Zealand) in 1977 from 'Satchmo'
× seedling. The buds are ovoid, opening
to large, cupped, double (39 petals)
blooms of vivid orange-red color with a
light fragrance. They are borne abun-
dantly in clusters on a compact, bushy
plant with medium green, glossy foliage.
It won the James Mason Medal (England) as well as gold medals in New
Zealand and at Portland. Louis
Armstrong died in 1971.

VANITY
Hybrid Musk

This rose has every reason to be vain! It
was bred by Pemberton (England) in
1920 from 'Château de Clos Vougeot' ×

Rosa 'Vanity'

seedling. It is a very tall, spreading
plant, but is not well branched or thickly
foliaged. To improve the bushiness, a
cluster of three can be planted, and this
will grow into a huge, thick mound of
color. The widely spaced clusters of
flowers are almost single and have been
described as light crimson or rose-pink.
Either way, they are spectacular in full
bloom, smothering the plant, with its
background of dark green foliage. They
also give off a strong, musk rose fragrance. 'Vanity' tolerates light shade and
poor soil.

Rosa 'Voodoo'

Rosa 'Victor Borge'

VICTOR BORGE
(Michael Crawford)
Large-flowered/Hybrid Tea

'Victor Borge' has very large, pale salmon to orange blooms, with a pale yellow/orange reverse. It is only slightly fragrant. It has dark green, semi-glossy foliage. The mostly single blooms are borne on long stems, with an abundance of large thorns. It is a vigorous plant of medium height. Named after the irrepressible concert pianist and entertainer Victor Borge, who shares this rose with popular English singer and actor Michael Crawford, this rose looks wonderful in the garden, especially if it is planted alongside red roses such as 'Etoile de Hollande'.

VOODOO
(AROmiclea)
Large-flowered/Hybrid Tea

'Voodoo' was bred by Christensen (United States) from (('Camelot' × 'First Prize') × 'Typhoo Tea') × 'Lolita'. The vibrant orange and yellow-orange flowers are crisp and clear. The fully double blooms have little or no scent. The bush is a medium height and with its upright nature, is an easy plant to care for and maintain with a quickness to reshoot after flowering. The glossy leaves are thick and hard, with good resistance to disease; abundant thorns protect the stocky tough plant. Black spot will need to be watched for late in the season when the best blooms are being produced. It is an ideal plant for a massed individual plantings as the color is sometimes difficult to blend. 'Voodoo' won the All-American Rose Selection in 1986.

WENLOCK
English Rose

'The Knight' × 'Glastonbury' were the parents of this Austin rose bred in 1984. It has a wonderful scent that is fitting to a crimson-red rose. The shapely bush is upright and is easily pruned into a small shrub. The red strains of David Austin Roses tend to be weaker growers in comparison to his pinks. The fully double flowers come on short stems and the bush is an ideal border or low hedge choice as it does not become obtrusive in the garden. Repeat flowering is quick and it will produce a mass of bloom to start the flowering season in spring. Care is needed to keep it disease-free and healthy all season as the large leaves can become infected in cooler regions.

Rosa 'Wenlock'

Rosa 'Westerland'

WESTERLAND
(KORwest, KORlawe)
Cluster-flowered Climber

This Kordes bred rose was released in 1969. Its parents were 'Friedrich Worlein' × 'Circus'. 'Westerland' is a bright apricot-orange that is a colorful addition to any garden. The double flowers have a ruffled look and the petals have a slightly serrated edge and a pleasant scent. Clusters of the flowers appear regularly on the bush and it has a very quick repeat-flowering cycle. The bush grows 8–10 feet (2.4–3 m) tall, and in mild climates can be trained as a 15 foot (4.5 m) high climber. It was the Anerkannte Deutsche Rose in 1974.

Rosa 'Whisky'

WHISKY
(Whisky Mac)
Large-flowered/Hybrid Tea

Tantau bred this rose from undisclosed parents in 1965. The buds are ovoid, developing into large, double (30 petals), very fragrant flowers with ruffled petals. They have been described as bronze yellow in color, perhaps reminiscent of a fine malt whisky. The plant is upright and bushy with dark green, glossy foliage. It must be the color and delicious perfume that make this variety popular, because it is not very free-flowering, is prone to mildew and consistently dies back, making the bush quite short-lived, even when well grown. When it does produce its best, however, the results are enough to compensate for the frustration. The well known rosarian Jack Harkness described it as a triumph of color over common sense!

WHITE LIGHTNIN'
(AROwhit)
Large-flowered/Hybrid Tea

Swim (United States) bred this rose in 1980 from 'Angel Face' × 'Misty'. It produces large, double, pure white blooms on a strong and vigorous bush. The scent is strong and long lasting, and the flowers are popular for picking. The bush is healthy and able to resist most diseases with minimal attention through the season. Repeat flowering is quick, making this a great addition to any garden. It won the All-American Rose Selection gold medal in 1981.

WHITE MEIDILAND
Ground Cover

'White Meidiland' was bred by Meilland (France) in 1987, from undisclosed parents. It is another of the Meilland landscaping roses, developed for

Rosa 'White Lightnin''

roadways, parks or low maintenance gardens. They become a little thatchy after a couple of years without pruning and can be rejuvenated by a lawn mower set high or a slasher. They are generally grown on their own roots (that is, from cuttings), so this does not damage the plant and there is no risk of destroying the bud union. 'White Meidiland' is a dense, prostrate plant, covered with small, double, creamy white flowers with a light, fruity fragrance. The foliage is bright green and glossy.

WINCHESTER CATHEDRAL
English Shrub

A sport from 'Mary Rose', 'Winchester Cathedral' was released by David Austin in 1988. The growth and

Rosa 'Winchester Cathedral'

Rosa 'White Meidiland'

Rosa 'Wise Portia'

Rosa 'Windrush'

flowers are the same as 'Mary Rose' except for the color. One would expect an exceptional rose from such an origin, and it is. The flowers are white, with a hint of buff at the center. They are carried freely and continuously throughout the season on a bushy shrub which grows to about 5 feet (1.5 m) tall. The flowers are very fragrant. It is one of the best whites among the English roses. It was named on behalf of the Winchester Cathedral Trust, to help raise money for the restoration of the cathedral.

WINDRUSH
English Shrub

A good garden rose, 'Windrush' was bred in 1984 from seedling × ('Canterbury' × 'Golden Wings'). It is different from many of the English roses, having only a small number of petals, but it was the intention of the breeder to produce a single-flowered English rose, having the refinement of the wild roses, which 'Golden Wings' displays most admirably. 'Windrush' would appear to be an improvement on its parent, being stronger, more bushy and more free-flowering. The large flowers are not quite single. They are a pale lemon color with a cluster of prominent stamens in the center of the blooms. They have inherited the fragrance of the Scottish Briar and are borne on a shrubby plant about 5 feet (1.5 m) tall.

WISE PORTIA
English Shrub

Named after Shakespeare's Portia the wise heroine of *The Merchant of Venice*, this rose was bred in 1982 from 'The Knight' × 'Glastonbury'. The large flowers are a mixture of mauves and purples, which may vary in intensity according to the season. Their form is old-fashioned, reminding one of the Gallicas, with a delightful and strong, old rose fragrance. They are borne freely on a compact, bushy plant that is not as robust as the later English roses, having dark green, semi-glossy foliage. However, it responds well to a little pampering and, with liberal feed, water and protective spraying, will reward the dedicated enthusiast.

CHAPTER 4

Miniature Roses

A true Miniature rose should be a miniature version of a Hybrid Tea (Large-flowered) Rose, with small flowers and leaves on a small compact bush. Although all true miniatures descend from *Rosa rouletii*, today's diversity of breeding must be borne in mind, and each new rose is individual.

The story of *R. rouletii* is as romantic as the Swiss village where it was found. In 1917, Colonel Roulet, while walking through the Swiss village of Mauborget, noticed a potted pink rose of small proportions on a window ledge. Upon returning to Geneva, he described the rose to a nurseryman friend, Henry Correvon. They returned to find the village had burned down, but fortunately they were able to find the rose growing in a nearby village, where people said it had been growing for 100 years. Cuttings were taken and the rose was named *R. rouletii* after Colonel Roulet. It is believed to be a variant of the old Chinese rose, *R. chinensis minima*.

The first hybrids of this rose came from a Dutchman, Jan de Vink, in 1936. This first rose was called 'Peon' and was later marketed in the United States under the name 'Tom Thumb'. As a novelty, it was very popular, and over 60 years later, it still is. Another of the early Miniature rose hybridists was Pedro Dot of Spain, who produced such varieties as 'Baby Gold Star', 'Perla de Montserrat', 'Perla de Alcanada' and 'Si'.

Although these roses had their admirers, it was not until Ralph Moore of the United States began to produce larger, well-formed blooms, that the Miniature rose came into its own. A legend in the rose world, he started his work in the 1930s, and is today still working at his dreams. His innovations have produced extraordinary results.

In 1948, Moore became fascinated with Moss roses. For 20 years, he trialed, learned, observed and planned until, in 1969, he introduced 'Fairy Moss'. This was followed by 'Dresden Doll' and 'Lemon Delight'. Breeding with the old Hybrid Perpetual 'Ferdinand Pichard' in 1975, he introduced the first striped Miniature rose, 'Stars 'n' Stripes'. Now we are seeing the fruits of other dreams, with Ralph's introduction of the Hybrid Rugosa 'Linda Campbell', an extraordinary rose with stems like velvet.

Other breeders have benefited from the pioneering work done by Ralph Moore, using his hybrids to produce, among others, striped roses of all classes.

Miniatures are usually classified as **Miniatures** and **Climbing Miniatures**, but for ease of identification, we have divided them into four sections — the micro-miniatures, the medium-sized miniatures, the large-sized miniatures and the climbing miniatures.

The **Micro-miniatures** were the first Miniature roses, and include such varieties as 'Tom Thumb', 'Si' and 'Trinket'. These roses, as the name implies, have very tiny flowers and leaves. What they lack in form, they make up for in daintiness. In a squat, decorative pot, in the rock garden or planted around a small statue or pond, they are a delight.

The **Medium-sized Miniatures** make up a diverse and popular group, with flowers which are approximately 1–2 inches (2.5–4.5 cm). The bushes vary in height from 18–24 inches (45–60 cm). The flower shapes range from high, pointed centers (Hybrid Tea shape) to single (five petals) and Floribunda types, which can resemble a water lily, a dahlia or even a camellia. With such a wide choice, collecting can become a great hobby. In this group, **Ground Cover** types such as 'Pincushion' and 'Green Ice' are found. These roses can also look delightful in hanging baskets. There is also a large selection of compact border or pot roses, which make a great display and are easy to care for. They are often sold under a collective name, such as the Minijets (Meilland), Bouquet Collection and the Select Range. The taller garden varieties, such as 'Love Me', 'Minnie Pearl' and 'Jean Kenneally', are also excellent for cut flowers.

The **Large-sized Miniatures** are another type of miniature rose. With the breeding of roses crossing many cultivars and species, there are some truly lovely roses that do not fit clearly into any modern class. Instead of dismissing them, the World Federation of Rose Societies has generally classified them as **Dwarf Cluster-flowered Roses**. However, in America, where miniatures are extremely popular, these are mostly classified as 'large miniatures'; whereas in Britain, where miniatures are not widely grown, the term 'patio rose' has been coined. Some of the best are 'Tinkerbell', 'Mini Champagne', 'Opal' ('Little Opal') and 'Gem' ('Little Gem'). Like all miniature roses, if conditions are kind, these will grow well, either in the garden or in a pot.

Finally, there are the **Climbing Miniature Roses**. Roses in all their shapes, sizes, colors and perfumes, intrigue, fascinate and sometimes obsess people. Climbing roses are different, as it is not usually the individual flowers that capture one's attention — it is more their effect. They lift the eye, give height to a garden, provide privacy with its ensuing peace and, most of all, give off an aura of magic. Often overlooked in town gardens, they can be the backbone of even the smallest garden. Some excellent Climbing Miniature Roses, for a 6 feet

Rosa 'Loving Touch'

(1.8 m) high suburban fence, include 'Work of Art', 'Hi Ho', 'Little Girl' and 'Softee'. Short pillar roses to 5 feet (1.5 m) include 'Sun 'n' Sand', 'Hurdy Gurdy' and 'Golden Gardens'.

Very new on the market are a group of **Climbing Patio Roses** in vibrant colors, bred by Chris Warner in England. They grow to about 8 feet (2.4 m) high and 'Warm Welcome' is an excellent example of these.

Another exciting addition to the climbing range are the German-bred **Super Cottage Climbers**. These roses are true ramblers with all the grace and beauty of the old-fashioned rambling roses, but with many more attributes. Their ability to repeat flower, their manageable size, mostly only to 10 feet (3 m), and their resistance to disease, make them highly desirable. Their flexible growth makes them the perfect rose for aches, pillars and low fences.

Miniature roses do well in containers, and can look particularly effective in hanging baskets. They are good for people who have small gardens, or who live in apartments. Miniature roses add a special charm to any garden.

BABY GRAND
(POUlit)
Miniature

Bred from 'Egeskov' × seedling by Poulsen (Denmark), this rose has clear pink flowers which are borne in small clusters. Each lightly fragrant bloom contains 25–40 petals and is very long lasting. They open to flat, quartered flowers which are reminiscent of many old garden roses. In hot climates, the pink becomes much deeper. It has small, medium matte green foliage on a low, compact, well-rounded plant. It is extremely disease-resistant. This is a charming, old-fashioned kind of rose which looks wonderful in a container where it can fill the space with flowers.

BEAUTY SECRET
Miniature

This lovely rose was bred from 'Little Darling' × 'Magic Wand' by Moore (United States). It is considered the classic miniature rose of the mid-1960s. The cardinal red flowers are high-centered with a characteristic point to the terminal edge of the petals. Grown on a vigorous bushy plant, the florets are mainly grouped in clusters of 4–10 blooms on strong straight stems. The color is fast and the blooms last a reasonably long time on the bush without serious fading. So attractive and well liked was this variety that when the ARS award program started in 1975, this rose was instantly honored.

BLACK JADE
(BENblack)
Miniature

This rose is very close in color to black. It was bred by Benardella (United States) in 1985 from 'Sheri Anne' × 'Laguna'. The vigorous, upright plant supports clusters of 5–10 blooms on very strong, straight stems. The florets have good exhibition form. When the bloom is fully open, it sports very attractive bright golden yellow stamens, which contrast with the very dark red petal color. It has a fairly rapid repeat bloom cycle. So dark is the bloom that some show judges use a flashlight to shine into the bloom center to properly observe the actual form. The very glossy foliage provides a natural barrier to mildew and other diseases.

Rosa 'Beauty Secret'

Rosa 'Black Jade'

Rosa 'Carrot Top'

CARROT TOP
(POUltop)
Miniature

The fire engine orange color certainly makes this rose stand out in the garden crowd! The very shapely buds hold their brilliance from beginning to end on an attractive rounded bush surrounded with dark green foliage. The plant itself is very clean, easy to maintain and not too susceptible to diseases. The flowers have a high center and although there are not very many petals (20–25), they hold their form well for exhibition. An excellent repeat bloomer, the plant is almost always in flower. The blooms have a slight fragrance. It was bred by Olesen (Denmark) from undisclosed parents.

CHILD'S PLAY
(SAVachild)
Miniature

This is one of the few miniature roses which is an AARS winner. The charming white blooms are framed with a delicate pink edge. Florets (20+ petals) come singly or in small clusters of 3–6 blooms with excellent exhibition form—high centered with moderate stem length and small foliage. Low growing and round with a bushy growth habit, the plant is vigorous and bloom production is very fast. It is an excellent variety for garden display, especially along a driveway or border as the plant is always in bloom. It was bred by Saville (United States) in 1991 from 'Yellow Jewel' × 'Tamango'.

DOUBLE JOY
Miniature

This rose from Ralph Moore (United States) was bred in 1979 from 'Little Darling' × 'New Penny'. It has elegant, long pointed buds which reveal pink double flowers (35 petals) with some fragrance. The blooms have an unusual capacity to hold their color in even the hottest climates. The flower form is strictly for garden display and the foliage is small with an attractive matte texture. In general, the bush is easy to maintain and disease-resistant. This compact bush bears prolific sprays, each with 5–12 florets and is a wonderful addition to the garden. On occasions a cluster can win at a rose show.

Rosa 'Figurine'

Rosa 'Double Joy'

DRESDEN DOLL
Miniature

The flowers of this rose are a soft but delicate dusty pink. The cupped blooms are small, with only 18 petals, and have a medium fragrance. When fully opened the blooms display another attractive feature—golden stamens—which add to the quality and appearance of the florets. The bush is compact and throws lots of large clusters that are architecturally attractive, but quite large for a miniature. In fact, the plant seems to want to grow outward rather than upward. This rose has won its share of awards at rose shows in the fully opened bloom class. It is a second generation of repeat flowering moss miniatures borne from 'Fairy Moss'. It was bred by the great Ralph Moore.

FIGURINE
Miniature

'Figurine' was bred in 1991 by Benardella (United States). Its parents are 'Rise 'n' Shine' × 'Laguna'. It has long, high-pointed, perfect buds, opening to a beautiful, moderately full flower. The flowers are ivory white tinged with pink. They are borne singly and in small clusters. 'Figurine' makes a wonderful, upright, bushy shrub to about 18–22 in (45–55 cm). It is a

Rosa 'Dresden Doll'

Rosa 'Foxy Lady'

Rosa 'Holy Toledo'

Rosa 'Hot Tamale'

perfect rose for the show bench and a great favorite with florists. From the Benardella Collection, this is one of the most beautiful. It is a great garden plant and makes an excellent potted rose.

FOXY LADY
(AROshrim)
Miniature

'Foxy Lady' was bred by Christensen (United States) in 1980 from 'Gingersnap' × 'Magic Carrousel'. The ovoid buds reveal pointed, double flowers with 25 petals that are coral-pink and white. The petals of the medium-sized florets overlap, and the foliage is attractively small compared with the bloom size. Regarded by many growers as 'a real beauty', the color can be salmon and cream in some warmer climates. Bloom production is sparse. Some people regard the choice of an adult name for a miniature rose somewhat peculiar.

HOLY TOLEDO
(ARObri)
Miniature

The flowers of 'Holy Toledo' are an eye catching apricot-orange with a yellow-orange reverse. The florets are double (28 petals), imbricated and are suitably complemented by small, dark green, disease-resistant foliage. It is a vigorous

and bushy plant. This Miniature rose is admired mainly for its wonderful color range, pretty flower shape, growth habit and clean foliage. The unique color combination is striking and needs to be seen to be believed. The blooms can come in large trusses on very strong stems which are resistant to damage by wind or rain. This award-winning rose has maintained its popularity worldwide for two decades. It was bred by Christensen (United States) from 'Gingersnap' × 'Magic Carrousel'.

HOT TAMALE
(JACpoy)
Miniature

These flowers are a striking yellow-orange blend that age dramatically to yellow-pink providing almost an electric glow to the blooms. This attractive color combination lasts for a long time, even in the midday sun of southern California. The florets have consistent Large-flowered form making 'Hot Tamale' a frequent winner on the show tables. The blooms are borne mostly singly but small clusters can develop in cooler climates. They have a delicate light fragrance. The foliage is semi-glossy, dark green and disease-resistant on a compact, tall growing plant. This rose was a sensation at the Royal National Rose Society's National Miniature show in St. Albans, England in 1997 where a basket of over beautiful 100 blooms caught everyone's attention. 'Hot Tamale' won the American Rose Society Award of Excellence in 1994.

Rosa 'Jean Lajoie'

Rosa 'Lavender Jewel'

JEANNE LAJOIE
Miniature Climber

An excellent repeat flower rose, 'Jeanne Lajoie' was bred in 1975 by Sima (United States) from ('Casa Blanca' × 'Independence') × 'Midget'. The long, pointed, mid-pink buds open to double pink flowers borne in clusters. It will climb to 6 feet (2 m) and will need staking to lattice or posts.

LAVENDER JEWEL
Miniature

Another Ralph Moore rose, 'Lavender Jewel' was bred in 1978 from 'Little Chief' × 'Angel Face'. The pointed buds open to Large-flowered-shaped blooms with high centers. They are lavender to mauve. It is a great pity it does not carry the perfume of its father, but sadly, perfume is a recessive gene, not often found in Miniature roses. 'Sweet Chariot' and 'Moon River' are two glorious exceptions. This rose makes a nice show rose. It is a healthy, compact bush, about 12–15 in (30–40 cm).

LEMON DELIGHT
Miniature

Long, pointed, mossy buds open to reveal wonderful 10-petalled small blooms that

Rosa 'Lemon Delight'

Rosa 'Magic Carrousel'

Rosa 'Minnie Pearl'

are a bright butter yellow. Rose growers bubbled with enthusiasm over this variety when it was released, because it has a wonderful garden display. The lovely lemon florets have a strong lemon fragrance. The plant is free blooming, vigorous, bushy and upright and very hardy. The color is generally fast in most climates and the mossing adds an extra charm. This rose is another outstanding achievement by Ralph Moore—this time using 'Fairy Moss' × 'Gold Moss'.

LOVING TOUCH
Miniature

A rose that lives up to its name, 'Loving Touch' was bred in 1983 by Jolly (United States) from 'Rise 'n' Shine' × 'First Prize'. The large, pointed buds open to medium, double, soft apricot flowers. They are borne singly and in small clusters. It is very healthy rose, which repeats very quickly. It makes a beautiful pot specimen and a great garden rose, and will grow up to 18 in (45 cm). Its elegant beauty and gentle color makes it a 'must have' rose.

MAGIC CARROUSEL
Miniature

If Ralph Moore produced no other rose, he would be remembered just for this one, which he bred in 1972 from 'Little

Rosa 'Loving Touch'

Darling' × 'Westmont'. Its double flowers are white edged with pink and are produced in clusters both large and small. 'Magic Carrousel' is always in flower and is a large, healthy bush, growing 3–4 feet (90–120 cm) high. The young leaves are a bronze-green. It is one of the easiest and most rewarding roses to grow, and makes a lovely hedge. Another good beginner's rose, it benefits from a good pruning.

MINNIE PEARL
Miniature

'Minnie Pearl' was bred in 1982 by Saville (United States) from ('Little Darling' × 'Tiki') × 'Party Girl'. The buds are long and pointed, opening to high-centered, Large-flowered-shaped blooms, which are light pink with a darker pink reverse to the petals. They are borne singly and in clusters. The plant grows to a height of 24–30 in (60–75 cm). It is an excellent show rose and also very popular with florists as a cut flower. A healthy, bushy plant, it is excellent for garden or pot. 'Minnie Pearl' has been one of the top exhibition roses in the United States.

ORANGE HONEY
Miniature
Another Ralph Moore Miniature, this rose was bred in 1979 from 'Rumba' × 'Over the Rainbow'. The pointed buds open to high-centered, double flowers in a lovely soft orange-yellow color. The flowers have a soft fruity scent, and last well when cut. The healthy, bushy, spreading plant grows 18–23 in (45–55 cm). Because it is an easy-to-grow garden rose, it is popular with amateur rose growers. 'Orange Honey' produces its best colors when grown in light shade.

PINSTRIPE
(MORpints)
Miniature
A wide variety of vivid red and white stripes distinguish this rose. In fact no two blooms look alike. The well-formed, double, fragrant blooms are extremely long lasting with small color differences developing as they move to fully open. The most beautiful bloom stage is when the florets are fully open, revealing their distinctive color striping. The flowers are borne singly or in small clusters of 3–5 blooms. The foliage is medium green and disease-resistant and the plant has a low mounded habit.

POPCORN
Miniature
When Morey (United States) bred this rose in 1973 from 'Katharina Zeimet' × 'Diamond Jewel', he could not have given it a better name. The small, single, white flowers with their prominent yellow stamens are borne in clusters on a dwarf, bushy plant to a height of 12 in (30 cm). It is the perfect border rose. It is also lovely grown in planter boxes. 'Popcorn' is easy to grow and is very healthy. No fancy pruning is necessary with this rose. A quick, short back and sides is all that is required.

PRIDE 'N' JOY
(JACmo)
Miniature
This is a very appropriately named rose, with ovoid buds which open to bright,

Rosa 'Orange Honey'

Rosa 'Popcorn'

Rosa 'Pride 'n' Joy'

Rosa 'Rainbow's End'

medium orange flowers with an orange-cream reverse that fades to salmon-pink. The double (30–35 petals) florets have a fruity fragrance and can have good, high, well-formed centers that tend to open too quickly for exhibition. The foliage is dark green, clean and disease-resistant. This is a vigorous, spreading, compact bush with lots of blooms all year long. It is a wonderful cut flower because of the contrast of the bright orange color against dark, glossy foliage. It was hybridized by the master of Floribundas, the late Bill Warriner of Jackon & Perkins, using 'Chatem Centennial' × 'Prominent', and won the All-American Rose Selection in 1991.

RAINBOW'S END
Miniature
'Rainbow's End' was bred in 1984 by Harm Saville (United States) from 'Rise 'n' Shine' × 'Water Color'. The pointed buds open to deep yellow, double, Large-flowered-shaped flowers. A distinctive red edge forms as the flower ages, older flowers becoming completely red. It is a lovely show rose and also makes a great cut flower. It is a healthy, upright bush growing to some 12–16 in (30–40 cm). Watch out for black spot.

RED CASCADE
Miniature Climber
Another Ralph Moore Miniature, 'Red Cascade' was bred in 1976 from (*R. wichuraiana* × 'Floradora') × 'Magic Dragon'. The pointed buds open to double, deep red flowers. They are borne in clusters on a lax, dense bush with arching canes. The flowers have only a slight fragrance. It is an excellent Miniature Climber, grown through a low fence or as a free standing hedge, and also looks very effective in a hanging basket. 'Rad Cascade' won an American Rose Society Award of Excellence in 1976, and it is still going strong.

Rosa 'Rise 'n' Shine'

Rosa 'Snow Bride'

RISE 'N' SHINE
Miniature

'Rise 'n' Shine' has been popular since its introduction in 1977 by Ralph Moore (United States) and it is still one of the best yellow Miniatures around. Its parents are 'Little Darling' × 'Yellow Magic'. The long pointed buds open to fully double, rich yellow flowers. They are sometimes only cream. In spite of this color variation, they are beautiful roses for the show bench and are a popular picking rose. It is a good, healthy bush, growing to a height of 12–16 in (30–40 cm) and has glossy foliage. It seems to do well in most climates, but can be prone to black spot.

SNOW BRIDE
(Snowbride)
Miniature

This rose was bred by Jolly (United States) in 1982 using 'Avendel' × 'Zinger'. Its lovely creamy white flowers with excellent Large-flowered form make it suitable for exhibition. The blooms occur one to a stem or in large clusters. As the petals reflex in a classic manner it maintains its form for days. The foliage is small dark green and glossy on a compact, vigorous plant. This outstanding white Miniature has been popular since its introduction because of its ability to consistently produce beautiful weather-proof blooms on a healthy plant. In some climates, it may need some protection from powdery mildew. It has won many trophies and prizes at rose shows in the USA and the UK.

STARINA
(MEIgabi, MEIgali)
Miniature

The parents of this Meilland-bred rose are ('Dany Robin' × 'Fire King') × 'Perla de Monsterrat'. The flowers are bright orange-scarlet-vermilion borne singly or in small clusters. They are beautifully formed exhibition type, double florets and are complemented by small, glossy green foliage. It has a dwarf habit. This rose is the classical Miniature rose of the 20th century, defining the standard for what is expected of Miniature roses. In spite of its age it remains on the lists of top Miniature roses throughout the world.

Rosa 'Starina'

Rosa 'Winsome'

SWEET CHARIOT
(MORchari, Insolite)
Miniature

These flowers are a lavender to purple blend aging gracefully to a superb mixture of lavender hues. The florets have 40 petals with an old garden type informal form, and come in large clusters that take several weeks to bloom out. One very distinguishing feature is its overpowering perfume. No matter where it is planted in the garden the heavy damask fragrance can be detected even by the most insensitive noses! Foliage is small, medium green on an upright, vigorous, spreading plant. It has been used as a hanging basket with great success, as the canes arch downwards to cover the container, and the clusters hang out, spreading their fragrance to the surrounding air. It is another rose from Ralph Moore, this time using 'Little Chief' × 'Violette'.

WINSOME
(SAVawin)
Miniature

Saville (United States) bred 'Winsome' in 1984 from 'Party Girl' × 'Shocking Blue'. The flowers are purple-red and have over 40 petals. They have no

Rosa 'Sweet Chariot'

fragrance and are borne singly on an upright bush with medium, semi-glossy green foliage. The blooms can be larger in cooler climates where a darker shading effect on the petals makes it even more attractive for lovers of this color class. When fully open the flowers are further enhanced by the bright golden yellow stamens. It is an extremely vigorous plant and also self-cleaning —spent blooms fall off by themselves and start the next bloom cycle. It does not fade. It won the ARS Award of Excellence in 1985.

Cultivation Table

The following table provides the appropriate information about the cultivation requirements of all the roses described in this book.

It is made up of facts gleaned from the personal experience of some prominent rosarians, and, although opinions on certain facts about certain varieties will always differ, it is as accurate as reasonably possible and is an excellent guide for beginners.

Variations in geographic locations and climate will mean differences in growth habits, especially size.

The sizes shown are for warm to sub-tropical climates, and can be reduced by as much as 30% for colder areas. Growers should consult their local nurseries if in doubt about the characteristics of particular roses.

It must also be pointed out that virtually every variety of rose requires sunlight. Where it is shown that a rose is shade tolerant, it is exactly that.

Roses do not like shade, although some varieties manage to do better in it than others.

Rose

Rose	SLIGHT FRAGRANCE	MODERATE FRAGRANCE	STRONG FRAGRANCE	ONCE-FLOWERING	REPEAT-FLOWERING	RECURRENT BLOOMS	SUITABLE FOR CUT FLOWERS	SUITABLE FOR EXHIBITION	SUITABLE FOR CONTAINER GROWING	CAN BE GROWN AS A PILLAR OR CLIMBER	SUITABLE FOR BEDDING/MASS PLANTING	SUITABLE FOR HEDGING	GROUND COVER OR BORDER	DECORATIVE FRUIT	REQUIRES FULL SUN (6 HRS*)	KEEP OUT OF HOT SUN (MORNING SUN ONLY)	SHADE TOLERANT	PREFERS WARM CLIMATE (OR SHELTERED SUN) FROST TENDER	TOLERATES POOR SOILS	BLOOMS HATE WET WEATHER	CAN BE PRONE TO DIE BACK	PRONE TO BLACK SPOT	PRONE TO MILDEW	PRONE TO RUST	AVERAGE PLANT SIZE—IMPERIAL HEIGHT × WIDTH	AVERAGE PLANT SIZE—METRIC HEIGHT × WIDTH
Abraham Darby		X		X											X							X			6 x 5	1.8 x 1.5
Adolf Horstmann		X		X	X	X									X										4 x 3	1.2 x 1
Agnes		X		X							X						X		X						2 x 2	2 x 1.8
Aimée Vibert		X		X													X		X						14 x 10	4 x 3
Alba Maxima		X	X														X		X						8 x 6	2.5 x 2
Albéric Barbier	X			X													X		X						20 x 14	6 x 4
Albertine		X	X												X									X	27 x 14	7 x 4
Alchymist		X		X													X		X		X				15 x 10	4.5 x 3
Alec's Red		X		X	X	X									X										5 x 4	1.5 x 1.2
Alexander				X					X							X		X							6 x 5	2 x 1.5
Alfred de Dalmas		X		X							X				X				X						3 x 30"	1 x 0.75
Alister Stella Gray		X		X											X				X						16 x 10	5 x 3
Alpine Sunset		X		X		X	X	X		X					X										3 x 3	1 x 1
Altissimo					X										X				X						15 x 10	4.5 x 3
Amadis	X		X												X										14 x 10	4 x 3
Ambassador				X	X										X										5 x 4	1.5 x 1.2
Amber Queen	X			X	X	X	X	X	X						X							X			4 x 3	1.2 x 1
Ambridge Rose		X		X	X	X	X	X							X										3 x 3	1 x 1
Amelia		X	X												X										4 x 3	1.2 x 1
America		X		X											X				X						16 x 10	5 x 3
Anaïs Ségales		X	X												X				X						4 x 6	1.2 x 2
Angel Face		X		X	X	X	X								X							X	X	X	3 x 30"	1 x 0.75
Anna Olivier	X			X	X										X										3 x 3	1 x 1
Anna Pavlova		X		X	X										X					X	X				5 x 4	1.5 x 1.2
Anne Harkness				X			X		X	X					X										3 x 3	1 x 0.9
Antigua	X			X	X										X								X	X	6 x 3	2 x 1
Aotearoa (New Zealand)		X		X	X	X	X								X										5 x 4	1.5 x 1.2
Apricot Nectar		X		X	X					X					X										5 x 4	1.5 x 1.2
Archiduc Joseph (Monsieur Tillier)	X			X		X									X				X						6 x 4	1.8 x 1.2
Arthur Bell		X		X											X										4 x 3	1.3 x 1
Autumn Delight	X			X	X		X								X										4 x 3	1.2 x 1
Autumnalis	X			X														X							12 x 6	3.5 x 2
Baby Grand	X			X		X		X								X									18" x 12"	0.45 x 0.3
Ballerina	X			X				X							X		X		X						7 x 5	2.1 x 1.5
Bantry Bay	X			X											X				X						15 x 10	4.5 x 3
Baronne Edmund de Rothschild		X		X	X	X									X										6 x 5	1.8 x 1.5
Baron Girod de l'Ain		X	X				X								X								X		5 x 3	1.5 x 1

Rose

Rose	Slight Fragrance	Moderate Fragrance	Strong Fragrance	Once-Flowering	Repeat-Flowering	Recurrent Blooms	Suitable for Cut Flowers	Suitable for Exhibition	Suitable for Container Growing	Can Be Grown as a Pillar or Climber	Suitable for Bedding/Mass Planting	Suitable for Hedging	Ground Cover or Border	Decorative Fruit	Requires Full Sun (6 hrs+)	Keep Out of Hot Sun (Morning Sun Only)	Shade Tolerant	Prefers Warm Climate (or Sheltered Sun) Frost Tender	Tolerates Poor Soils	Blooms Hate Wet Weather	Can Be Prone to Die Back	Prone to Black Spot	Prone to Mildew	Prone to Rust	Average Plant Size—Imperial Height × Width	Average Plant Size—Metric Height × Width
Baronne Henriette de Snoy		X				X									X					X					5 x 4	1.5 x 1.2
Baronne Prévost			X		X				X						X								X		6 x 4	1.8 x 1.2
Beauty Secret		X			X		X		X						X										18" x 12"	0.45 x 0.3
Belle Amour		X		X														X	X						6 x 4	1.8 x 1.2
Belle de Crécy			X	X							X				X				X	X				X	4½ x 3	1.4 x 1
Belle Poitevine			X		X							X						X	X						7 x 6	2.1 x 1.8
Belle Portugaise		X	X	X					X									X	X	X				X	20 x 15	6 x 4.5
Belle Story		X		X			X	X							X										4 x 4	1.2 x 1.2
Betty Prior	X					X					X				X										4 x 4	1.2 x 1.2
Bewitched		X			X		X	X							X		X							X	6 x 4	2 x 1.2
Big Purple		X			X		X								X										5 x 4	1.5 x 1.2
Bill Warriner	X				X				X						X										5 x 3	1.5 x 1
Bishop Darlington	X				X					X					X										6 x 4	1.8 x 1.2
Black Jade		X			X		X	X							X										18" x 12"	0.45 x 0.3
Blanc Double de Coubert		X		X								X		X	X				X						6 x 5	1.8 x 1.5
Blaze	X				X					X					X										15 x 10	4.5 x 3
Blue Girl		X			X		X	X							X							X	X	X	6 x 3	2 x 1
Blue Moon		X			X		X								X										6 x 4	1.8 x 1.2
Blush Damask		X	X												X			X	X					X	4½ x 3	1.4 x 1
Blush Noisette		X							X	X		X			X										10 x 5	3 x 1.5
Blush Rambler	X			X						X					X				X						12 x 12	3.5 x 3.5
Bonica					X				X		X	X			X				X						3 x 4	1 x 1.2
Bonn					X							X			X				X						7 x 5	2.1 x 1.5
Botzaris		X	X										X				X		X						4 x 3	1.2 x 1
Boule de Neige		X	X		X										X										4 x 3	1.2 x 1
Bourbon Queen		X	X						X								X		X						7 x 4	2.2 x 1.2
Brandy		X			X		X	X							X										5 x 4	1.5 x 1.2
Brass Band		X			X		X	X	X						X										4 x 3	1.2 x 1
Breath of Life		X			X		X			X					X										12 x 12	3.5 x 3.5
Brown Velvet	X				X		X								X										4 x 4	1.2 x 1.2
Buff Beauty		X			X					X		X						X							6 x 6	2 x 1.8
Bullata		X	X	X														X	X	X				X	5 x 4	1.5 x 1.2
Capitaine John Ingram		X	X						X						X				X						4 x 3	1.3 x 1
Cardinal de Richelieu		X	X						X										X						4 x 3	1.2 x 1
Cardinal Hume		X			X								X					X							3 x 4	1 x 1.3
Carefree Beauty		X			X							X			X										4 x 4	1.2 x 1.2
Carefree Delight	X				X						X	X	X		X										4 x 4	1.2 x 1.2

Rose

	Slight Fragrance	Moderate Fragrance	Strong Fragrance	Once-Flowering	Repeat-Flowering	Recurrent Blooms	Suitable for Cut Flowers	Suitable for Exhibition	Suitable for Container Growing	Can Be Grown as a Pillar or Climber	Suitable for Bedding/Mass Planting	Suitable for Hedging	Ground Cover or Border	Decorative Fruit	Requires Full Sun (6 hrs+)	Keep Out of Hot Sun (Morning Sun Only)	Shade Tolerant	Prefers Warm Climate (or Sheltered Sun) Frost Tender	Tolerates Poor Soils	Blooms Hate Wet Weather	Can Be Prone to Die Back	Prone to Black Spot	Prone to Mildew	Prone to Rust	Average Plant Size—Imperial Height × Width	Average Plant Size—Metric Height × Width
Carrot Top	X			X		X	X	X																	12" × 12"	0.3 × 0.3
Casino		X			X										X										12 × 3	3.5 × 3
Catherine Deneuve			X		X		X								X										5 × 4	1.5 × 1.2
Cécile Brunner		X				X			X						X										4 × 3	1.2 × 1
Cécile Brunner, Climbing			X	X						X					X				X						20 × 20	6 × 6
Celebrity	X				X		X	X							X										5 × 4	1.5 × 1.2
Celestial			X	X											X				X						6 × 4	1.8 × 1.2
Céline Forestier		X			X										X				X						10 × 5	3 × 1.5
Celsiana			X	X								X			X				X						5 × 4	1.5 × 1.2
Champagne Cocktail		X			X					X					X										4 × 3	1.2 × 1
Champion of the World	X				X				X						X	X									4 × 3	1.2 × 1
Champney's Pink Cluster		X			X										X				X						14 × 6	4 × 2
Chapeau de Napoléon			X	X											X				X						6 × 4	1.8 × 1.2
Charles Austin		X			X					X					X										7 × 5	2.2 × 1.5
Charles de Mills			X	X			X			X		X			X				X						4½ × 4	1.4 × 1.2
Charlotte Armstrong		X			X		X	X							X										5 × 4	1.5 × 1.2
Chaucer		X			X										X				X						5 × 4	1.5 × 1.2
Cherish	X				X		X	X	X						X										4 × 4	1.2 × 1.2
Chevy Chase	X			X			X		X						X									X	15 × 10	4.5 × 3
Chicago Peace	X				X										X							X			5 × 4	1.5 × 1.2
Child's Play	X				X		X	X	X		X				X										12" × 12"	0.3 × 0.3
Chloris		X	X																X	X					5 × 4	1.5 × 1.2
Christian Dior					X		X	X							X						X			X	5 × 4	1.5 × 1.2
Chrysler Imperial		X			X										X										5 × 4	1.5 × 1.2
Circus					X										X										4 × 3	1.3 × 1
Clair Matin	X				X												X		X						10 × 6	3 × 2
Claire Rose			X		X				X						X					X					7 × 6	2.2 × 1.5
Cocktail				X					X						X		X								7 × 6	2.2 × 1.5
Color Magic		X			X	X									X								X		5 × 4	1.5 × 1.2
Commandant Beaurepaire		X			X												X		X						5 × 5	1.5 × 1.5
Compassion		X			X		X								X										10 × 5	3 × 1.5
Complicata		X	X														X		X						12 × 6	3.5 × 2
Comte de Chambord		X			X		X	X							X				X						4 × 3	1.2 × 1
Conditorum		X	X					X							X				X						4½ × 3	1.4 × 1
Constance Spry			X	X						X					X				X					X	10 × 5	3 × 1.5
Cornelia		X			X												X		X						5 × 6	1.5 × 1.8
Cramoisi Supérieur					X										X			X							3 × 30"	1 × 0.75

Rose

Rose	SLIGHT FRAGRANCE	MODERATE FRAGRANCE	STRONG FRAGRANCE	ONCE-FLOWERING	REPEAT-FLOWERING	RECURRENT BLOOMS	SUITABLE FOR CUT FLOWERS	SUITABLE FOR EXHIBITION	SUITABLE FOR CONTAINER GROWING	CAN BE GROWN AS A PILLAR OR CLIMBER	SUITABLE FOR BEDDING/MASS PLANTING	SUITABLE FOR HEDGING	GROUND COVER OR BORDER	DECORATIVE FRUIT	REQUIRES FULL SUN (6 HRS+)	KEEP OUT OF HOT SUN (MORNING SUN ONLY)	SHADE TOLERANT	PREFERS WARM CLIMATE (OR SHELTERED SUN) FROST TENDER	TOLERATES POOR SOILS	BLOOMS HATE WET WEATHER	CAN BE PRONE TO DIE BACK	PRONE TO BLACK SPOT	PRONE TO MILDEW	PRONE TO RUST	AVERAGE PLANT SIZE—IMPERIAL HEIGHT × WIDTH	AVERAGE PLANT SIZE—METRIC HEIGHT × WIDTH
Dainty Bess		X			X		X								X					X					6 x 4	1.8 x 1.2
Dapple Dawn	X			X						X					X					X					6 x 6	2 x 2
Deep Secret			X		X		X								X					X					4 x 3	1.2 x 1
Delicata			X		X				X		X							X		X					3 x 3	0.9 x 0.9
Desprez à Fleurs Jaunes	X			X						X								X		X					20 x 10	6 x 3
Devoniensis		X		X											X		X								8 x 5	2.5 x 1.5
Diamond Jubilee		X		X			X	X							X							X			5 x 4	2.5 x 1.5
Don Juan			X		X					X					X										12" x 12"	0.3 x 0.3
Dortmund	X					X				X					X					X					6 x 5	2 x 1.5
Double Delight			X		X		X								X										5 x 4	1.5 x 1.2
Double Joy		X			X		X	X							X										18" x 12"	0.45 x 0.3
Dove	X				X		X								X										4 x 5	1.5 x 1.8
Dresden Doll		X			X		X	X							X										12" x 12"	0.3 x 0.3
Dublin Bay						X									X						X				8 x 6	2.5 x 2
Duchesse de Brabant		X					X		X						X										3 x 3	1 x 1
Duchesse de Brabant Climbing		X					X								X										12 x 6	3.5 x 2
Duchesse de Montebello			X	X			X		X						X										4½ x 3	1.4 x 1
Duet							X	X							X										5 x 4	1.5 x 1.2
Echo	X		X												X					X					5½ x 5	1.6 x 1.5
Edelweiss	X				X				X	X	X				X										3 x 3	1 x 0.9
Eden 88	X				X					X					X										12" x 12"	0.3 x 0.3
Electron		X			X		X	X			X				X			X							5 x 4	1.5 x 1.2
Elina	X				X		X	X	X						X										5 x 4	1.5 x 1.2
Elizabeth Harkness	X				X		X	X							X										5 x 4	1.5 x 1.2
Elizabeth of Glamis		X			X		X								X								X		4 x 4	1.3 x 1.2
Ellen			X		X		X								X										4 x 3	1.2 x 1
Ellen Willmott	X				X			X							X										5 x 4	1.5 x 1.2
Empress Joséphine		X		X								X						X	X						5 x 4	1.5 x 1.2
Ena Harkness		X			X		X	X	X						X				X						4 x 3	1.2 x 1
Erfurt					X							X						X	X						4 x 5	1.3 x 1.5
Escapade	X				X						X				X										4 x 5	1.3 x 1.2
Etoile de Hollande			X		X		X								X										12 x 6	3.5 x 2
Europeana	X				X		X				X				X										4 x 3	1.2 x 1
Eva				X									X								X				7 x 6	2.2 x 1.8
Evelyn		X		X			X				X				X										8 x 6	2.4 x 1.8
Evelyn Fison	X				X							X			X										4 x 3	1.3 x 1
Eye Paint					X							X			X										4 x 4	1.3 x 1.2

Rose

	Slight Fragrance	Moderate Fragrance	Strong Fragrance	Once-Flowering	Repeat-Flowering	Recurrent Blooms	Suitable for Cut Flowers	Suitable for Exhibition	Suitable for Container Growing	Can Be Grown as a Pillar or Climber	Suitable for Bedding/Mass Planting	Suitable for Hedging	Ground Cover or Border	Decorative Fruit	Requires Full Sun (6 hrs+)	Keep Out of Hot Sun (Morning Sun Only)	Shade Tolerant	Prefers Warm Climate (or Sheltered Sun) Frost Tender	Tolerates Poor Soils	Blooms Hate Wet Weather	Can Be Prone to Die Back	Prone to Black Spot	Prone to Mildew	Prone to Rust	Average Plant Size — Imperial (Height × Width)	Average Plant Size — Metric (Height × Width)
F.J. Grootendorst		X		X			X				X				X		X								4 x 3	1.2 x 1
Fair Bianca		X		X				X		X					X										3 x 3	1 x 1
Fantin-Latour			X	X													X		X						5½ x 4	1.6 x 1.2
Felicia		X				X					X						X		X						4 x 5	1.2 x 1.5
Felicité et Perpétue	X		X														X		X						14 x 10	4 x 3
Felicité Parmentier			X	X			X										X		X						4½ x 3	1.4 x 1
Ferdinand Pichard		X		X											X			X	X		X				5½ x 4	1.6 x 1.2
Figurine					X	X	X								X										30" x 12"	0.8 x 0.3
Fimbriata		X		X			X				X				X		X								4 x 4	1.2 x 1.2
First Kiss	X			X			X		X						X										4 x 3	1.2 x 1
First Love	X			X		X									X										5 x 4	1.5 x 1.2
First Prize	X			X		X	X								X										5 x 4	1.5 x 1.2
Fisher Holmes		X		X			X								X							X	X		3 x 3	1 x 1
Flamingo	X			X		X									X										5 x 4	1.5 x 1.2
Flower Carpet					X								X		X		X								3 x 10	1 x 3
Foxy Lady	X			X			X								X										12" x 12"	0.3 x 0.3
Fragrant Cloud (Duftwolke)			X	X		X	X								X										5 x 4	1.5 x 1.2
Francis E. Lester		X	X							X							X		X						14 x 16	4 x 5
François Juranville	X				X	X				X	X				X										25 x 10	8 x 3
French Lace			X	X		X	X								X						X				5 x 4	1.5 x 1.2
Friesia (Sunsprite)		X		X		X	X		X		X				X										4 x 3	1.3 x 1
Fritz Nobis			X							X							X		X						6 x 5	1.8 x 1.5
Frau Dagmar Hastrup	X			X		X							X	X	X		X		X						30" x 4	0.8 x 1.2
Général Jacqueminot		X	X												X						X			X	5 x 3	1.5 x 1
Général Kléber		X	X								X				X				X						6 x 4	1.8 x 1.2
Georg Arends			X	X		X									X				X						6 x 5	1.8 x 1.5
Georges Vibert		X	X				X								X				X						3 x 3	1 x 1
Gertrude Jekyll			X	X		X						X			X										4 x 3	1.3 x 1
Ghislaine de Féligonde		X			X					X			X	X	X		X								8 x 3	2.4 x 1
Glamis Castle			X	X		X	X		X		X				X										3 x 3	1 x 1
Gloire de Dijon		X		X						X					X				X			X	X		12 x 6	3.5 x 2
Gloire de France		X	X														X		X						3 x 4	1 x 1.3
Gold Medal	X			X		X	X	X							X										5 x 4	1.5 x 1.2
Golden Celebration			X	X		X									X										6 x 6	1.8 x 1.8
Golden Showers	X			X													X		X						13 x 6	3.8 x 2
Golden Wings				X		X							X		X		X		X						6 x 5	1.8 x 1.5
Graham Thomas		X		X		X						X			X		X		X						7 x 6	2.2 x 2

Rose

Rose	Slight Fragrance	Moderate Fragrance	Strong Fragrance	Once-Flowering	Repeat-Flowering	Recurrent Blooms	Suitable for Cut Flowers	Suitable for Exhibition	Suitable for Container Growing	Can Be Grown as a Pillar or Climber	Suitable for Bedding/Mass Planting	Suitable for Hedging	Ground Cover or Border	Decorative Fruit	Requires Full Sun (6 hrs+)	Keep Out of Hot Sun (Morning Sun Only)	Shade Tolerant	Prefers Warm Climate (or Sheltered Sun) Frost Tender	Tolerates Poor Soils	Blooms Hate Wet Weather	Can Be Prone to Die Back	Prone to Black Spot	Prone to Mildew	Prone to Rust	Average Plant Size—Imperial Height × Width	Average Plant Size—Metric Height × Width
Granada		X		X		X									X										4 x 3	1.2 x 1
Great Maiden's Blush			X	X		X											X	X							6 x 5	2 x 1.5
Gruss an Aachen			X		X				X		X							X							3 x 3	1 x 1
Guinée			X		X					X					X										15" x 12"	0.4 x 0.3
Handel					X					X					X					X					12 x 6	3.5 x 2
Harry Wheatcroft					X		X								X										5 x 4	1.5 x 1.2
Hawkeye Belle		X			X		X	X							X										4 x 4	1.2 x 1.2
Helen Traubel		X			X										X										5 x 4	1.5 x 1.2
Helmut Schmidt	X				X		X	X							X										5 x 4	1.5 x 1.2
Henri Martin		X	X												X								X		5 x 4	1.5 x 1.2
Henry Kelsey	X				X					X	X				X										10" x 10"	0.25 x 0.25
Heritage		X			X										X										5 x 4	1.5 x 1.2
Hermosa	X					X			X									X							3 x 2	1 x 0.6
Hippolyte		X	X												X										4 x 4	1.2 x 1.2
Holy Toledo	X								X	X	X				X										18" x 12"	0.45 x 0.3
Honor	X						X	X	X						X										5 x 4	1.5 x 1.2
Honorine de Brabant		X		X								X						X	X	X					6 x 5	2 x 1.5
Hot Tamale	X						X	X	X						X										18" x 12"	0.45 x 0.3
Iceberg	X						X	X			X				X										5 x 4	1.5 x 1.2
Iceberg Climbing	X				X													X							15 x 10	4.5 x 3
Iced Ginger	X						X	X			X				X										4 x 3	1.2 x 1
Ingrid Bergman					X			X							X										4 x 4	1.2 x 1.2
Intrigue (Lavaglut)	X				X							X			X										4 x 4	1.3 x 1.2
Intrigue (JACum)			X		X			X							X										4 x 3	1.2 x 1
Ipsilante		X	X									X			X				X						4 x 3	1.3 x 1
Irene Watts	X					X		X	X						X										3 x 2	1 x 0.6
Irish Elegance	X				X										X									X	5 x 4	1.5 x 1.2
Irish Rich Marbled		X	X						X					X			X	X							4 x 3	1.2 x 1
Ispahan			X	X				X							X										4 x 3	1.2 x 1
Jacqueline du Pré		X			X								X		X			X							5 x 4	1.5 x 1.3
Jacques Cartier			X		X		X	X							X			X	X						3 x 30"	1 x 0.8
James Veitch			X		X			X							X								X		3 x 3	0.9 x 0.9
Jean Ducher		X								X					X										5 x 4	1.5 x 1.2
Jeanne Lajoie					X					X					X										10 x 6	3 x 2
John F. Kennedy			X		X		X								X										5 x 4	1.5 x 1.2
Joseph's Coat	X				X					X					X					X					7 x 6	2.1 x 2
Joyfulness	X				X		X	X	X						X					X					5 x 4	1.5 x 1.2

Rose

	SLIGHT FRAGRANCE	MODERATE FRAGRANCE	STRONG FRAGRANCE	ONCE-FLOWERING	REPEAT-FLOWERING	RECURRENT BLOOMS	SUITABLE FOR CUT FLOWERS	SUITABLE FOR EXHIBITION	SUITABLE FOR CONTAINER GROWING	CAN BE GROWN AS A PILLAR OR CLIMBER	SUITABLE FOR BEDDING/MASS PLANTING	SUITABLE FOR HEDGING	GROUND COVER OR BORDER	DECORATIVE FRUIT	REQUIRES FULL SUN (6 HRS+)	KEEP OUT OF HOT SUN (MORNING SUN ONLY)	SHADE TOLERANT	PREFERS WARM CLIMATE (OR SHELTERED SUN) FROST TENDER	TOLERATES POOR SOILS	BLOOMS HATE WET WEATHER	CAN BE PRONE TO DIE BACK	PRONE TO BLACK SPOT	PRONE TO MILDEW	PRONE TO RUST	AVERAGE PLANT SIZE—IMPERIAL HEIGHT × WIDTH	AVERAGE PLANT SIZE—METRIC HEIGHT × WIDTH
Judy Garland			X		X		X	X								X									4 x 4	1.2 x 1.2
Julia's Rose	X				X		X		X						X								X		4 x 3	1.2 x 1
Just Joey		X				X	X								X										6 x 4	1.8 x 1.2
Kardinal					X		X	X							X										5 x 4	1.5 x 1.2
Kathleen		X			X						X				X					X					6 x 6	2 x 1.8
Kathleen Harrop			X		X														X	X					12 x 6	3.5 x 2
Kathryn Morley			X		X		X								X										6 x 4	1.8 x 1.2
King's Ransom	X				X		X								X										5 x 4	1.5 x 1.2
Königen von Danemarck			X							X					X										6 x 3	2 x 1
Kronenbourg			X		X		X								X							X	X		5 x 4	1.5 x 1.2
Kronprinzessin Victoria			X			X									X			X						X	4 x 3	1.2 x 1
La France		X			X				X						X							X	X	X	4 x 3	1.2 x 1
La Reine Victoria		X			X				X						X							X	X		5 x 3	1.5 x 1
La Sevillana						X						X			X				X						4 x 5	1.2 x 1.5
La Ville de Bruxelles		X	X												X				X	X				X	5 x 3	1.5 x 1
Lady Hillingdon		X			X										X										6 x 5	1.8 x 1.5
Lady Hillingdon Climbing		X			X		X	X		X					X				X						10 x 6	3 x 1.8
Lady of the Dawn	X				X							X			X										5 x 5	1.5 x 1.5
Lady Mary Fitzwilliam	X					X									X										4 x 3	1.2 x 1
Lagerfeld		X			X										X										5 x 4	1.5 x 1.2
Lamarque		X			X														X						16 x 10	5 x 3
Las Vegas	X				X		X	X							X										6 x 5	1.8 x 1.5
Lavender Jewel	X					X							X		X										12" x 12"	0.3 x 0.3
Lavender Lassie		X			X															X	X				6 x 6	1.8 x 2
Lavender Pinocchio	X					X			X						X										4 x 4	1.2 x 1.2
L. D. Braithwaite		X			X		X								X										5 x 5	1.5 x 1.5
Leander			X		X					X					X										10 x 14	3 x 4
Leda (Painted Damask)		X		X				X							X					X					4 x 3	1.2 x 1
Lemon Delight		X			X				X						X										12" x 12"	0.3 x 0.3
Lilac Rose		X			X		X		X			X			X										4 x 4	1.2 x 1.2
Lili Marlene	X				X		X	X			X				X										4 x 3	1.2 x 1
Lilian Austin		X			X				X				X		X										3 x 30"	1 x 0.8
Livin' Easy			X		X		X				X				X										4 x 3	1.2 x 1
Lord Penzance		X		X										X				X			X		X		8 x 5	2.5 x 1.5
Louise Odier		X			X				X				X												3 x 3	1 x 1
Loving Touch	X					X	X	X	X						X										19" x 19"	0.5 x 0.5
Lucetta		X			X														X						5 x 5	1.5 x 1.5

Rose

	Slight Fragrance	Moderate Fragrance	Strong Fragrance	Once-Flowering	Repeat-Flowering	Recurrent Blooms	Suitable for Cut Flowers	Suitable for Exhibition	Suitable for Container Growing	Can Be Grown as a Pillar or Climber	Suitable for Bedding/Mass Planting	Suitable for Hedging	Ground Cover or Border	Decorative Fruit	Requires Full Sun (6 hrs+)	Keep Out of Hot Sun (Morning Sun Only)	Shade Tolerant	Prefers Warm Climate (or Sheltered Sun) Frost Tender	Tolerates Poor Soils	Blooms Hate Wet Weather	Can Be Prone to Die Back	Prone to Black Spot	Prone to Mildew	Prone to Rust	Average Plant Size—Imperial Height × Width	Average Plant Size—Metric Height × Width
Madam Plantier			X	X						X						X	X								12 x 6	3.5 x 2
Madame Alfred Carriere			X		X											X	X								16 x 10	5 x 3
Madame Butterfly			X		X		X								X										5 x 4	1.5 x 1.2
Madame Caroline Testout	X				X										X										4 x 4	1.3 x 1.2
Madame Gregoire Staechelin		X		X												X	X								14 x 14	4 x 4
Madame Hardy			X	X								X				X	X								6 x 5	1.8 x 1.5
Madame Isaac Pereire			X		X						X				X									X	6 x 5	2 x 1.5
Madame Legras de St. Germain			X	X					X		X					X	X								8 x 6	2.5 x 1.8
Madame Louis Lévêque			X		X										X							X	X		4½ x 3	1.4 x 1
Madame Pierre Oger		X			X										X										4½ x 4	1.4 x 1.2
Magic Carrousel					X	X	X		X		X				X										3 x 19"	1 x 0.5
Maigold		X		X													X		X						14 x 10	4 x 3
Maman Cochet	X				X		X								X										4 x 3	1.2 x 1
Margaret Merrill		X			X		X	X	X		X				X										4 x 3	1.2 x 1
Margo Koster					X				X		X				X								X		4 x 3	1.2 x 1
Marguerite Hilling	X				X							X			X		X								10 x 6	3 x 2
Maria Callas		X			X		X	X							X										5 x 4	1.5 x 1.2
Marie Lambert	X				X		X		X						X										4 x 3	1.2 x 0.9
Marjorie Fair					X														X				X		4 x 6	1.2 x 2
Martha		X		X												X	X								10 x 6	3 x 1.8
Mary Rose		X			X		X					X			X										6 x 5	2 x 1.5
Masquerade					X												X					X			5 x 4	1.5 x 1.2
Matangi					X							X	X		X										4 x 4	1.2 x 1.2
Medallion		X			X		X	X							X										6 x 4	1.8 x 1.2
Meg		X			X					X					X	X									12 x 10	3.5 x 3
Mermaid		X			X													X						X	50 x 20	15 x 6
Michèle Meilland	X				X		X	X							X										4 x 4	1.3 x 1.2
Minnie Pearl					X	X	X	X	X		X				X										30" x 19"	0.8 x 0.5
Mischief					X		X	X							X									X	5 x 4	1.5 x 1.2
Mister Lincoln			X		X		X	X							X										6 x 5	1.8 x 1.5
Montezuma	X				X										X									X	5 x 4	1.5 x 1.2
Moonlight		X			X											X	X								6 x 5½	1.8 x 1.6
Moonsprite			X		X	X			X						X										4 x 3	1.2 x 1
Mount Hood		X			X		X								X										5 x 4	1.5 x 1.2
Mrs Foley Hobbs		X			X										X									X	4 x 4	1.2 x 1.2
Mrs Herbert Stevens			X		X										X										4 x 4	1.3 x 1.2
Mrs John Laing			X		X		X					X			X									X	5 x 4	1.5 x 1.2

Rose

Rose	SLIGHT FRAGRANCE	MODERATE FRAGRANCE	STRONG FRAGRANCE	ONCE-FLOWERING	REPEAT-FLOWERING	RECURRENT BLOOMS	SUITABLE FOR CUT FLOWERS	SUITABLE FOR EXHIBITION	SUITABLE FOR CONTAINER GROWING	CAN BE GROWN AS A PILLAR OR CLIMBER	SUITABLE FOR BEDDING/MASS PLANTING	SUITABLE FOR HEDGING	GROUND COVER OR BORDER	DECORATIVE FRUIT	REQUIRES FULL SUN (6 HRS+)	KEEP OUT OF HOT SUN (MORNING SUN ONLY)	SHADE TOLERANT	PREFERS WARM CLIMATE (OR SHELTERED SUN)	FROST TENDER	TOLERATES POOR SOILS	BLOOMS HATE WET WEATHER	CAN BE PRONE TO DIE BACK	PRONE TO BLACK SPOT	PRONE TO MILDEW	PRONE TO RUST	AVERAGE PLANT SIZE—IMPERIAL HEIGHT × WIDTH	AVERAGE PLANT SIZE—METRIC HEIGHT × WIDTH
Mrs Oakley Fisher	X			X			X								X										X	4 x 4	1.2 x 1.2
Mrs Sam McGredy	X				X				X						X											4 x 3	1.3 x 1
Mutabilis					X													X		X						5 x 4	1.5 x 1.2
Nevada	X			X								X			X					X						10 x 6	3 x 2
New Dawn		X			X					X								X		X						10 x 8	3 x 2.5
Officinalis (Gallica Officinalis)		X	X	X							X		X	X	X					X						4½ x 5	1.4 x 1.5
Oklahoma		X			X		X	X							X											5 x 4	1.5 x 1.2
Old Blush		X			X				X						X					X						6 x 5	2 x 1.5
Old Master					X				X						X											4 x 3	1.2 x 1
Olympiad					X		X	X							X											5 x 4	1.5 x 1.2
Omar Khayyam		X	X												X											3 x 3	1 x 1
Ophelia		X			X		X								X											5 x 4	1.5 x 1.2
Ophelia Climbing		X			X					X					X					X						15 x 12	4.5 x 3.5
Orange Honey		X			X				X						X											19" x 19"	0.5 x 0.5
Oranges 'n' Lemons					X						X				X											4 x 3	1.2 x 1
Othello		X			X					X					X								X	X		6 x 5	2 x 1.5
Papa Gontier	X				X										X											4 x 3	1.2 x 0.9
Papa Meilland			X		X		X								X								X	X		5 x 4	1.5 x 1.2
Paradise		X			X		X	X							X											5 x 4	1.5 x 1.2
Parfum de l'Hay		X			X							X				X	X							X	X	4½ x 4	1.4 x 1.2
Parkdirektor Riggers	X				X					X					X					X						16 x 12	5 x 3.5
Pascali					X		X								X											6 x 4	2 x 1.2
Paul Neyron		X			X		X		X						X											4 x 3	1.2 x 1
Paul Shirville		X			X		X								X											5 x 4	1.5 x 1.2
Paul Transon	X				X										X			X	X							10 x 8	3 x 2.5
Pax	X				X							X				X	X			X						6 x 6	2 x 1.8
Peace	X				X										X					X						5 x 4	1.5 x 1.2
Peace Climbing	X				X					X					X					X						16 x 12	5 x 3.5
Penelope		X				X						X				X	X			X						5 x 6	1.5 x 2
Perdita		X			X		X								X											5 x 4	1.5 x 1.2
Perle d'Or	X					X			X						X											5 x 3	1.5 x 1
Petite de Hollande		X	X						X						X					X						4 x 3	1.2 x 0.9
Phyllis Bide	X				X					X								X		X						10 x 6	3 x 2
Piccadilly	X			X			X								X					X			X		X	4 x 3	1.3 x 1
Pierre de Ronsard	X				X	X				X	X				X											5 x 4	1.5 x 1.2
Pink Grootendorst				X	X	X						X														4 x 3	1.2 x 1
Pink La Sevillana					X						X				X											4 x 5	1.2 x 1.5

Rose

	Slight Fragrance	Moderate Fragrance	Strong Fragrance	Once-Flowering	Repeat-Flowering	Recurrent Blooms	Suitable for Cut Flowers	Suitable for Exhibition	Suitable for Container Growing	Can Be Grown as a Pillar or Climber	Suitable for Bedding/Mass Planting	Suitable for Hedging	Ground Cover or Border	Decorative Fruit	Requires Full Sun (6 hrs+)	Keep Out of Hot Sun (Morning Sun Only)	Shade Tolerant	Prefers Warm Climate (or Sheltered Sun) Frost Tender	Tolerates Poor Soils	Blooms Hate Wet Weather	Can Be Prone to Die Back	Prone to Black Spot	Prone to Mildew	Prone to Rust	Average Plant Size—Imperial Height × Width	Average Plant Size—Metric Height × Width
Pink Parfait	X				X										X										5 x 4	1.5 x 1.2
Pink Peace			X		X	X									X					X		X			5 x 4	1.5 x 1.2
Pinstripe		X			X				X		X				X										18″ x 12″	0.45 x 0.3
Playboy					X					X	X				X										4 x 3	1.2 x 1
Playgirl	X				X				X	X	X				X										4 x 3	1.2 x 1
Polar Star					X		X								X				X						5 x 4	1.5 x 1.2
Polka	X				X					X	X				X										10 x 8	3 x 2.8
Pompon Blanc Parfait		X	X															X		X					4 x 3	1.2 x 1
Pompon de Bourgogne		X	X												X										30″ x 24″	0.8 x 0.6
Popcorn		X				X	X		X						X										19″ x 19″	0.5 x 0.5
Portrait		X			X		X								X										5 x 4	1.5 x 1.2
Precious Platinum	X				X		X								X										5 x 4	1.5 x 1.2
Président de Sèze			X	X				X							X					X	X				4½ x 3	1.4 x 1
Pretty Jessica			X		X										X										4 x 3	1.2 x 1
Pride 'n' Joy		X			X		X		X		X				X										18″ x 12″	0.45 x 0.3
Prince Charles			X	X														X	X						5 x 4	1.5 x 1.2
Princess de Monaco	X		X		X		X								X										5 x 4	1.5 x 1.2
Priscilla Burton	X				X								X	X	X										4 x 3	1.2 x 1
Pristine		X			X		X								X										5 x 5	1.5 x 1.5
Prosperity		X				X				X		X			X		X								6 x 5	2 x 1.5
Prospero			X		X			X							X							X	X		3 x 4	1 x 1.2
Purple Tiger	X				X				X						X						X				3 x 3	1 x 0.9
Quatre Saisons			X	X											X				X						6 x 5	1.8 x 1.5
Queen Adelaide (Yves Piaget)		X			X			X							X						X				4 x 4	1.2 x 1.2
Queen Elizabeth	X				X						X				X				X						6 x 5	2 x 1.5
Queen Margrethe		X			X		X	X							X										3 x 3	1 x 1
Queen Nefertiti		X			X										X										5 x 4	1.5 x 1.2
R. Banksiae Banksiae		X	X															X							27 x 16	7 x 5
R. Banksiae Lutea		X	X															X							27 x 16	7 x 5
R. Bracteata		X		X													X	X							10 x 10	3 x 3
R. Centifolia			X	X														X	X	X				X	6 x 5	1.8 x 1.5
R. Centifolia Muscosa			X	X											X				X	X				X	6 x 5	1.8 x 1.5
R. Chinensis Viridiflora					X			X		X					X				X						3 x 3	1 x 1
R. Davidii Elongata		X	X											X			X	X	X						14 x 6	4 x 2
R. Ecae			X						X									X							5 x 3	1.5 x 1
R. × Ecae Golden Chersonese			X															X	X						6 x 5	2 x 1.5
R. Elegantula Persetosa			X												X			X	X						6 x 5½	1.8 x 1.6

Rose

	Slight Fragrance	Moderate Fragrance	Strong Fragrance	Once-Flowering	Repeat-Flowering	Recurrent Blooms	Suitable for Cut Flowers	Suitable for Exhibition	Suitable for Container Growing	Can Be Grown as a Pillar or Climber	Suitable for Bedding/Mass Planting	Suitable for Hedging	Ground Cover or Border	Decorative Fruit	Requires Full Sun (6 Hrs+)	Keep Out of Hot Sun (Morning Sun Only)	Shade Tolerant	Prefers Warm Climate (or Sheltered Sun) Frost Tender	Tolerates Poor Soils	Blooms Hate Wet Weather	Can Be Prone to Die Back	Prone to Black Spot	Prone to Mildew	Prone to Rust	Average Plant Size—Imperial Height × Width	Average Plant Size—Metric Height × Width
R. Filipes 'Kiftsgate'		X	X											X			X		X						33 x 20	10 x 6
R. Foetida	X		X															X						X	8 x 5	2.5 x 1.5
R. Foetida Bicolor	X		X															X	X					X	8 x 5	2.5 x 1.5
R. Foetida Persiana		X	X															X	X					X	6 x 5	1.8 x 1.5
R. Gallica	X		X									X			X				X						4½ x 3	1.4 x 1
R. Gigantea		X	X												X				X						50 x 16	15 x 5
R. Glauca	X		X											X	X				X						6 x 5	2 x 1.5
R. Holodonta (R. Moyesii Rosea)	X		X											X		X			X						12 x 6	3.5 x 2
R. Hugonis	X		X											X	X				X						8 x 5	2.5 x 1.5
R. Laevigata	X		X												X	X			X						20 x 16	6 x 5
R. × Macrantha		X	X										X	X					X						5 x 6	1.5 x 2
R. Macrophylla	X		X										X	X					X						16 x 10	5 x 3
R. Majalis	X		X										X	X					X						6 x 5	2 x 1.5
R. Moschata		X	X															X	X						10 x 6	3 x 2
R. Moyesii			X											X	X				X						12 x 6	3.5 x 2
R. Moyesii 'Geranium'			X											X	X				X						10 x 6	3 x 2
R. Moyesii 'Highdownensis'			X											X	X				X						10 x 6	3 x 2
R. Mundi (R. Gallica Versicolor)		X	X									X	X		X				X						4½ x 5	1.4 x 1.5
R. Nitida			X					X							X	X			X						4 x 3	1.2 x 1
R. Pimpinellifolia			X						X			X			X				X						4 x 4	1.2 x 1.2
R. Pimpinellifolia 'Altaica'			X									X			X				X						5 x 4	1.5 x 1.2
R. Roxburghii	X		X												X				X						8 x 8	2.5 x 2.5
R. Rugosa		X				X						X		X	X				X						6 x 6	2 x 1.8
R. Rugosa Alba		X				X						X		X	X				X						6 x 6	2 x 1.8
R. Sericea Pteracantha			X												X				X						10 x 6	3 x 2
R. Setigera	X		X							X			X		X				X						5 x 6	1.5 x 2
R. Villosa Duplex			X											X	X				X						6 x 5	2 x 1.5
R. Wichuraiana	X		X							X					X				X						6 x 22	2 x 6.5
R. Willmottiae	X		X										X		X				X						6 x 6	2 x 2
R. Woodsii var. Fendleri	X		X										X		X				X						6 x 6	2 x 2
R. Xanthina 'Canary Bird'	X		X												X				X						8 x 6	2.5 x 1.8
Rainbow's End					X		X	X	X		X		X		X										12" x 12"	0.3 x 0.3
Rambling Rector		X	X											X	X				X						28 x 16	7.5 x 5
Raspberry Ice (Hannah Gordon)					X						X							X							5 x 4	1.5 x 1.2
Raubritter	X		X																X		X				4 x 5	1.2 x 1.5
Red Cascade				X					X						X										8 x 6	2.5 x 2
Red Cedar (Loving Memory)	X				X	X									X										5 x 4	1.5 x 1.2

Rose

	SLIGHT FRAGRANCE	MODERATE FRAGRANCE	STRONG FRAGRANCE	ONCE-FLOWERING	REPEAT-FLOWERING	RECURRENT BLOOMS	SUITABLE FOR CUT FLOWERS	SUITABLE FOR EXHIBITION	SUITABLE FOR CONTAINER GROWING	CAN BE GROWN AS A PILLAR OR CLIMBER	SUITABLE FOR BEDDING/MASS PLANTING	SUITABLE FOR HEDGING	GROUND COVER OR BORDER	DECORATIVE FRUIT	REQUIRES FULL SUN (6 HRS+)	KEEP OUT OF HOT SUN (MORNING SUN ONLY)	SHADE TOLERANT	PREFERS WARM CLIMATE (OR SHELTERED SUN) FROST TENDER	TOLERATES POOR SOILS	BLOOMS HATE WET WEATHER	CAN BE PRONE TO DIE BACK	PRONE TO BLACK SPOT	PRONE TO MILDEW	PRONE TO RUST	AVERAGE PLANT SIZE—IMPERIAL HEIGHT × WIDTH	AVERAGE PLANT SIZE—METRIC HEIGHT × WIDTH
Regensberg					X				X		X				X										4 x 3	1.2 x 1
Reine des Violettes		X		X		X					X				X										5 x 4	1.5 x 1.2
Remember Me	X				X										X										5 x 4	1.5 x 1.2
Rêve d'Or		X			X	X									X										14 x 10	4 x 3
Rise 'n' Shine	X				X	X	X		X		X		X		X										24" x 15"	0.6 x 0.4
Robusta		X			X							X							X		X				6 x 5	1.8 x 1.5
Rock 'n' Roll					X							X			X										4 x 3	1.3 x 1
Rose de Meaux		X	X					X							X										30" x 24"	0.7 x 0.6
Rose de Rescht			X	X											X										4½ x 3	1.4 x 1
Rose du Roi			X		X			X							X										3 x 30"	1 x 0.8
Roseraie de l'Hay			X			X						X	X		X				X		X				7 x 7	2.1 x 2.1
Royal Dane		X			X	X									X										5 x 4	1.5 x 1.2
Royal Highness			X		X		X	X							X							X		X	4 x 4	1.3 x 1.2
Sadlers Wells					X										X					X					5 x 5	1.5 x 1.5
Safrano	X				X										X										5 x 4	1.5 x 1.2
Sally Holmes							X	X	X									X							6 x 6	1.8 x 1.8
Sarabande	X				X				X		X				X										4 x 4	1.2 x 1.2
Sarah van Fleet		X			X						X				X										5 x 6	1.5 x 1.8
Savoy Hotel	X				X				X						X										5 x 4	1.5 x 1.2
Scabrosa		X			X						X				X										6 x 5	1.8 x 1.5
Scarlet Meidiland							X		X				X		X										30" x 4	0.75 x 1.3
Scarlet Queen Elizabeth					X										X										6 x 5	2 x 1.5
Scentimental		X	X		X	X				X					X										5 x 3	1.5 x 1
Schneezwerg		X			X									X			X		X						6 x 5	1.8 x 1.5
Sea Foam	X				X				X				X		X										3 x 8	1 x 2.5
Sexy Rexy					X			X	X	X					X										4 x 3	1.2 x 1
Sharifa Asma		X	X		X										X										5 x 4	1.5 x 1.2
Sheer Bliss		X			X	X									X										5 x 4	1.5 x 1.2
Shocking Blue		X	X		X	X	X	X							X										4 x 4	1.3 x 1.2
Shot Silk		X			X	X									X										4 x 4	1.3 x 1.2
Shot Silk Climbing		X			X										X										14 x 8	4 x 2.5
Showbiz					X			X	X						X										3 x 3	1 x 1
Silver Jubilee	X				X		X	X							X										4 x 4	1.3 x 1.2
Silver Moon	X			X														X							14 x 16	4 x 5
Simplicity	X					X			X		X	X			X						X				4 x 3	1.2 x 1
Singin' in the Rain	X				X		X	X	X						X										4 x 3	1.2 x 1
Sissinghurst Castle			X	X					X						X										4 x 3	1.2 x 1

Rose

	Slight Fragrance	Moderate Fragrance	Strong Fragrance	Once-Flowering	Repeat-Flowering	Recurrent Blooms	Suitable for Cut Flowers	Suitable for Exhibition	Suitable for Container Growing	Can be Grown as a Pillar or Climber	Suitable for Bedding/Mass Planting	Suitable for Hedging	Ground Cover or Border	Decorative Fruit	Requires Full Sun (6 Hrs+)	Keep Out of Hot Sun (Morning Sun Only)	Shade Tolerant	Prefers Warm Climate (or Sheltered Sun) Frost Tender	Tolerates Poor Soils	Blooms Hate Wet Weather	Can be Prone to Die Back	Prone to Black Spot	Prone to Mildew	Prone to Rust	Average Plant Size—Imperial Height × Width	Average Plant Size—Metric Height × Width
Snow Bride	X			X		X	X								X									X	18" x 12"	0.45 x 0.3
Sombreuil		X		X											X										10 x 6	3 x 1.8
Sonia		X		X	X										X										5 x 4	1.5 x 1.2
Soupert et Notting			X	X						X					X							X			3 x 30"	1 x 0.75
Souvenir de la Malmaison		X			X										X					X		X			6 x 5	1.8 x 1.5
Souvenir de Madame Leonie Viennot	X			X											X							X			14 x 10	4 x 3
Souvenir de St Anne's		X			X										X										5 x 4	1.5 x 1.2
Souvenir du Dr Jamain			X	X					X							X						X	X		8 x 4	2.5 x 1.2
Sparrieshoop	X			X		X	X		X								X		X						10 x 6	3 x 1.8
St. Cecilia			X	X		X	X								X										4 x 4	1.3 x 1.2
Stanwell Perpetual		X			X				X								X		X						8 x 6	2.5 x 2
Starina	X			X		X	X								X										12" x 12"	0.3 x 0.3
Striped Moss		X	X						X						X					X					3 x 30"	1 x 0.75
Sundowner		X		X		X			X						X										7 x 3	2.1 x 1
Sunflare	X			X					X		X	X	X		X										4 x 3	1.2 x 1
Sunny South		X			X						X				X				X						6 x 5	2 x 1.5
Super Star (Tropicana)		X		X		X									X									X	5 x 4	1.5 x 1.2
Susan Louise	X				X										X				X						6 x 5	2 x 1.5
Sutter's Gold		X		X		X	X								X										5 x 4	1.5 x 1.2
Swan	X			X		X									X										6 x 5	1.8 x 1.5
Sweet Chariot			X						X	X		X			X										18" x 12"	0.45 x 0.3
Symphony		X		X		X	X								X										5 x 4	1.5 x 1.2
Taboo		X		X		X	X		X		X	X			X										6 x 3	1.8 x 1
Talisman		X		X		X									X										4 x 3	1.3 x 1
Tamora			X	X		X									X										3 x 3	1 x 1
Tequila	X			X					X						X										4 x 3	1.2 x 1
Tequila Sunrise		X		X											X						X				4 x 3	1.5 x 1.2
The Bishop			X	X					X						X			X							4 x 3	1.3 x 1
The Fairy					X								X			X	X								3 x 6	1 x 2
The Miller			X	X					X						X		X								7 x 5	2.2 x 1.5
The Pilgrim			X	X	X				X						X										10" x 10"	0.25 x 0.25
The Prince			X	X	X		X								X										3 x 4	1 x 1.3
Timeless		X		X		X	X				X	X			X										5 x 3	1.5 x 1
Tineke				X		X	X								X										5 x 4	1.5 x 1.2
Thisbe		X			X												X		X						5 x 5	1.5 x 1.5
Titian	X				X						X						X		X						6 x 5	2 x 1.5
Tournament of Roses		X		X		X	X				X	X			X										5 x 3	1.5 x 1

Rose

	SLIGHT FRAGRANCE	MODERATE FRAGRANCE	STRONG FRAGRANCE	ONCE-FLOWERING	REPEAT-FLOWERING	RECURRENT BLOOMS	SUITABLE FOR CUT FLOWERS	SUITABLE FOR EXHIBITION	SUITABLE FOR CONTAINER GROWING	CAN BE GROWN AS A PILLAR OR CLIMBER	SUITABLE FOR BEDDING/MASS PLANTING	SUITABLE FOR HEDGING	GROUND COVER OR BORDER	DECORATIVE FRUIT	REQUIRES FULL SUN (6 HRS+)	KEEP OUT OF HOT SUN (MORNING SUN ONLY)	SHADE TOLERANT	PREFERS WARM CLIMATE (OR SHELTERED SUN) FROST TENDER	TOLERATES POOR SOILS	BLOOMS HATE WET WEATHER	CAN BE PRONE TO DIE BACK	PRONE TO BLACK SPOT	PRONE TO MILDEW	PRONE TO RUST	AVERAGE PLANT SIZE—IMPERIAL HEIGHT × WIDTH	AVERAGE PLANT SIZE—METRIC HEIGHT × WIDTH
Trigintipetala (Kazanlik)			X	X											X				X						5 x 4	1.5 x 1.2
Troilus			X		X	X									X										5 x 4	1.5 x 1.2
Trumpeter	X				X		X	X							X										4 x 3	1.3 x 1
Tuscany Superb			X	X					X		X				X				X						4 x 3	1.2 x 1
Vanity	X						X			X					X		X								7 x 5	2.2 x 1.5
Variegata de Bologna			X		X					X					X				X				X		6 x 5	1.8 x 1.5
Veilchenblau	X			X											X		X								10 x 6	3 x 2
Vick's Caprice	X				X				X						X				X						4 x 3	1.2 x 1
Victor Borge	X				X				X						X										5 x 4	1.5 x 1.2
Voodoo	X				X		X	X			X				X										5 x 3	1.5 x 1
Wenlock			X		X	X			X		X	X			X										5 x 4	1.5 x 1.2
Westerland		X			X				X						X										15 x 8	4.5 x 2.4
Whisky	X				X	X									X						X		X		4 x 3	1.3 x 1
White Lightnin'			X		X	X	X								X										5 x 3	1.5 x 1
White Meidiland						X			X				X		X				X						30" x 5	0.75 x 1.5
William Lobb			X	X						X					X				X						8 x 5	2.5 x 1.5
Winchester Cathedral			X			X									X										5 x 5	1.5 x 1.5
Windrush	X				X				X						X										4 x 4	1.2 x 1.2
Winsome	X				X		X	X	X						X										12" x 12"	0.3 x 0.3
Wise Portia			X		X	X		X							X										3 x 4	1 x 1.2
Yellow Charles Austin		X			X					X					X										7 x 5	2.2 x 1.5
York and Lancaster			X	X									X				X		X						6 x 4	1.8 x 1.2
Zéphirine Drouhin			X		X										X		X								12 X 6	3.5 X 2

INDEX